Embarcadero

Embarcadero

RICHARD H. DILLON

GREENWOOD PRESS, PUBLISHERS
WESTPORT, CONNECTICUT

131754

Dedicated to the memory of

JOSEPH HENRY JACKSON

1895-1955

Contents

NOTE

Eight pages of illustrations will be found following page 124.

Foreword

D URING the nineteenth century, indeed until the opening of the Panama Canal in 1914, San Francisco was less an American city, psychologically, than it was a Pacific city. Even after the railways spanned the Great Plains, the deserts and the Sierra, San Francisco was still a long way from Chicago and Philadelphia, Boston, Charleston and New York. For most western travelers it continued to mean the voyage around Cape Horn to establish intercourse with these points; the journey eastward overland was even more complex. The next city west, on the other hand, was Honolulu, where forty-niners had their laundry done rather than in chaotic, if closer, San Francisco; west of that was Yokohama, which again—like Samoa and Panama, Shanghai and Callao—was only at the foot of Sacramento Street where the bowsprit of a Pacific sailing vessel speared out across the drays, cargoes and foot traffic of the Embarcadero.

San Francisco's Embarcadero, or central waterfront, became the major maritime center of the Pacific following the Gold Rush period. It evolved from Yerba Buena cove in that tiny Spanish settlement in which, during the Mexican war of 1846, a party from the sloop-of-war *Portsmouth* planted an American flag and ended the Spanish era. The American era really began in 1849 when the Argonaut traffic exploded the port and the city.

During the second half of the nineteenth century San Francisco, and the Embarcadero, was also the point at which the famous overland trails continued west as maritime trails. The literature of the American West is, if anything, overcrowded with accounts of these overland trails which shaped the destiny of California. For the most part, curiously enough, tales from the maritime trails, though no less exciting, have been ignored in these same accounts of the American West. Yet this part of the story of westward migration bristles with as much tension and adventure, classic drama, incredible yarns and characters as the movement across the land ever offered to history.

Richard H. Dillon, one of the younger western historians and a collector of western maritime lore, has tapped much of the true adventure from this literary and historical Comstock in *Embarcadero*. It is not, of course, a history of the port—a saga in itself which has been well covered before. (Harold Gilliam's *San Francisco Bay*, for example; John Haskell Kemble's *San Francisco Bay: A Pictorial Maritime History* and William Martin Camp's *San Francisco: Port of Gold*, among others.)

Mr. Dillon is far more concerned here with a montage of drama, heroism, rascality and eccentricity, all of which originated on the Embarcadero at one point or another during its rough, brutal, infamous period. A period, in truth, which the respectable San Francisco of today might find it hard to believe ever happened.

It was a rough waterfront in its nineteenth century heyday, a notorious place where sailors were regarded as outcasts and incorrigibles. Seafaring men then were treated far worse than chattel in the ante-bellum South. This, too, was the era of crimps and shanghaiers, of brutal skippers and worse mates. The belaying pin was no joke in a time when desertions were the order of the day, when holding crews became a problem for ships headed back to Panama to pick up more rushers to the gold fields.

The notorious measures to recruit new crews began later in the wake of the Gold Rush, when San Francisco's harbor was jammed with up to 800 ships, many of them abandoned. These waterfront shenanigans continued for years in a tough city quarter completely on its own, crowded as it was with an international flotsam and jetsam and ignored by municipal authorities who preferred to look the other way rather than get clobbered themselves by members of a maritime underground they could not hope to apprehend.

(All this festered before the rise of the labor unions—themselves an important and often tragic part of the Embarcadero's story—which originated through the efforts of a hawk-faced Scandinavian named Andrew Furuseth, "Emancipator of Sailors," who in the 1880's laid the foundation for the Coast Seamen's Union, later the Sailor's Union of the Pacific and the International Seamen's Union.)

But Mr. Dillon is not so much concerned with the history of the Embarcadero here, as he is with some of the history-making maritime adventure which emanated from it. Mr. Dillon is plainly a teller of true sea tales from history and a very good one. A case in point is one of my favorites, Mr. Dillon's saga of Bernard Gilboy. A solo mariner far less well known in the files of classic seamanship than either Captain Bligh or Joshua Slocum, Bernard Gilboy nevertheless casually maneuvered an eighteen-foot skiff, rigged as a sloop, from the Embarcadero toward the Golden Gate one August day in 1882. In marvelously offhand fashion, Gilboy then took it all the way to Australia—a distance twice that between New York and Liverpool! Mr. Dillon thus rescues Gilboy's feat from oblivion, as he does again and again with other figures from a large cast of audacious, eccentric, twisted and heroic characters.

And the cast has been a huge one since Gaspar de Portola first stumbled into this bay in 1769, quite late in the history of exploration. Jack London, a denizen of this port for many years as wanderer, oyster pirate, sailor and connoisseur of its unique flavor, wrote countless vignettes of San Francisco maritime life

9

in his fiction. Yet nowhere in London's tales can one find more curious characters than the real-life people Mr. Dillon authenticates in these accounts. Bully Hayes, San Francisco's "own pirate," is good for a starter. Then Ben Boyd, something of an empire builder who sailed west from the Golden Gate once too often, in 1851, to end up as "long pig," a feast for the cannibal tribesmen of Guadalcanal. These and the many other stories Mr. Dillon relates all began in this port of gold—which was also a port of guano and copra and prostitutes from Peru, of coffee as well as coolies, but *always* the port of adventurers and misfits from the world around.

The port area has changed as the city around it has changed. The jerry-built, post-Gold Rush, once-improbable town that wallowed in a sea of mud, sand, dust, and frame structures is gone. Gone too is the waterfront's first jail which was, naturally enough, an abandoned ship. Mr. Dillon nostalgically mentions a sign on one busy corner of that former slaphappy metropolis, an image as grim as it is amusing and representative: THIS STREET IMPASSABLE, NOT EVEN JACKASSABLE. This is where the infamous Sydney Town flourished—later supplanted by the Barbary Coast, a citadel of depravity no less heinous than the waterfronts of Hamburg and Port Said and Marseilles, too.

But the port of San Francisco in a very few years forgot its casual beginnings as Yerba Buena cove. Forgot, too, the Spanish town from which hides and tallow were exported to the American Atlantic seaboard, as described in Richard Henry Dana's *Two Years Before the Mast*. It became a world port quickly, almost overnight, as great ports are built.

As a physical point of embarkation, the Embarcadero itself was established after the Gold Rush shipping emergency. The irregular harbor's shallows were filled in and a six-mile seawall, filled with debris from the city's hills, gave the waterfront a definition. The American name for it was East Street, happily abandoned much later for the Spanish designation which remains today, an eighteen-mile line of ship-berthing space, efficient, if less romantic and terrifying than in its formative years. The sailor saloons, dives, crimp boardinghouses and maritime jungle atmosphere has almost entirely evaporated from this geographical rim of San Francisco. And that is the best thing that happened in the history of the "port of gold."

Sail gave way to steam. Fleets of ferryboats came, then disappeared after the bay was laced with its series of dramatic bridges and faster transportation. Still, from modern San Francisco's hills, hotels and apartment houses, the bay remains in a series of joyous vistas, a blend of Naples and Hong Kong, even though the maritime activity on it has become almost too efficient for further romance. The Embarcadero, in the throes of perpetual modernization, has, to its enthusiasts, been partially and sadly defaced by a concrete skyway which rises higher than a Liverpool lime-juicer's spars. This obscures the classic Ferry Building, and removes the intimacy between the citizen and the harbor. Yet even now, in the era of Japanese motor ships and Liberian supertankers, any number of walks in the harbor region can stir a variety of thrills, as one responds to seascapes and bayscapes, and to the handsome natural endowment of a port which remains the best on the Pacific north of Cape Horn.

Only the carefully preserved Scottish-built *Balclutha*, pride of the San Francisco Maritime Museum, berthed at Fisherman's Wharf, lends a suggestion of the Embarcadero's once fantastic forest of rigging that even in historic photographs of the front is hard to comprehend. Yet from Fort Mason, the military docks set in a parklike cove near the Golden Gate bridge, to Fisherman's Wharf, then east and south along the finger piers which jut into the bay under Telegraph Hill, and south again to the liner docks at Mission Rock, and on once more to China Basin and the vast Naval shipyards at Hunter's Point the aroma of coffee and copra and bananas, and the movement of tugs, cargo vessels, aircraft carriers, railroad barges and other water-borne traffic continues to preserve the maritime flavor of this Pacific city at a continent's end.

And while the shenanigans practiced in a tough town on its own in the Embarcadero's more primitive days will not occur again, San Francisco is an ever-changing city, and so its Embarcadero must change with it. Further adventures will continue to spring from it, we have no doubt.

In the meantime, it is Mr. Dillon's exciting function in this book to rescue some of the best, if little-known, dramas which have already originated on these storied shores. Here is a fine young historian and collector of maritime narratives at work. I hope he will continue. The stories are there for the telling as this book will vividly attest.

WILLIAM HOGAN

Embarcadero

Chapter I

THE ODYSSEY OF BERNARD GILBOY

ZEALOUSLY partisan, maritime historians will wrangle for years over just which small-boat voyage of history is the greatest of all in daring and in execution. Many will vote for Lt. William Bligh's 3,618-mile voyage to Timor, with eighteen companions crowded into an open boat. Bligh did a masterful job of navigating through hostile waters, with bread and water on short rations, bringing his loyal *Bounty* crewmen to safety in forty-one days. Others will cite the similar exploit of the lifeboat crews of the S.S. *Trevessa* in the 1922 Indian Ocean shipwreck. Undoubtedly, there will be support for the two "Iron Men of the Atlantic," the Norwegian-Americans George Harbo and Frank Samuelsen, who *rowed* across the Atlantic in fifty-five days in 1896! Captain Joshua Slocum, the most famous and perhaps the greatest singlehanded navigator of them all, would certainly be a contender, as would Captain Romer, the German who sailed and paddled a kayak from Portugal to the West Indies in 1928.

Bernard Gilboy would have very few supporters for the crown, simply because his exploit of sailing seven thousand miles from San Francisco alone in one hundred and sixty-two days is so little known. Only in Australia is his great feat remembered and even there his name is unknown to all save the old-timers with long memories of conversations with their fathers.

It was on August 18, 1882, that a small knot of curious spectators lined the edge of the wharf as Bernard Gilboy cast off his lines. Word had got about that he and his tiny *Pacific* were bound for Australia, catching the one o'clock tide. Few reporters were present, for Gilboy had kept his actual destination secret until the moment of casting off his lines. A few friends knew he was attempting to sail Down Under alone. To those who asked him in idle curiosity where he was going, he answered offhandedly that he intended to cruise about outside the Heads.

Bernard Gilboy's departure from the Embarcadero went all but unnoticed. Two days after he set sail, the *Daily Alta California*—its editorial hair on end—was writing of the 16-ton *Spirit of the Waves*, commanded by Captain Lee and bound for Southern California on a hunting and fishing trip: "... we can not see much sport in such a small craft!" What would the *Alta* have had to say if their *Along the Wharves* reporter had been on Clay Street Wharf to watch the eighteen-foot *Pacific*'s departure?

The San Francisco *Daily Examiner* was the only newspaper not caught napping. It ran a piece on August 19th titled RECKLESS VOYAGING—AN ECCENTRIC MARINER SAILS IN AN OPEN BOAT FOR AUSTRALIA.

No little excitement was caused among the crowd of loungers who frequent the boat steps at the foot of Washington Street yesterday afternoon when a small skiff, rigged with two masts and flying at the fore a huge American flag, pulled out from the dock and a swarthy individual, who took great pains to keep his name concealed, arose in the stern and shouted, "All aboard for Australia!"

The little vessel, which measures only eighteen feet over all and is named the *Pacific*, arrived at the wharf Tuesday night and took on board a quantity of stores that were in waiting. Nothing was seen of the eccentric master until 2 o'clock yesterday afternoon, when he went to the boat and busied himself arranging his cargo of eatables. Without conversing with anyone or making his intentions known other than that he proposed sailing to Australia, he shifted his jib and mainsail and with a lively breeze, passed around the sea wall and out the Gate.

Inquiry at the Customhouse showed that he had not obtained clearance papers and will, perhaps, find difficulty in getting in a foreign port unless because of his curious motives in undertaking the hazardous voyage. He is known to have been for some time in the employ of the United Workmen's shoe factory and claims to have been once fifty days at sea in an open boat.

Why he should desire to make the dangerous trip unaccompanied to the Southern Continent is a mystery, and it is more than probable that before he is many days out he will tack for the California coast and consider himself lucky if he reaches it.

How little did the *Examiner* know Bernard Gilboy!

The *Morning Call* on Sunday, August 20, picked up the story from the *Examiner* and in the shipping news column, *The City Front,* reported:

"All aboard for Australia," shouted a man Friday morning as he drew out from the Washington Street wharf [Gilboy's log has it the Clay Street Wharf] in a small sloop. He passed on down the bay and out of the Heads. Nothing is known along the waterfront of the mysterious stranger, nor have any clearance papers been issued to him out of the Customhouse."

We would know nothing of Gilboy's great voyage if friends in Queensland and New South Wales had not urged him to write the story of his exploit. He obliged them by rewriting and expanding his log in a fifty-three page, paper-covered pamphlet titled *Voyage of the Boat "Pacific" from San Francisco to Australia.* Printed in Sydney by J. G. O'Connor in 1883, this little volume is very rare in American libraries.

Born in Buffalo in 1849, Bernard Gilboy had had some experience in sailing small boats after being impressed by the adventure of Alfred Johnson, the American fisherman who took a cutter-rigged dory across the Atlantic in 1876, soloing that great ocean fifty-one years before Lindbergh. Gilboy decided to sail across the Pacific Ocean in the smallest boat possible. He wanted it just big enough to hold him and supplies for a five months' voyage, and no more. Shipwrights Burns and Kneiss, of San Francisco, built the *Pacific* to his specifications—eighteen feet long and with a six-foot beam.

The little vessel was schooner-rigged, having a jib, a foresail and mainsail. It was decked over and had two hatches. The masts were stepped in watertight boxes so that they could be unstepped at any time without water getting into the hull. In an aftercompartment Gilboy kept his sextant, barometer, navigation books and charts in one locker, and food for a week in the other. He replenished the aftercompartment from the forward hold when necessary.

The *Pacific* was launched on Friday, August 3, 1882, and he had her ready for sea by the 17th. On that day he upped anchor and sailed down the Bay to the Clay Street Wharf, hoping to get his clearance papers from the Customhouse in time to catch the ebb tide at four o'clock. Gilboy realized it was late in the season to be starting for Australia and therefore decided not to take a shakedown cruise. He kept his real plan secret because he was afraid that if he revealed his destination to be Australia, his departure would be witnessed by a large crowd who might well see him return red-faced because of a need for refitting or repairing his untried craft.

Delayed by the red tape at the Customhouse, the impatient Gilboy had to postpone sailing on the 17th and instead slept ashore in a hotel. Next morning, August 18th, according to his story, he finally got his clearance and was ready to catch the one o'clock tide.

His cockleshell was deeply laden with supplies—fourteen ten-gallon casks of drinking water; one hundred and sixty-five pounds of bread in airtight cans; two dozen cans of roast beef; two dozen cans of peaches; twenty-four cans of milk; twenty-five pounds of sugar; three pounds each of coffee and tea; and, rounding out his "iron rations," two dozen one-pound cans of boneless pigs' feet! He took matches, nails, hammer and hatchet; a pistol and cartridges; a double-barrel shotgun and ammunition; candles and a lamp; a clock and a watch; rope; clothing; alcohol; an American flag—and, of all things, an umbrella.

He cast off his lines at 1 P.M. after calmly revealing his true destination. One of the crowd on the wharf warned him of the sailor's superstition that Friday was an unlucky day on which to start a voyage. (The *Pacific* was launched on a Friday, as well.) But the lone voyager replied, "I can't help it. I am ready for sea and one day is as good as another to me." He was to find that one day is not always as good as another in the Golden Gate.

Accompanied by three cheers from the little crowd, he sailed out into the Bay and over to Lime Point on the Marin County shore. Here he saw the fog closing in outside and decided to wait until the next day as the water was splashing over the boat "quite lively." He ran into Fort Baker's tiny harbor, little Horseshoe Bay between Lime Point and Point Cavallo, furled his sails and made everything secure. After cooking his first meal aboard the *Pacific* on his little kerosene stove, he turned in for the night.

Gilboy planned on catching the next afternoon tide out, but seeing a number of small boats sailing out in the morning, he started for Point Bonita, hoping to get into Bonita Cove in the lee of the long outermost headland protecting San Francisco Bay. In making a last tack before he got into the lee of the Point, where he would wait the ebb tide, he ventured too far and was caught in the flood tide. Beating against it until the

17

tide changed around three o'clock, he found himself back at Fort Point, the inner entrance to the Bay and the point on which the Golden Gate Bridge is now anchored.

The long, singlehanded voyage to Australia was beginning to look like a farce, for more than a day after he had cast off his lines he was almost back to the Embarcadero again. Gilboy recalled bitterly the ancient Friday sailing superstition of seamen. However, by six o'clock he was clear of land and heading southward with a west-southwest breeze and a heavy beam sea. At ten-thirty he sighted Farallon Light, but he was not to sight land again for thousands of miles.

Each night Gilboy hove to in order to sleep. He threw his canvas sea anchor overboard on the weather side of the boat, lowered his jib and foresail, fixed his mainsail and fastened his rudder amidships to keep the *Pacific*'s head steady to windward. Her one-man crew was thus able to sleep peacefully even in a heavy sea.

One week out, he took a bearing at noon to find himself 540 miles out of San Francisco. He enjoyed pleasant weather and favorable, steady trade winds with only a few rain squalls for the first few weeks. On Thursday, September 7, he sighted a sail but the ship did not speak him. The monotony of the voyage was next broken when he discovered gulls following the *Pacific* for the first time the next day.

Five days later, he was awakened by something hitting the boat. He grabbed up his fish spear and struck at a large sea turtle but it escaped him. The same day, as the boat was sailing before the wind, it again struck something and this time the *Pacific* was brought almost to a standstill. Gilboy was afraid that she had stove herself in, but she rode over the obstruction and a 2 x 6 scantling, about twenty-four feet long, bobbed up astern. No damage was done to the stout little craft.

Two evenings later Gilboy spotted a ship's lantern seven

miles or so astern. He fastened a lantern to the rigging himself and saw the other vessel alter its course. A school of whales came rushing up to the boat on the 14th and stayed a short while before swimming off, coming "so near that I didn't feel comfortable," he said later. Two days later it was a school of porpoises that came directly at the boat, surrounding it and even diving directly under the hull.

From September 20th, he had twenty-nine days of either head winds or calms, plus constant rain. He made less than two hundred miles of headway and his rations schedule was thrown off. He cut down to two meals a day, in compensation, without suffering. Since he did so little exercise, he found that he did not need much food. During this period he caught bonitas and boiled them in sea water. He found them a lot of trouble for rather dry eating. However, he was willing to cook almost anything that he could lay his hands on, to vary his monotonous diet, and he enjoyed a squid which jumped aboard. Most welcome were the tasty flying fish—some a foot long—which he found on deck from time to time. A second sea tortoise nosed about the boat one day and Gilboy, disdaining the spear which had been so ineffectual before, reached overboard, caught a hind flipper and jerked the beast aboard. He cut off its head and let the blood run off the deck and into the water.

Half an hour after the decapitation, a huge shovel-nosed shark approached the stern. It was some twelve feet long and three feet across the head. Gilboy noted in his log: *I have seen a great many sharks in different parts of the world, but this one was a monster as compared to any I had seen before, and the size of the ravenous brute for a moment startled me.* He thought of getting his revolver but he knew that he could not kill the shark with a pistol. It came within three feet of the boat but did not attack. *As he was passing, I mustered up courage enough to prick him a few times in the back with the fish spear. This did not seem to make any impression on him, as his skin seemed to be as hard as a board.*

The shark swam past the boat and then came back to the stern, rubbing his side against the lashed rudder so hard that Gilboy was afraid he would break it. (He had already hauled up his log line for safety.) Eventually the brute left.

When he finally regained the trade winds on October 20th, his clock was hardly going, although he kept a lamp burning beside it during the periods of humid weather. Had he not shipped his bread in airtight containers, it would have spoiled also in the wet month of calms, opposing winds and rain. Anxious to cross the Equator and make up for lost time, Gilboy cut down on his sleep, never taking more than four hours out of twenty-four and often doing with less than three. On fine mornings he would lash the tiller and let her run under jib and mainsail while he slept, trusting the weather and his luck. Friday, October 27, 1882 was a momentous day, for the *Pacific* crossed the Equator after logging 420 miles in the week's run.

On November 2nd, a swordfish—the first Gilboy had ever seen —followed the boat for an hour and several times darted under the bottom as though trying to strike it with its sword. The sharks also continued to trouble him; they would swim up to the stern when he was asleep just before daylight and, turning on their sides, strike the bottom a tremendous blow as they ran along the hull with open mouth, scooping in the small fish following the boat. The sharks occasionally raided the friendly and playful dolphins which followed the boat, also. Gilboy tried everything to keep them away, using the grains and his revolver; and he was finally able to write in his log that "the sharks, in time, became a little shy when they saw me about." When he went to sleep he set up a scarecrow at the tiller in the form of an old shirt to persuade the sharks that the master of the *Pacific* was still at the helm.

The ninetieth day out of San Francisco, November 17th, was

another momentous one, for about six in the evening Gilboy sighted a sail to southward and altered course to speak her. It was the barkentine *Tropic Bird,* commanded by Captain Burns, a few days out of Tahiti and bound for San Francisco. Captain Burns had thought the *Pacific* was a boat lost from a ship and was astonished to find Gilboy sailing alone from the Golden Gate to Australia. He gave him his correct longitude (149° 02′ W), a supply of oranges, limes and bananas, and a promise to report him in San Francisco.

On the twenty-fifth of November, a small fly made its appearance on board. The lonely Gilboy immediately adopted it as a pet and mascot of the expedition. The *Pacific* was fairly boiling along now, making 730 miles by observation and 610 by log during one week, the difference being due to the strong westerly current pushing her in its favor.

Gilboy sighted land on December 8th for the first time since San Francisco's Farallones. The isle was Eua, in the Tonga or Friendly Islands, situated to the east of Tonga-tabu. He sighted it when it was some twenty miles distant and ran the passage between it and Cattow (sic) Island. His latitude at noon was 21° 31′ S and 175° 03′ W; he was now making good time.

The day after passing the islands, Gilboy was again annoyed by a large swordfish knocking against the boat, but his real troubles began just after he crossed the international date line. A treacherous, heavy sea broke right under his rudder. Vainly he struggled to shift the helm but the *Pacific* shuddered and turned completely over! Gilboy surfaced on the weather side of the hull and crawled up on the bottom. He took off his oilskin coat and flannel overshirt and rolled them around his precious watch. Next, he dragged the sea anchor up onto the bottom of the boat, drew on the line till it was taut—the end being fastened to the deck—and, climbing over to the opposite side of the vessel, pulled on the line with all his might.

Had there been any sea it would have helped him rock the

21

Pacific over but the sea moderated and he began to feel that his gargantuan task was hopeless. Still, Gilboy knew that righting the *Pacific* was his only chance for survival—alone, soaked, without food or water, on the bottom of an overturned boat in the middle of the Pacific—so he kept at it till he ached all over from fatigue and strain. After a full hour's work, the *Pacific* began to right herself.

He got her upright and started to cut the shrouds which held the masts in place but she turned turtle again. This time, however, he was able to right the waterlogged vessel easily. When her deck was once again topside, he unshipped both masts and made them fast to the sea-anchor rope. He then threw them overboard, with all the spars and tackle, on the weather side to form a drag and keep her head to sea while he bailed out the hatches with a sugar box.

Gilboy actually made little headway, for the swell dashed more water into the boat than he was able to bail out. Luckily (and luck surely rode with him in the *Pacific*'s cockpit all the way across the Pacific Ocean) the heavy kegs and boxes in the forward compartment worked their way up into the forepeak so that the aftersection was raised a bit, making his bailing more effective.

The lone navigator had capsized about 1,430 miles from Sandy Cape, Australia, which he admitted "was quite a distance to go without a compass and [only] a short stock of provisions." He still had his sextant and his patent log but missed his compass greatly. On cloudy nights with no stars visible, or when the days were overcast and he could not find the sun, he had to heave to until he could get his bearings. Moreover, since he could no longer steer a straight course or figure his longitude, even with the log he could not keep an accurate record of the distance he was sailing on his now erratic course.

He had lost a lot of his canned meat and fish when he capsized, and sea water and kerosene got into his next-to-last can of bread. When he checked his very last can of bread he found that it was wet with sea water, but he managed to eat it up.

Daylight on the 14th of December showed that the mainmast and sail had worked adrift and were lost, as was the bundle of clothing containing his watch. Gilboy reset his sea anchor, dried out his clothing and re-stored his boxes and casks. Then he re-shipped the foremast and spliced the cut-up rigging. Replacing his rudder (also lost in the capsizing) with a steering oar lashed to a spare boom for added length, he got under way. He found that he was exhausted, however, and could not keep his eyes open. Heaving-to was no easy matter now, with mainmast and mainsail gone. He tried her with stern to windward without success and finally rigged up the studding sail to an oar set as far aft as possible. This answered for a mainsail when the *Pacific* was hove to.

For several days he dried clothing and when he got his stove going and had a hot meal, he began to feel like his old self again. Five o'clock one afternoon a swordfish, which had been follow-ing him, struck the *Pacific* with its sword, putting it right through the bottom and giving the boat another jerk as it pulled it out again. Gilboy could hardly believe that the fish had been able to pierce the tough new hull, thinking the sword had pene-trated only part way. Cans knocking together in the forward compartment warned him, however, that the boat was taking in water. After heaving to, he opened the main hatch and found ten inches of water in the boat. He bailed and plugged the leak, near the keel, with lamp wick and rags and got under way again. It continued to leak for the remainder of the voyage but he kept the pump rigged in the afterhatch and, since the plug did not come out, it caused him little anxiety.

On December 21st he saw another swordfish swimming about the boat. The fish fouled itself in the log line and, in trying to pull free, nearly cut the line in two as it made off. Two days later a large shark paid Gilboy a visit, coming up close to the

23

boat and holding its head out of the water as though "he was looking for someone, or was surprised at the rig of the boat." Gilboy struck him a few times with an oar and off he went.

The day before Christmas he sighted Fearne Island, about 1,200 miles from Australia. All he had left in the way of provisions was twelve pounds of canned meat and fish, half a gallon of alcohol and ten gallons of water. He mused, correctly, "The chances of sighting a ship, I think, are poor." .

By keeping in the same latitude however (22° 30′ S), he hoped to meet a ship and get provisions. If he sighted no sail, he planned to continue on the same parallel until he fell in with Nouméa, New Caledonia. He proceeded according to this plan until he sighted Walpole Island, one hundred and fifty miles east-by-south of New Caledonia. But off Walpole Island a heavy norther came up and blew for four days. Though hove to, the *Pacific* was carried far to the south. It appeared that his luck was changing—for the worse. A New Caledonia landfall was now impossible.

Christmas Day was pleasant and clear, with a gift of steady trades. Gilboy dined on beef, liquor and water, and memories of former Yuletide feasts. He sighted Matthew Island, as barren as Fearne had been, off the southern tip of New Caledonia. It was a volcanic isle some three hundred and fifty feet high, without vegetation.

The *Pacific* nearly stranded on hidden reefs off the southeast end of Matthew Island where Gilboy tried to run a pass between the island and a small islet offshore. He found he could not go between and had to sail around the north end of Matthew Island, one hundred miles out of his course. The time he wasted he could ill afford.

The island was so thickly girdled with reefs extending as far as eight or ten miles out to sea that he decided it was not safe to sail after sunset. The following night his log line was caught

24

in one of the ubiquitous reefs and the line parted, leaving him with no way to reckon the distance he would cover.

Still dogged by the barren guano island, Gilboy tried on the 28th to clear the west end but suddenly ran into breakers. It was too late to haul around so he kept the courageous *Pacific* before the wind, her bow heading directly for the reef. Clambering clumsily over the reef like some sea monster, she shipped tons of water and almost capsized, losing her sea anchor overboard. Luckily, one sea took her through the breakers into relatively smooth water about a fathom deep on the other side of the reef.

Gilboy came to anchor and fell asleep. At 2 A.M. he awoke to hear the *thump-thump* of the boat's bilge and keel striking on the bottom. It was low tide and the rocks of the ocean floor were gnawing at the little schooner. He weighed anchor and poled the *Pacific* by moonlight to a deeper pool with a sandy bottom and then fell asleep again.

After sighting a false cape, he found Matthew Island extending still farther westward, but by the night of December 30th he finally cleared the island. In sailing along the shore line for thirty or forty miles, he had hoped to find some coconuts but was unable to spot even a single tree on the barren lava slopes.

The last day of 1882 a small, dark sea bird came flying about the boat, trying to alight on the gaff or the mast but unable to do so because of the rocking motion. Finally, it landed on Gilboy's head! He slowly reached up to capture it but it escaped. Miraculously, as his provisions were giving out, more and more birds (perhaps boobies) visited him. Three more landed on his head and he caught and ate them all. Another three landed on the boat; he caught two but the other escaped after he had wounded it with his revolver.

The capture of the birds cheered him up, as a similar occurrence was to cheer Eddie Rickenbacker, Hans Christian Adamson, and their raft companions some sixty years later in World

War II. With a little food in his stomach, Gilboy was able to console himself further with the old saw "Darkest is the hour before the dawn." He was now down to only four pounds of beef, one quart of alcohol, and ten gallons of water.

On Saturday, January 13, 1883, he wrote in his log: *At about 3 P.M. today I ate the last of my meat, which was about two ounces.* He had lived for a week on two pounds of beef, three sea birds and a flying fish, alcohol and water.

Gilboy found himself very weak now and a further blow came when his steering oar worked loose during the night and drifted off. No fatalist, the tenacious Gilboy did not lose hope of averting disaster as many would have done. He fashioned a rudder out of locker doors and part of his fish spear and was delighted to find that this makeshift rudder worked far better than the steering oar.

On January 18th he sighted Middle Ballona Reef, caught a bird and ate half of it (except for the feathers) and saved the other half for the following day. His hopes of finding coconuts on the reef were in vain. Nothing showed above the sea but bare patches of sand. Although he had no hooks, the resourceful Gilroy tried to catch some of the small fish which swam around the boat. He made a rude spear from a pair of dividers and a stick, but the flimsy device did not work.

His entry for January 21st was: *I am so hungry today that I picked the largest barnacles off the boat, chewing them and spitting them out again.* Two teaspoons of liquor remained and four and a half inches of water in the ten-gallon keg. Monday, January 30, he let the boat steer itself. He could no longer stand to the tiller. He had at last reached the point where all hope of avoiding starvation and death seemed lost.

As he grew weaker and weaker, he could only keep watch. Suddenly, off to leeward, he sighted a sail about eight miles distant. Finding new strength in his despair, Gilboy altered course and waved his open umbrella to attract the attention of the vessel. The umbrella slipped from his weakened grasp and fell overboard. He then fastened the American flag to the end of a stick and waved it, and fired six shots from his revolver, all without effect. Still persevering, the lone mariner finally hauled down his jib, made the flag fast to it, upside-down, and ran it up again. About two o'clock he saw the ship tack. He slumped down in the cockpit, drained of strength, and watched his rescuer beat to windward, slowly drawing up on the *Pacific*. He had won his battle.

Around five o'clock, the schooner drew alongside and a line was thrown to him. He crawled forward, exhausted and starving as he was, and took a turn in the line. Several hands jumped down to look after his boat and the captain of the schooner shouted down to Gilboy to come up as soon as he could. He managed to climb the Jacob's ladder somehow and staggered aft on the schooner's deck, falling against the cabin. He was helped farther aft to a skylight where he lay down and was given soup, bread and tea by the seamen.

Gilboy found that he was hardly able to talk but he managed to tell Captain Boor, of the *Alfred Vittery*, on which he found himself, that he was out of San Francisco and bound for Australia. The captain and crew and the ninety-five Melanesians aboard (recruited Solomon Islanders for the plantations of Queensland) were amazed at his courage and daring. They gathered about him, chattering excitedly in English, pidgin and Solomon Islands tongues.

The *Alfred Vittery* picked Gilboy up only 160 miles off Sandy Cape, that point of land in Queensland almost 7,000 miles from San Francisco. The doughty Gilboy, first to sail alone across the mighty Pacific, was then one hundred and sixty-two days out of San Francisco.

When the schooner dropped her hook in the Mary River, February 2, 1883, Gilboy went ashore and stayed in Maryborough at the Melbourne Hotel. He was feverish and exhausted, partly from talking so much during the days since his rescue. Soon he was taken to a hospital in Maryborough for three weeks of rest and quiet. His normal weight was 177 pounds. On landing he weighed only 148, and his weight skidded down to 134 pounds before he began to convalesce. Talking caused him great pain after his long months of silence, affecting his lungs and head particularly, but from the end of March 1883 he began to recover his strength.

Gilboy went to the seashore, enjoyed Australian hospitality, and made arrangements to exhibit his boat in Sydney. He was frequently asked whether he had not been bothered by lonesomeness. He answered that he felt depressed and lonely for the first month but his mind was fully occupied after that.

Captain Burns of the *Tropic Bird* did not fail to report him, and a newspaper account of the *Pacific* and her skipper had appeared on page three, column six, of the San Francisco *Daily Evening Bulletin* for Tuesday, December 19, 1882. There, buried amidst the advertisements for rattan chairs and Siberian Balsam (*cures catarrh, asthma, croup ...*) was a tiny story titled "A Little Craft in Mid-Ocean."

> Tidings of the dory *Pacific*, that sailed from this port in August bound for Australia, have been brought in by the barkentine *Tropic Bird* that arrived yesterday from Tahiti. Following is the entry on the log made November 17: Latitude 14 degrees 50 minutes south, longitude 149 degrees 5 minutes west; light, variable winds, freshening somewhat toward night. About sunset we discovered a small sailboat off our starboard bow. As we came up abreast of her we hove to and waited for her to come up, thinking she might be in need of some assistance. It was nearly dark before she was near enough to be plainly distinguished, when we made out a small schooner-rigged boat, decked over and with the Stars and Stripes flying from her mizzen gaff. In answer to our captain's "Boat ahoy!" a strong voice came back: "This is the boat *Pacific*, ninety days out from San Francisco and bound for Brisbane, Australia." In answer to our in-

quiries the captain said his name was Bernard Gilboy, and that he was making the voyage entirely alone, just to see what could be done. His boat, he said, was less than two tons' burden— 1⅞ exactly. He reported having experienced fine weather throughout the voyage, except between latitude 5 and 8 degrees north, where he had headwinds and calms and was delayed twenty-nine days. He seemed cheerful and sanguine of success and did not want any assistance.

A great news story went begging in Gilboy's feat. Singlehanded, he took a boat from San Francisco to Queensland— 6,441 miles in one hundred and sixty-two days, averaging about 40 miles per day on short rations and plagued with storms, capsizings and puncturing swordfish. In the long run, of course, Gilboy's seemingly bad luck was really just the contrast of a series of unfortunate incidents silhouetted against the good fortune which rode in the cockpit of the *Pacific* with him all the way and brought him safely to Queensland. If Gilboy's feat was not the greatest sea voyage of all time, surely it was the luckiest.

After he regained his health, he returned to San Francisco where he is believed to have exhibited his boat at Woodward's Gardens and to have signed on the traditional cable cars as a gripman. He was soon back at sea, however, with a berth in the coasting trade. By 1897 he was first mate of the collier *Mackinaw*, commanded by Captain Littlefield, on the San Francisco–Puget Sound run.

An old-time sailor in San Pedro, California, remembers Gilboy. When Thorwald Olesen, then just a green young A.B., came aboard the *Mackinaw* and asked for a berth, Gilboy looked him over sharply and asked if he was a sailor.

"Yes, sir," answered Olesen.

"Very well," said Gilboy. "Then take off your coat and get to work on that coal scattered on deck."

It was not until several months later, when Gilboy left the *Mackinaw*, that Olesen learned of the mate's historic small-boat voyage of 1882. Gilboy was no braggart. On the contrary, he hardly mentioned his exploit even to his friends. Some of Olesen's new shipmates mentioned that "First" had once made a long ocean voyage in a small boat, but nobody knew the details.

One of the hoariest old kettles which ever called at the Embarcadero after the turn of the century was the *Centennial*. She was an old iron steamer, built at the Thames Iron Works, London, as a sidewheeler in 1859. First named the *Delta*, she became the *Takasaga Maru* before being renamed the *Centennial*. She did a bit of everything in her time and when found to be a misfit for handling lumber in the Pacific coastal trade, she was put on the Alaska run during the Klondike Gold Rush, under the command of Captain Strand.

Gilboy joined her as first mate after spending some time on the *Argyll* and was with her for the opening of the Russo-Japanese War. Strand took her across the Pacific a couple of times to Siberian ports, running the Japanese blockade, but became ill and had to give up the command. Gilboy was promoted to master and took her back once again on June 12, 1905, with a cargo of salt for Nikolayevsk, calling at Dutch Harbor en route.

A Japanese patrol vessel put a shot across her bows and seized her as a contraband carrier. She was tied up in Japan while the case was wrangled in the court of chancery. Finally, the Americans proved to the satisfaction of the Japanese that the *Centennial* had attempted to call at Siberian coast ports only after the cessation of hostilities and was, therefore, not a blockade runner, and the Japanese authorities released the ship.

The Charles Nelson Company had bought the old tub from the Alaska Steamship Company but now, in turn, sold her to Captain Kane of Seattle, subject to her safe arrival in Puget Sound from Japan. Chartered to Barneson-Hibbard Company, Gilboy took the *Centennial* from Mororan for San Francisco via Hakodate on February 24, 1906, with a crew of thirty and a cargo of sulphur—and disappeared.

On March 27, 1906, the San Francisco *Chronicle* expressed some worry over her, saying that "her non-arrival is beginning to occasion some comment." She was next posted on the overdue ships lists and her reinsurance rates went up. It was assumed that she had caught fire in mid-ocean, since no trace of her was found. Finally she was written off, although it is said Lloyd's never tolled the bell for her.

The *Coast Seamen's Journal* took notice of her disappearance on April 11, 1906, by stating:

> Forty-six days have passed since the steamer *Centennial* left the port of Mororan for San Francisco, and nothing has since been heard of the vessel. The belief is current that the *Centennial* has been lost. The owners and charterers of the steamer do not share this view, but almost everybody has expressed the opinion that the old *Centennial* has gone down. She is believed by some shipping men to have put into Dutch Harbor, Alaska, but there is no particular ground for this belief. The rate of reinsurance is now 60 per cent and it is expected to advance rapidly.

Only one man of the crew could be found, the first officer, Mr. McCarran. He had overstayed his leave in Japan and Gilboy had sailed without him.

In 1913 the *Centennial* burst back into the news again, this time on the front pages. The *Examiner* for October 24th carried a headline LONG-LOST "CENTENNIAL" SIGHTED. The vessel was found, frozen solid in the ice of the Okhotsk Sea west of Sakhalin Island, by Captain E. Hieber, the American pilot of a Russian exploring expedition.

With her flush deck and antiquated, sharp—almost clipper—bow, it had to be the old *Centennial*. Her name was partly obliterated and her iron was rusted. There was no one aboard, dead or alive. Her lifeboats were gone and it was assumed that Gilboy and his crew had apparently abandoned her to her icy tomb.

Hieber reported the finding to G. A. Griffin, an engineer in the Philippine Coast Guard, who passed the word on to the Marine Engineers Beneficial Association in San Francisco. The books were finally closed on the *Centennial*.

Thus, Bernard Gilboy met death mysteriously aboard his first command—if we except his tiny *Pacific*, in whose cockpit he fought the sea so successfully twenty-four years earlier.

Chapter II

SAN FRANCISCO'S OWN PIRATE

BULLY HAYES, San Francisco's own pirate, has been known erroneously for some time as America's last pirate and, even in global terms, as "the last of the pirates." Actually, Captain Hayes was only the Pacific's penultimate pirate, but the gentleman who dubbed him "last of the pirates"—H. H. Romilly, Britain's Deputy Commissioner for the Western Pacific—cannot be blamed for this miscarriage of notoriety.

However, Bully Hayes was by all odds the greatest of the latter-day pirates. Robert Louis Stevenson wrote of him, in the Prologue of *The Wrecker: Talk in the South Seas is all upon one pattern. It is a wide ocean but a narrow world. You shall never talk long and not hear the name of "Bully" Hayes.*

Bully's connections with San Francisco were strong. It was on a voyage out of San Francisco that William Henry Hayes, to give him his real name, really got his start, and it was on a passage from Frisco that he met his bloody finish.

Will Hayes began a long career of blackbirding, barratry and piracy in a most landlubberly fashion. The first time he came to the attention of the law was in 1852, when he mistook a neighbor's horse for his own and made off with it. This incident occurred in Cleveland, the same city where Hayes was born in 1829, the son of an honest saloonkeeper. Luckily, there was a

33

legal flaw in the indictment and the apprentice horse thief escaped punishment for his felony. He did not tarry long in Ohio, however, but undertook a long ocean voyage for his health. He got his sea legs on the passage of the bark *Canton* from New York to Melbourne, where he arrived in August 1853, and he was to fish in the troubled waters of the South Pacific for the next twenty-four years, until a fear-crazed Scandinavian cook crushed his skull off Jaluit.

The name of Bully Hayes soon became synonymous in the South Seas for shady dealing, maritime swindling and blackbirding. This last, the traffic in enslaved islanders for the plantations of Fiji or Queensland, was not his own invention, although his success in the dirty business was enough to suggest a pioneering start. Blackbirding was simply a later spasm of the moribund African slave trade, begun by Peruvians who raided Polynesia for natives to work the deadly guano deposits of the Chincha Islands off the coast of Peru. Bully Hayes proved himself an apt pupil of the *Latinoamericanos* and profited—in more ways than one—by their example.

"The bird is flown" was the phrase used to describe San Francisco's first real acquaintance with Bully Hayes. Thus the San Francisco *Daily Evening Bulletin* of August 31, 1859, summed up succinctly its story on his running away with the brig *Ellenita,* paying off his numerous creditors with a glimpse of her fore-tops'l.

This was Bully's first big *coup.* After a half-dozen years of petty oceanic thievery in Australasian waters he appeared in San Francisco, where he picked up the *Ellenita,* a 350-ton coasting-trade brig, from a San Franciscan named Morrison for $800. He paid $500 in cash, which he had somehow run up from a skinny bankroll of $50 borrowed from the Reverend Samuel Damon of Honolulu. Hayes then laid in stores of provisions, wines, liquors, fancy furniture and carpets, all on credit. He neglected to pay Morrison for a cargo of beans and other vegetables he took aboard and the $300 he owed on the vessel slipped his mind as well. He did remember to overhaul the *Ellenita,* placing her on the Steuart Street ways of Tichenor & Company, on credit.

He then advertised her as bound for Melbourne and the San Francisco *Daily Alta California* for forty-two days carried an announcement of the imminent departure of the fast-sailing clipper packet *Ellenita.* Hayes played his cards astutely, placating his creditors, save for the man who filled his water casks and libeled the brig for his $80 bill. The captain moved his sailing date up from July 25th to August 5th to August 15th to August 22nd and, finally, to September 1st. He retained a "Philadelphia" lawyer to delay the libeling of the brig, now technically in the custody of the United States Marshal, and then proceeded to borrow money from the shyster himself.

A number of people, heeding his marathon ads in the *Alta,* had booked passage for Melbourne and Sydney, tempted by the promise that he would "take cabin and steerage passengers at reduced rates." One Sunday evening Hayes invited a number of the *Ellenita's* passengers to attend church with their captain. During the services he slipped out, raced down to the Washington Street Wharf and caught the brisk evening tide.

Making sure that one of the few passengers remaining on the ship was a woman—for Bully Hayes was desolate without female companionship—he cleared the Heads instead of the Customhouse and stood for the Farallon Islands and points much farther west. When U. S. Marshal Solomon discovered that his "bird had flown," he started in pursuit aboard the steam tug *Martin White.* Bully crowded on sail, however, and the brig showed her heels to the tossing steamer.

It was believed that Captain Hayes would head for Tahiti to pick up a cargo of oranges for the Sydney market, but on September 15, 1859, the *Ellenita*, flying the flag of New Granada, showed up at the tiny port of Kahului, Maui, in the Hawaiian Islands. There Hayes negotiated for a load of cattle for Nouméa, New Caledonia.

Sheriff Peter H. Treadway of Maui hurried across the island to arrest him for a baker's dozen of violations of Sandwich Island customs regulations, including entering a closed port, failing to enter at the Customhouse of the Kingdom of Hawaii at Lahaina, and smuggling goods into Kahului on the side. He was met by a smiling, apologetic Hayes who asked him to stay on board overnight and then pilot him into Lahaina next day. They had a drink on it, supped, and then had a few more drinks.

When Treadway awakened next morning, he found the brig ready for sea and Hayes wasting no time in informing him that the *Ellenita*'s destination was New Caledonia and that he could either go ashore in the boat alongside or, for a consideration, take passage to *L'Oceanie Française*. The irate sheriff, no match for the burly Hayes and his crew, went ashore and watched the brig squaring away before a fresh wind. In his hurried departure, Captain Hayes forgot to pay for the fresh provisions he had taken aboard in Kahului, to the sum of about $100.

The editor of the Sydney *Morning Herald* quoted a story in the San Francisco *Daily Evening Bulletin* concerning Hayes' running off with the *Ellenita*. Shortly thereafter a letter-to-the-editor appeared in the Sydney paper, over Hayes' signature. In it he claimed that the *Ellenita* had sprung a dangerous leak and thus forced him to push for the nearest port—Kahului—to make repairs. There a jolly but overzealous and acute sheriff (the adjectives are Bully's) had tried to arrest him. Since Hayes had only a cargo of beans, potatoes and onions, surely not the type of contraband worth an honest smuggler's time, he *did not choose to be arrested upon an unfounded suspicion of a bare intention. . . .* Therefore, he concluded, *for the sake of my passengers, and knowing that in some places the most senseless and disgraceful customs laws prevailed, I thought it better to evade an arrest which I thought morally wrong, productive of only vexation and delay.*

Once well away from Kahului, however, the *Ellenita* ran into real trouble. Dirty weather hit the old coasting brig and opened her seams some seventy miles from the Navigator's Islands, as the Samoan group was then called. Bully ordered all hands and passengers to the pumps, but the water kept gaining. Finally, he put together a raft made of the boom and a spare topmast, with planks nailed across and three water casks lashed on top.

The raft floated too low, so Bully had a deck made of cabin doors and other light wood stripped from the sinking brig. He and the mate and two seamen stayed aboard, hoping the *Ellenita* would remain afloat, but she filled almost to the upper-deck beams and began to go down by the head. Bully then jettisoned her anchor, but this did little good and she continued to settle until the water was over the forecastle deck. The captain called the boat alongside and the four men got off, joining the twenty-one others already in the boat and raft. Just after they left her, the brig went down headfirst, her stern davits and main-topgallant yard finally sinking out of sight.

Hayes took the raft in tow of the single boat but cut it adrift during the night. The raft and the small boat soon drifted apart but Hayes had his boat crew pull to windward, knowing that they would find the drifting raft after daylight. When they did fall in with it again, they found that the heavy seas had knocked off much of the deckwork.

Bully put all of the men out of the boat save himself and the oarsmen. Shaking a fist the size of a picnic ham, he threatened to throw overboard one gentleman who dared protest the transfer. Taking with him the women and most of the crew, eleven persons in all, he placed the thirteen remaining men and a thirteen-year-old boy aboard the raft. Since the boat had a supply of water, Bully contented himself with some bread and

37

meat from the raft's stores. He also took the navigational instruments, except for a quadrant for the use of the raft's crew which was soon lost overboard.

Before parting company with the raft, he shot the sun and gave the men their position. The *Ellenita* had foundered in latitude 12° 48′ South and longitude 172° 25′ West. Ten passengers, the steward, the cook, a boy and one (!) seaman he left to manage the disintegrating raft. They had sixty gallons of fresh water and some bread.

For the first three days after the boat left the men on the raft, the weather was so rough that many articles which they tried desperately to save were washed overboard, including blankets and clothing. The castaways tried frantically to paddle to the island of Savaii, which they sighted on the fourth day, but it was far to windward and they made no headway. That evening the raft gave a heavy roll and nearly capsized; the men rushed to the upper side to balance it but this made things worse, for it rolled wildly to that side, taking them into the water to their waists. The raft continued to wallow from side to side for ten minutes, as they frantically rushed from one point to the other in attempts to balance it. All the while sharks circled the raft with its frightened, scrambling complement.

That night some of the men became mentally unbalanced and talked of going to this San Francisco hotel or that one to get a good meal. Two of them, in going to their fanciful hotel, walked overboard two or three times but each time miraculously caught hold of the raft and got on board again. One fellow, thinking that he was on one of the islands among the natives, went up to one of his companions and demanded a native drink.

Finally setting a small sail, the men steered the cumbersome craft as much to southward as they were able, until they fell, too weak to stand to the helm. On the eighth day they caught a shark and fresh meat supplemented their scanty rations. It was caught by tempting it alongside with a ham bone tied on a small line. The shark followed close to the raft and one of the men managed to slip a noose over its head. The famished survivors no sooner hoisted it aboard than it was cut open, the blood drunk and much of the flesh torn off and eaten, while the rest was still flopping about on the raft's deck.

The raft's water allowance was cut in half at this time, for the casks were getting low and what water remained was brackish, what with the sea washing over the raft and leaking into the kegs. The group suffered dreadfully from thirst since everything they had to eat, including their bread and drinking water, was drenched with salt water.

Some began to drink sea water while others, including the captain's steward, drank their own urine. During this period several strong squalls caught the raft, carrying away much of what remained of its deck and sending water crashing over everyone night and day.

On the twelfth day they caught another shark, more welcome than the first. It was laid on its back and cut open carefully so that the gall would not become mixed with the blood. Then the men went down on their knees, dipping up the blood with their cupped hands to drink it. The shark, together with a piece of ham and some preserved oysters, lasted two or three days.

By this time a large portion of the deck was washed away and there was not enough room for all to stand on the raft. Most of the men began to suffer with salt-water boils and the feet and legs of some were completely raw. A large empty cask lashed forward was cut open and two men got into it. One had had his leg injured while building the raft, the other complained of pains in both legs. Another, smaller barrel with one head knocked in was lashed upright and served as a shelter for one or two others when the sea was not too heavy.

The men in the large barrel had such a comfortable place on cold nights that others thought that they would like to share it.

Those who entered it without being invited caused rows in the "cabin," as it was called. Knives were frequently drawn, but no stabbings occurred.

Finally it was agreed that the boy deserved a place in the barrel and threats were made to knock in its head if he were not admitted. He was accordingly let in but the others kicked him about so much that he was often only too glad to get out again onto the open deck. Quarrels and brief scuffles were common, with the sounds coming up through the bunghole like the voices of a ventriloquist, thrown from a distance.

The privations, fatigue and exposure led the men into strange delusions. Some thought they heard roosters crowing and people talking, others heard bells ringing. The steward told a man that he had seen the women and children who went in Bully Hayes' boat and had heard them talking as plain as they did in the "cabin," and he was certain that they had all been lost at sea.

The steward warned his listeners not to tell anyone because they might think he was superstitious. He continued to talk in his strange, rambling way until the fifteenth day when he died, completely insane, calling out frequently to the man who was keeping his head out of the water: "Kill me! Kill me if you want to!" He was left a short time, a prayer was said, and he was thrown over the side.

The sixteenth day another shark was spotted at dusk but in the darkness the men were unable to catch it. The next morning, however, they discovered that it had followed them all night, and they caught it and quickly devoured it. Someone spied what he thought was land and everyone waited eagerly for the clouds to clear from the horizon. In a short while everyone was on his feet, satisfying himself that it was really land at last.

The raft was to windward of the isle, which turned out to be Wallis Island, with the wind from the north and east, but light. All who could stand were called upon to steer; those who were willing to work but could not haul themselves to their feet did their best at paddling the clumsy craft.

The men fell back exhausted so frequently that it took two days and two nights to close with the island. The second evening they were close enough to the shore to be able to see fires burning on the island, and at daylight they were within half a mile of the beach.

Now the fickle wind played a trick on them, shifting suddenly around to the south. The raft, with its disheartened crew, began to drift away from land. Exhausted men who had been helpless for hours dug strength out of desperation and seized their paddles again.

Natives were spied running along the shore. One of them raised a flag and waved to the men on the raft. A group of islanders on the beach launched a canoe in the lagoon behind the reef. They paddled to the reef that separated them from the castaways and held up coconuts and other fruit. One of the men jumped overboard from the raft as the canoe reached the reef but was unable to swim any distance and clambered back again.

Although they were drifting away from the coral reef, the men kept at their paddling. When all hope seemed lost and, one by one, they dropped exhausted over their paddles, two of the natives plunged into the surf and swam to the shipwrecked company of the *Ellenita.*

Seeing the wretched condition of the crew, they called another native out to assist them and tried to paddle the crazy raft. They were able to make little if any progress, however, and they bent some lines together and swam to shore with one end. When they found a foothold, they hauled away until the raft reached the reef.

The islanders carried those survivors who could not walk, including the man with the broken leg, across the reef to the canoes in the placid lagoon. The rest of the company stumbled their way across the sharp coral, assisting one another as best they could. The canoes carried them to the small island, where they remained overnight. Next night they were taken to the main island of the lagoon where they were treated very kindly by the French missionaries and natives.

Shortly thereafter, H.M.S. *Elk* arrived at Wallis Island to rescue the castaways. The commanding officer had learned of the raft from Bully Hayes, who had arrived in Samoa. The navigation officer of the *Elk* figured that the raft would drift toward Wallis Island and steered a zigzag course, posting lookouts constantly at the masthead. The *Elk* had reached Wallis earlier without sighting the raft and sailed on to Ivalan in Fiji. Now it returned to Wallis, where it was met by islanders in canoes shouting "They're found! They're found!"

Even though Bully had deserted his passengers in their hour of need, the safety of their lives was due to his warning the *Elk* that they were adrift. Afraid to go to Apia and the authorities himself, he had prevailed upon a trader at Savaii to sail in a whaleboat to inform the *Elk*'s commander of the wreck. Had not Bully notified H.M.S. *Elk*, and had not the natives been told to keep a sharp lookout by the warship, there would have been little chance of the raft's crew surviving. The island with which they fell in was a small uninhabited one some miles from Wallis itself. Without assistance from the natives, the men would have not been able to conquer drift, wind, surf and reef. They would have been driven farther to leeward and to starvation.

Bully and his boat's crew had an easier passage but a rum go of it once they reached land. They came ashore at Satou on the island of Savaii. Here the natives threatened them and plundered their goods. They seized all of Hayes' money, some $220, and his clothes. A pistol-wielding chief threatened to relieve Bully of his life and charged him fifty cents a bucket for drinking water (doubtless charged to Bully's $220 Satou account).

This incident, with the resultant loss of face to Europeans, led the British and American consuls to draw up a joint letter to the ruling chiefs of Savaii. They claimed compensation for the injuries done to American and British citizens from the brig. Some of the money demanded was actually paid, but the letter, a curious document in Samoan (and translated literally into English), was actually of little effect.

Legend has it that Bully, for his part, did not forget Satou and the tough old chief. He is said to have squared things with the Savaiians by marking Satou for one of his first blackbirding raids.

Bully had an elephantine memory for wrongs done him, but on the other hand, he never forgot a favor. From Salaibra, on Savaii, he wrote a letter to the editor of the Sydney *Morning Herald* thanking publicly all the Europeans of Savaii who had helped him and his castaway crew. He singled out Abraham Hort particularly, calling attention to the fact that the latter "walked 35 miles at night over stones and quagmires in the bush to offer us a passage in his vessel to Apia, though he himself was bound up to Sydney. . . ."

When H.M.S. *Elk* reached Samoa there was talk of apprehending Hayes and taking him to Sydney. But the consuls—and almost everyone else—were so afraid of him that no charges were preferred and the *Elk* sailed without him. Much later, H.M.S. *Herald* took him to Sydney on a charge connected with the foundering of the *Ellenita,* but the case broke down and he was released. The captain of the *Herald* was mildly reprimanded for exceeding his duty and Hayes went free, in the words of the Auckland *Star,* "as he always did."

On the beach and down-and-out, Hayes was not at loose ends for long. He took the brig *Antonio* to Sydney from Savaii, arriving in time to celebrate New Year's Day 1860, doubtless with borrowed funds. He soon engaged in his highly successful career of polished and proper piracy, participating in a number of mercantile, maritime and marital adventures which, though most profitable, did not take him to San Francisco.

Bully was shipwrecked four more times before his 1876 return to Frisco. He was married, formally and otherwise, any number of times, and was often chased by British or American gunboats. He flourished in the blackbirding and Chinese coolie traffic and twisted the Kaiser's imperial mustache by raiding and destroying the German Consulate at Apia, Samoa, in 1870. According to some optimistic newspaper accounts, he was hanged by the neck until dead from a yardarm of H.M.S. *Blanche,* at anchor at Tokelau. As in Mark Twain's case, the reports of his passing were somewhat exaggerated.

When he did return to the Golden Gate, he was as changed as the city he had left at the tail end of the Gold Rush days. Still the toughest town on the Pacific littoral, its rougher element was now grouped in small cankers on the body of the respectable city. While he had been away, San Francisco had grown into the Athens of the Pacific Coast, wealthy, cultured and dignified. Bully could always find his kind, however, in the ulcerous *barrios* of the Barbary Coast, the Embarcadero, the Tenderloin and South of the Slot. Here the raffish seamen and blowsy female barflies brawled as they had done ever since the Gold Rush.

Hayes, now a forty-seven-year-old balding and barrel-chested veteran, soon tired of the Barbary Coast. He began to look around for a ship and, as always, found one.

In October 1876 a San Francisco businessman named Moody engaged Captain Hayes to take his cutter *Lotus* on a tramp trading voyage to Singapore, Manila and the Carolines. The gentleman and his attractive wife, Jennie Ford Moody, planned to go along just for the trip.

On October 9th, with Moody and his wife aboard, the ship was ready for sea when Hayes suddenly recalled that he had left the chronometer ashore in Charlie Pace's clock shop on

44

Battery Street, where it was being corrected. Since the captain was so busy getting everything shipshape for the voyage, the owner volunteered to pick it up at the shop. He wasted considerable time haggling with Pace, who insisted he had never seen Captain Hayes' chronometer. Finally, Moody gave up and returned to the Embarcadero just in time to catch a glimpse of the *Lotus*'s canvas silhouetted against the dark Sausalito hills where they plunge into the Golden Gate. While Moody wrung his hands and tore his hair, Hayes conned the *Lotus* through the Gate and slipped out into the open Pacific.

Unfortunately, the log of the *Lotus,* like the logs of all Bully's ships, has not come to light. We must therefore piece together the story of his last voyage from reports in the San Francisco *Daily Alta California,* the *Hawaiian Gazette,* and the *Australian Sketcher.*

By a process of elimination, Bully was forced to call at the tiny port of Kawaihae on the "Big Island" of Hawaii. He was afraid to enter at Honolulu because he was sure he would be remembered there. (The supercargo of the *Orestes,* Mr. Clement, had had to remove Hayes from command of the vessel in 1858 before he stole the ship and its cargo!) Kahului and Lahaina were closed to Bully because of his scrape with Sheriff Treadway of Maui in the former port.

At Kawaihae, Hayes took on water and fresh provisions on January 1, 1877, and set sail for a leisurely cruise. At Samoa he persuaded a Dr. Ingolls to sail with him to the Westward Isles to treat one of the kings there. He promised him a fee of $2,000, to be paid shortly.

During his lazy tramp cruise Hayes enjoyed the company of Jennie Ford Moody while the acting mate and the two *kanaka* forecastle hands worked the ship. Besides the acting mate, Peters, and the two crewmen, Hayes had signed on a cook-steward who has been identified as being Dutch, German and Scandinavian by varying accounts, and a thirteen-year-old cabin boy destined to become an (un-named) Australian Member of Parliament.

Off and on Hayes quarreled with his new steward, who was anything but the placid and stolid "Dutchman" of tradition. Finally, off Jaluit, Bully became completely exasperated with the cook's lubberly handling of the tiller. He cursed and upbraided him for his inept steering and was answered in kind by the hot-headed seaman. When Bully started up the companionway only a few minutes after threatening to shoot the cook, the "Dutchman" let go the tiller and rushed at him. He struck him on the head with the boom crutch, and rolled the captain—still alive—over the side into the sea.

Acting mate Peters, asleep below, awoke during the commotion and came on deck. When he realized what had happened, he put the *Lotus* about. But the water revealed nothing and he could not find Bully Hayes' body. As soon as it became obvious that his captain was lost overboard, Peters brought the cutter back to Bonham Island as fast as she could sail. There, however, the cook-steward prudently jumped ship and escaped, never to be heard of again. Bully Hayes' bones lie many fathoms below the surface of the restless Pacific, off Jaluit atoll in the Marshalls.

Epilogue

Toward the end of March 1877, the American ship *Maggie Johnston* called at Bonham. The German trading concern, Copelle & Co., asked Captains Henry and Bliven to take charge of the *Lotus* since Peters, although acting mate, had signed no articles and therefore had no control over the vessel. There was a rumor already making the rounds that certain individuals hoped to seize the *Lotus* and use it for inter-island trading. Accordingly, the two American captains placed her papers in the Copelle & Co. safe, left acting mate Peters in command and, after holding an inventory, deposited her cargo in the Copelle warehouse. The *Lotus* was then moored in the harbor to a 1,600-pound anchor, her sails unbent and stored in the warehouse.

It was long thought that the *Lotus* later drifted from her moorings and was destroyed on Bonham reef, and there are maritime historians today who share this belief. Actually, the *Lotus* had a long and colorful career after Hayes' murder, falling into the hands of King John of Ailinglap Island in the Ralik chain of the Marshalls. This was discovered when Will Jackson, a castaway from the American vessel *Rainier*, wrecked on its maiden voyage January 3, 1884, on Ujae atoll, reached Jaluit. He found the *Lotus* there, commanded by the son of the King of Ailinglap.

Jackson persuaded King John to allow him to take the *Lotus* to Ujae to pick up the other castaways from his ship; but at the last minute, influenced by a renegade *kanaka* from the *Rainier*, the king decided "schooner no go!" Jackson stole a canoe, paddled out to the *Lotus* and forced the twenty or so islanders on the ship to jump overboard at pistol point. Peace was restored by a copra trader named Ryan just as Jackson was about to cut the anchor rope and sail the *Lotus* to Ujae alone. The King gave him a crew of thirty-five men to man the vessel and they set sail.

A squall hit the *Lotus* and would have overturned her had not her main halyard been carried away, dumping the mainsail. The *kanakas* became frightened and wanted to turn back but Jackson bullied them into continuing. Near Lae another squall hit the cutter and, as the mariner from Bath reported, "blowed the outer jib to ribbons. So we were minus one sail." This was too much for the natives, who finally overpowered Jackson, locked him below decks and turned back toward Lae. He yelled at them repeatedly through the cracks in the hatchway, shouting that if they did not stop and pick up the shipwrecked crew of

47

the *Rainier,* "a man of war would come and 'bum-bum' them all." The Marshall Islanders respected a gunboat's cannonading, if nothing else. Once again they came about, and this time finally ran for Ujae. Here the King, showing off his new United States Navy commander's uniform, paddled out to greet Jackson, whom the natives had released from his prison. He had news for the American: the U.S.S. *Essex* had already rescued his fellow shipmates from the *Rainier.*

Jackson let the *Lotus* sail from Ujae without him, and took passage to Jaluit alone on Ryan's copra schooner *Francisco.* But he had not seen the last of the *Lotus.* At Jaluit the King of Ailinglap employed him as a carpenter and he worked the cutter over, putting in new beams, calking her and making a new set of canvas. The King offered him command of his royal schooner but Jackson declined, musing "I might wake up some fine morning to find I had been killed!" Jackson was one down-Easter who did not trust Marshall Islanders, even those of kingly station.

Eventually Jackson sailed aboard the schooner *Klaluk* bound from the Gilberts for San Francisco. He never knew that the *Lotus,* "formerly a San Francisco yacht of 12 tons or so," had been Bully Hayes' bloody ship, and nothing more is known of the cutter's fate.

No one knows either what became of the unnamed Dutch or Scandinavian cook who ended the career of the last of the *great* pirates. (Bully Hayes was a more polished and accomplished performer than men like Alex Maclean or Lucky Blackburn.) The two *kanakas* and the cabin boy never emerged from blessed anonymity. Peters drifted off into obscurity. A Jennie Ford was listed as a "domestic" in the 1878 San Francisco City Directory and this might conceivably be Mrs. Moody, who could have made her way back to San Francisco. She does not appear in later directories, however, and either she moved on or was taken back by a forgiving husband.

48

Of all the characters in the drama of Bully Hayes' last voyage, we know for sure the fate of only the eclipsed star of the piece. Bully Hayes' bones, all that remains of the master of the *Lotus*, the *Ellenita,* the *Rona* and the *Leonora,* lie many fathoms below the surface of the restless Pacific, off Jaluit atoll in the Marshalls.

Chapter III

THE *SAGINAW'S* GIG

JUST one day after Commander David G. Farragut was succeeded in the command of the Mare Island Navy Yard by Captain R. B. Cunningham, a letter was dispatched from Washington stating that the Navy Department had decided to have a side-wheel steamer built there "for service in the China seas."

The matter of availability of timber for ship construction had already been explored, with live oak and native California bay (laurel) considered best for the hull. General Vallejo had recalled that a 250-ton ship was built of laurel in California during the Mexican period, thirty years earlier, and was still in use. Farragut sent an assortment of West Coast woods to Washington on the *Vincennes* and by an Act of Congress dated June 12, 1858, the construction of the steamer was authorized.

Built of California laurel, she was a lightly rigged vessel of 508 tons, 155 feet long and mounting a 32-pound Parrott pivot gun and two boat guns. She was entirely a West Coast ship from stem to stern. Her boilers and other iron engine parts were fabricated by Peter Donahue's Union Iron Works in San Francisco under the first such Navy contract let on the Pacific Coast.

Winter rains slowed down her construction but, dressed in a fresh coat of black paint, the *Toucey* (named for the Secretary of the Navy) slid gracefully into the waters of the Napa River

51

on March 3, 1859. Her launching was viewed by hundreds of visitors from Vallejo, San Francisco, and elsewhere, many of whom jammed the steamers *Wilson G. Hunt, Carquinez* and *Active* on the river.

The California christening champagne had hardly spattered the bows before a letter was on its way west from Washington with orders that the vessel's name be changed to *Saganaw.* This was done, with a misspelling to add spice, and the side-wheeler lived out her active life as the *Saginaw.*

She dropped down to San Francisco for her engines, borrowed anchors and cables from the *John Hancock* (her own had not yet arrived from Boston) and, with coal borrowed from the Pacific Mail Steamship Line, was ready for her trial run. This was a great success. The *Saginaw* plowed through choppy seas on the broad bay and the yard engineer, Mr. Sewell, reported her boilers steamed in great style on "pure sea water." Her commander, James Findley Schenck, was satisfied she was ready for duty and he took her out the Gate on March 5th, bound for China.

The *Saginaw* returned home in plenty of time to participate in the alarums and excursions of San Francisco's Civil War jitters, as we will see in the account of Asbury Harpending's privateer plot. But her chief ordeal was yet to come.

When the little side-wheeler put into San Francisco Bay in the winter of 1869–70, she was a tired ship. Sent to Mare Island after a plodding cruise on the west coast of Mexico, she brought home a weakened crew. In Manzanillo her men had contracted "coast fever," with twenty-five hands down at one time. Luckily, only one death resulted. She had then labored up the coast under sail, for her engines were disabled, and was so long in reaching the Golden Gate that when she finally did arrive there was not a half-day's supply of provisions aboard. The officers had been on ship's grub along with the grumbling crew for many days.

An immediate refitting was necessary for the *Saginaw* because she had been chosen by the Government to take charge of operations at Midway Island which were expected to turn that lonely mid-Pacific atoll into a coaling station for the Pacific Mail Steamship Company's Orient liners. Lt. Commander Montgomery Sicard, commander of the *Saginaw,* was to superintend the work of deepening and widening the one channel through the island's enclosing reef. A contract for the work was let to an experienced Boston engineer and the *Saginaw* was charged with the transportation of workers and materials to the island.

A schooner, loaded with supplies for the contractor, was sent ahead and on February 22, 1870, the *Saginaw*'s paddles chunked past Mile Rock, shrouded in fog, and bit into whitecaps spawned by a stiff southeaster. Fourteen days out, mostly under sail, she sighted the Island of Molokai. The next day, March 9th, she ran into Honolulu harbor and her arrival was duly noted in the April 1 issue of *The Friend.*

The *Saginaw* was, of course, no stranger to Honolulu. The same paper had given her an enthusiastic *aloha* on March 20, 1859, when the paint was still fresh and crisp on her paddle boxes. Schenck, with fifty-nine officers and men, had spent ten days in Honolulu at that time before continuing on to Hong Kong. *The Friend* had described her then:

> Her model is a most beautiful one, and as a specimen of naval architecture, she reflects credit on California shipbuilders. She was built at Mare Island and is intended especially for the service of the American Minister in China. She has more the appearance of a merchantman than of a war steamer.

The *Saginaw* spent only six days in Honolulu on her March 1870 visit, refitting and obtaining fresh fruit and other provisions. She then sailed for Midway and reached the island on March 24th, easing through Seward Roads into Welles' Harbor at eight in the evening. Commander Sicard discovered that there was hardly enough room in the anchorage (called a "harbor" in rank optimism) to swing his ship. The officers and crew inspected Midway with a jaundiced eye and found it even worse than they had anticipated. To the crew it was just a barren, desolate island of blowing and drifting sand. The only evidences of life were goonies, or brown albatrosses, and a few seals.

(Captain N. C. Brooks of the Hawaiian bark *Gambia* had discovered the two little sandspits in their coral-reefed lagoon on July 9, 1859. He mapped them, raised the U. S. flag over them and shyly dubbed them Brooks Island and Brooks Shoal. They were again visited in August 1867 when the U.S.S. *Lackawanna* surveyed and charted them.)

The day after the *Saginaw* arrived at Midway Island, the contractor's schooner *Kate Piper* came to anchor. She was just in time to be greeted by a fierce gale which whipped up at dusk. It blew so hard that the little *Saginaw*, with both anchors down, was forced to work her engines constantly to keep from being piled up on the waiting reef.

During April the reef and the bar were surveyed while the contractor's house was built. (It was later used, for years, by other work parties and shipwrecked survivors—from the *General Siegel* and the *Wandering Minstrel*—and probably still stands today.) The scow for the divers was completed and launched also.

Since Sicard was charged with the task of making monthly progress reports, he took the side-wheel steamer on several back-and-forth trips to Honolulu. These voyages were made mostly under sail and proved to be as monotonous as duty on station at Midway. The old *Saginaw* was not only underpowered in her engines but was also a poor sailor. On one passage she met headwinds and made only twenty miles in two days! The only solace in her voyages was the mail for the lonely men which she picked up in Honolulu.

The steamer returned to Midway for the last time on October

12, 1870. The appropriation of $50,000 had been spent in blasting a channel, divers having tried to dislodge the coral blocking the "harbor" entrance by detonating canisters of powder. About five tons of rock had been blasted loose and broken up in this fashion. The work was carried on in intermittent fashion during September and October when weather permitted, but frequent strong westerly gales blew right into the mouth of the harbor and made work dangerous when not impossible. Blowing sand made goggles constantly necessary for the workmen. Six months of powder and labor resulted in a passage through the reef only fifteen feet wide and four hundred feet long. It was obvious to all that the $50,000 appropriation would be just a drop in the bucket. The estimated essential width of the channel was one hundred and seventy feet.

Paymaster George H. Read voiced the opinion of other officers when he wrote that he thought the underwater jungle of jagged reefs around Midway would make a poor anchorage for large steamers. The sea broke heavily on the reef and the mouth of the lagoon faced the west where the prevailing winds piled up water, making the entrance to the sheltered lagoon impassable for a vessel except with a smooth sea.

On Friday, traditionally a bad day to sail, October 28, 1870, the *Saginaw* flew her homeward-bound pennants and put to sea with the contractor's working party. The house had been shut up and the scow dragged high up on the beach beyond the reach of the sea. When the steamer reached the open sea, Captain Sicard ordered her headed to the westward under reduced steam. With topsails set, she sailed under a light easterly breeze to call at Kure Island or, as it was more commonly called, Ocean Island. Vague reports of a wreck on the atoll had reached Sicard and he wished to determine if any castaways were marooned on the lonely island. Further, he wished to verify its position by steaming around it before continuing on to San Francisco.

Ocean Island lay some fifty miles to the west of Midway and was almost a dead-ringer for the latter in general appearance. Charles Darwin had singled it out in his book *The Structure and Distribution of Coral Reefs,* published in 1842, as a prime example of the true coral atoll as distinguished from the "high" island girdled by a reef: To seafarers, however, Ocean Island was best known as a navigational hazard. The British ship *Gledstanes* ran on its reef at midnight July 9, 1837. All of the crew were saved but one seaman who, drunk (if we can believe the temperance-advocating *Friend* of Honolulu), jumped overboard and drowned. Captain J. R. Brown and his crew were on the island for five months, during which time they built a schooner from parts of the wreck. The captain, chief mate, and eight seamen then sailed to Hawaii. The officers and men left on the atoll suffered greatly until they were rescued by a vessel sent for them by the British consul in Honolulu.

Captain Brown described the island as lying in latitude 28° 22′ North and 178° 30′ West. About three miles in circumference, it was made up of decomposed coral and shells with a fringe of low bushes growing in the sandy soil near the shore. It abounded with sea birds during certain seasons of the year and hair seals were also found on its beaches. The highest point on the island was only about ten feet above sea level and the only fresh water was seepage after heavy rains.

Another wreck occurred on Ocean Island the very year that Darwin's book mentioned the barren spot. The whaleship *Parker* of New Bedford had lost her captain, Prince Sherman, when his boat capsized and was stove December 14, 1841. George W. Smith, first officer, took the command but held it only until September 1842 when he ran the *Parker* onto Ocean Island's treacherous reef. Four of his men drowned but twenty-three survived. The ship, with its cargo of 2,000 barrels of sperm oil and 1,000 barrels of right whale oil, was a complete loss. The castaways spent eight days and seven nights on the reef, days of extreme hunger and thirst, until they were able to drift across the lagoon on a raft to the island itself. They warped in and found the remains of the *Gledstanes* and, like the *Saginaw's* crew twenty-eight years later, used it for a supply of firewood and building materials. The only living things they found were sea birds, seals and a dog from the *Gledstanes*. The cur had gone wild but was caught after some weeks and eaten to vary their diet. During their stay on the atoll the crew killed sixty seals and seven thousand birds for food. From the wreck of the *Parker* they got copper with which they made cooking utensils. One hundred and twenty sea birds were sent off with messages for help attached to their legs. After six months of constant watch, a lookout spied a sail. Signals were made and on April 17, 1843, the *James Stewart*, Captain Smith, took off the *Parker's* Captain Smith and three men, leaving twenty on the island but well supplied with food and clothing. Smith expected to bring the *Stewart* back shortly to pick up the rest of the men but another vessel, the whaleship *Nassau*, Captain Weeks, came by on May 2nd and took them off.

The officers and men of the *Saginaw* were not exhilarated at the prospect of going home. They dreaded the long, tedious passage of more than 3,000 miles to San Francisco. It would have to be made under sail to conserve coal, they knew, and in a headwind the old *Saginaw* had a tendency to make "eight points to leeward" (that is, go sideways). Ocean Island would be the only break in the voyage until Honolulu and the men looked forward to seeing the island the next morning if only for that reason. "Lights out" was sounded at 9 P.M. and the ship was left in the care of the lookouts who called "All's well!" every half-hour. With the *Saginaw* traveling at about three knots, Sicard expected to raise Ocean Island by dawn. He should have plenty of time to circumnavigate the island and to get a good offing before the next night fell.

About 3 A.M., those of the sixty-four man crew and fifteen

57

civilians of the contractor's party who were asleep were rudely awakened by a commotion on deck and the sound of running feet. The captain's voice cut through the babble, ordering the topsails to be taken in and the topsail halyards cut away. According to the coxswain, the "crew became paralyzed [but] owing to the exertions of the officers who worked bravely and well, the sails were taken in." Orders to furl the topsails were obeyed but the sails became unmanageable and the task was given up.

The steamer had been making a steady three knots, with fires banked and topsail and jib set, when Sicard came on deck at 2 A.M. Mr. Garst, officer of the deck, relieved Mr. Coles and informed the captain of breakers ahead. Sicard immediately gave the orders to take in sail.

Suddenly the ship struck, but easily. However, the first shock was followed by another, and another, each stronger than the preceding one. The *Saginaw* was being tossed in the breakers that smashed on the reef of Ocean Island. The swells lifted and dropped the steamer with tremendous thumps which shook the whole ship.

Paymaster Read, like Coxswain Halford, noted the terror on board ship at the moment of the disaster and compared it with the shock effects of an earthquake tremor. The good old *Saginaw* had been cursed and belittled by her crew for years but she had always gotten through safely. Now she was dying under their feet.

Sicard's orders to take in sail were followed by an attempt to back engines. The steam pressure was too low to do more than turn the paddle wheels over a few times and this did not even overcome the momentum of the ship, much less fight the current setting in toward the reef.

Some of the crew skulked below decks, looted the wardroom liquor cabinet and became drunk on the officers' ale and claret, quite unable to work.

The pounding of the jagged reef against her laurelwood hull ripped the *Saginaw* open within an hour and water rushed into the engine room and put out the fires. Coxswain Halford later recalled the situation: "The vessel could not have been saved; even if she had got off the reef, she would have sunk like a stone."

The night was clear and starlit but land could not be seen and it was thought at first that they had struck some outlying, uncharted reef. The boats were launched in the lee of the *Saginaw* and the crew anxiously waited for daylight.

Sicard's crisp commands restored order out of confusion after some of the crew rushed to lower the launch, the largest boat, which was hanging at the starboard quarter. When it was only partially lowered a towering comber smashed it into kindling against the ship's side. This was a great loss, for Sicard had counted on the launch to save them should a long voyage be necessary.

The same wave carried off one of the Marine guards who had been on the bulwarks but, miraculously, tossed him back into the lee of the ship. His cries attracted rescuers who hauled him aboard at the stern, waterlogged and bruised but otherwise unharmed.

The Negro wardroom steward quieted many jumpy nerves by sitting on a hatch of the hurricane deck, whistling "Way Down Upon the Suwanee River," while his double irons, placed on him for some offense, were chiseled off. Once free, he busied himself rescuing food supplies and comported himself so well that Captain Sicard did not renew his confinement on the island.

The ship had struck bow-on but gradually swung around, although both anchors had been let go. For a time she lay broadside to the reef but then shifted until her stern, where most of the men were huddled, overhung the reef. The bow lay directly to seaward for an hour while the vessel seesawed with the waves. Then the forward section broke off and disappeared in the deep water outside the reef. The aftersection tipped over onto the inner side of the reef and the smokestack toppled over the side. Sicard ordered the starboard (seaward) shrouds cut to allow the mainmast to follow the stack. The mast was then used by the men as a bridge to the reef. Four boats were saved: the double-ended whaleboat used as the captain's gig, one of the cutters, the dinghy, and an iron lifeboat belonging to the contractor. Dawn showed the men that they had an island nearby where they could rest, at least. Sicard realized that it was Ocean Island.

Two very sick men were taken ashore, then four or five others who were not quite so ill. A line of men was next formed across the reef and provisions were passed hand to hand to the four boats in the lagoon and thence to the island itself. The men had their feet and ankles lacerated by the sharp coral as they stood in waist-deep water but were cheered by their luck in being wrecked on an island rather than a submerged rock or shoal just awash. The line passed supplies ashore until five in the afternoon when orders were given to abandon the wreck. As the sun set, all hands were piped to supper by the boatswain. The meal consisted of a half-teacup of water, a tiny piece of boiled pork and another of boiled mutton, and half a cake of hardtack for each man.

After dinner, all hands were mustered on the beach to hear a prayer of thanksgiving led by Captain Sicard, for their deliverance from the sea. He then apprised them of their situation, explaining that Navy Regulations held him responsible for law and order among his castaway crew just as aboard ship. He promised that officers and men would share alike the stores which were salvaged. He then dismissed them to get some rest.

After fourteen hours of hard labor on the reef, in the lagoon and on the beach, the men dropped where they stood and fell asleep.

The next day was Sunday but the Sabbath was not kept. Light

winds and calm seas left the wreck in position for still further salvage. Bread, even tiny fragments, and bags of flour were spread out to dry in the sun. The hair seals and goonies were found to be easily captured and killed to supplement their rations. The men were ordered not to collect the goony eggs, however, for fear of driving the birds away from the island.

Only a few water kegs were recovered for the ninety-three men and it looked as if a supply of drinking water would be the major problem of the castaways. Wells were dug immediately but the water was found to be too brackish for drinking.

One party stripped the bones of the old *Gledstanes* for firewood, while another foraging party revisited the wreck of the *Saginaw*. When they returned they joined the others in a dinner of scouse, a Navy dish composed of pork, potatoes and hardtack. A campsite was laid out with sails and awnings for cover, and a small boiler, used by the contractor to supply power for lifting coral fragments into the scow at Midway, was landed. A barrel of sperm oil and a lantern were also found and brought ashore with clothing, blankets, and the carpenter's chest.

The wreck of the *Saginaw* was stripped hurriedly but thoroughly for they feared she might be swept off the reef at any moment. For the time being, everything retrieved from her was piled helter-skelter on the beach—rigging, crockery, sails, canned goods and tools.

One match was saved from the wreck and a fire carefully started and nursed along. The small boiler was set up on the beach and connected to some distilling coils, canvas hose and a length of the pilothouse speaking tube. The fire was stoked, the steam was passed under the cooler water of the lagoon and condensed to return to a bucket on the beach. The immediate problem of drinking water was thus solved. Coffee was served with a quarter-ration of scouse but the hardtack was spoiling rapidly. Paymaster Read opened a wet bag of flour and found to his delight that it was all sweet and sound except for an outside

61

crust formed by the action of the sea water. A barrel of beans was also found in good condition and put in the custody of a sentry.

On November 1st, the crew was formed into watches and messes, each provided with a tent. They were all given jobs to prevent their brooding over their misfortune. The next day a high wind came up with a heavy rain and the men were kept busy—and wet to the skin—in just saving the tents.

The derelict *Saginaw* was now completely robbed of her contents, but the captain desired to use her timbers to build a seaworthy boat in which to send word to Hawaii of the fate of his ship and her complement. Sicard ordered his senior officers to file a secret, written opinion on the feasibility of such a plan.

Pieces of the *Saginaw* began to break off and were retrieved once the storm allowed the boats to be launched in the lagoon. The captain, Coxswain Halford, and the crew of the gig went to a nearby sandspit for driftwood and were caught by the storm and marooned there, huddled under their upturned boat. When the storm abated they returned not only with wood but, even more welcome, with some large sea turtles. Rats—descendants of castaways from the *Gledstanes* and *Parker*—robbed the men of their precious macaroni, and a storehouse was built on posts with inverted pans on them to keep the rodents off. The drinking-water problem was eased when fifty gallons of rainwater were caught during the storm. An extra cupful per man was doled out.

Sicard decided to use the gig to make an attempt to reach the Sandwich Islands, 1,100 miles ESE as the albatross flies but more like 1,800 miles by a boat at the mercy of wind and current. The boat was carried well up on the beach and set in a cradle. Her sides were raised eight inches amidships, tapering back to four inches at bow and stern. She was decked over, fitted with two masts and sails, and four square hatches with covers were fitted into her deck. In these the men could sit and row if the wind should be too light or contrary for sail. New sails were sewed on the island and the cutter's spars were used to give the gig as much sail as she could carry.

Lt. John G. Talbot, a clean-shaven (before the wreck) young man in a hirsute age, volunteered the day after the wreck to make the cruise to Hawaii for help. Several crewmen immediately volunteered to go with him and soon so many had stepped forward that it was necessary to pick and choose in order to get the men most likely to stand up well under the fatigue and exposure of a small-boat journey. The men were all aware that the "forlorn hope" expedition would be made in a frail and almost open boat, whereas the *Gledstanes'* crew had spent five months in building a seaworthy boat for their escape.

Still, life on Ocean Island went on. A large part of the *Saginaw* hurricane deck floated ashore one day and was greeted happily as a source of timber and nails for boatbuilding. Goonies were cooked all day long by Solomon Graves, cabin cook and "King of the Galley," but they were still terribly tough. Seal meat was even worse; it was parboiled overnight and fried in the morning. Smokers were generously given stogies by Passed Assistant Engineer Blye whose box of five hundred Manila cigars had been rescued.

The mainmast was laboriously raised on the highest point of the island as a lookout and a signal station but one of the guys parted and it crashed down. As it was being set up again, one of the men scooped up some of the water which had collected in the bottom of the hole dug to take the butt of the mast. "Boys!" he shouted. "Fresh water, by God!" They had found a pocket of sand-filtered rainwater only twenty feet from the salt water of the beach. The water was welcome in their sparse and tedious diet—Adam's ale, boobies or goonies, pork scouse, salt beef, dough balls of moldy flour, seal meat and sea turtle. The men decided not to eat the highly colored fish of the lagoon for fear they were poisonous relatives of the West Indian parrot fish. Should their provisions give out, they planned to start on the rats first, rather than the gaudy fish of the lagoon. The hated rodents swarmed over the island and the crew was engaged in a constant running battle with them.

On Sunday, November 13, the ship began to break up rapidly. Two days later the gig was finished and launched. Talbot was given letters by many of the men, while Read gave him his revolver and $200 in gold coin for possible expenses.

Calm weather, moonlit nights and balmy days (70° by day and 50° by night) compensated somewhat for stomachs either empty or rebellious from eating seal meat. Some men played chess with a set made of goony bones and blocks of wood while Mr. Main made a sextant from the face of the *Saginaw's* steam gauge, bits of a broken stateroom mirror, and scraps of zinc. Its scale was drawn on the zinc with a cambric needle and the instrument, when tested, was found accurate enough for navigation of the boat. Other officers made a duplicate of the official chart of the central Pacific and copied all the necessary tables from the *Nautical Almanac*. Read selected the best-preserved supplies from the storehouse to supply Talbot and his crew with thirty-five days of half-rations.

Wednesday, November 16, was chosen as the day to sail but bad weather blew up and the sailing date was postponed to fair (but unlucky) Friday, November 18, 1870. The men surrounded the twenty-two-foot gig and carried it bodily into the water. She was anchored and the stores passed out to her while James Butterworth, passed assistant engineer, put on the finishing touches by screwing oarlocks to the gunwales.

Ten casks of water were issued the gig, with five days' rations of hardtack in tins plus ten days' ration of the same in canvas bags, two cans of cooked beans, three tins of "boiled wheaten grits," one ham weighing about eight or ten pounds, six tins of preserved oysters, ten pounds of dried beef, five pounds of butter, twelve pounds of white sugar, one gallon of

64

molasses, four pounds of tea and five pounds of coffee. A small, tin oil-burning stove was improvised for the gig. Read was about to place aboard twenty-five pounds of boiled rice in tins when he noticed that one of the cans was swollen. The cans were opened and the rice was found to be spoiled. Five large cans, weighing five pounds each, of dried potatoes took the place of the rice; the cans were scalded and sealed.

There was little conversation at the last meal before the gig sailed. Read reported Talbot the most unconcerned of all, but knew he was putting on a good show of confidence to encourage those who had to stay behind. He gave Read his will, to be forwarded to his family in Kentucky if he should not survive the voyage. Letters were placed aboard the gig together with official papers and a bill of exchange for £200 sterling, all sealed airtight in a tin box.

As the time of departure, 4 p.m., drew near, prayers and good-byes were said. The five men shook hands with their comrades and waded out into the chest-high water to the gig, stepped the masts, spread the miniature sails and stood out across the lagoon and through the channel in the reef. Those on shore gave them three cheers and a tiger and watched them disappear on the northern horizon.

There had been intense rivalry in Camp Saginaw for the honor of being chosen to risk one's life in the gig, two men even wrestling for the chance of going. The loser was to waive all claims to the winner. Actually, it was up to one man besides Captain Sicard to choose the crew—the doctor, Assistant Surgeon Adam Frank.

The first man selected was an easy choice. William Halford was not only the regular coxswain of the gig, familiar with its handling, but he was a strapping young man of twenty-eight and the best seaman on the *Saginaw*. (Not all sailors, especially in the steam navy, were good *seamen,* it must be remembered.) Halford recalled in later years, "I knew it was going to be a

65

hard trip and I suppose the others knew it also. I had had two experiences of this kind before, one in the South Atlantic and one in the North Atlantic, but not for so long a distance."

Accompanying Talbot and the young coxswain were Quartermaster Peter Francis of Boston and two landsmen from G. W. Townsend's contract party, specially enlisted as seamen by Lt. Commander Sicard for the period of one month: James Muir of Glasgow, and John Andrews from Manila and the principal diver of the work party. They were chosen over the regular crewmen because, in Sicard's words, "They were men of such fine qualities and endurance that I thought it proper to let them go."

After the gig sailed, the men left on Ocean Island kept occupied building the schooner upon which they would have to depend should the gig fail them. The keel was hewed from the *Saginaw*'s topmast, and old deck planks were ripsawed in two with a salvaged bucksaw and handsaw to make the planking for the hull. It was forty feet long, flat-bottomed, with a centerboard. Captain Sicard first experimented with models and was advised by one of the contractor's carpenters who had had experience in boatbuilding. He also ordered the cutter fitted out for a passage to Midway where he planned to erect a sign to indicate to any search vessels where the *Saginaw*'s crew was shipwrecked.

Christmas and New Years came. Talbot had been gone forty-three days. But, on Tuesday, January 3, 1871, the island was turned into bedlam.

At three-thirty Paymaster Read was working alongside Mr. Mitchell, one of the contractor's carpenters. He had just handed him a nail when he noticed the carpenter squinting and staring intently to seaward. Read looked too and on the horizon saw something which made his heart pound. It was a sail! Or was it just a cloud? It began to grow in size and density and Mitchell said quietly, not wishing to give a false alarm (Sicard had issued orders warning against this), "Paymaster, I believe that is the smoke of a steamer."

The carpenter looked again. "I am sure of it."

Before he or Read could sing out, a shout arose that all the island could hear, "Sail ho!"

All "alarms" were supposed to be reported quietly to Captain Sicard for verification. But now the order was forgotten and Sicard's face was beaming with joy; he paid no attention to the violation of his order. This was no false alarm. He ordered Read to the lookout with his glasses.

Read trained his binoculars on the shadow on the horizon which was growing into the outlines of a steamer, trailed by a long thin line of smoke. She was heading westward and not directly toward Ocean Island. Read felt his heart thumping in anxiety over whether it might pass them by.

Above his head the distress flag waved, as if encouraging the steamer to come in. When she arrived at a point almost due north of Camp Saginaw, she changed course, her masts came into line and it was obvious to Read that she was running down to the island. He shouted the news to the men below and slid down the Jacob's ladder, pale and speechless.

It took him some time to recover his voice but at last he stammered out his report to Lt. Commander Sicard and the eavesdropping men. By the time he was through, the steamer was in plain sight from ground level and the rough navy men were embracing one another, many with tears coursing down their cheeks as they cried and laughed in the hysteria of relief.

Sicard ordered Read at once to break out the best meal he could concoct from their limited supplies and the castaways dined in style on boiled salt pork, flour, beans and coffee. Read recalled, "I felt as I might after a Delmonico dinner."

The vessel was recognized as the *Kilauea,* the King of Hawaii's own steamer. Coming within half a mile of the reef where the *Saginaw's* bones lay, she dipped her ensign and then steamed slowly away. It was too late in the day for her to risk the dangers of the reef in any attempt to effect a rescue at night. The *Saginaw*'s crew realized that they would have to wait until morning for deliverance from their sandspit prison. That night the men danced around a huge bonfire on the highest point of the island, cheering and singing while all night they fed the fire with timbers once almost worth their weight in gold.

At daybreak the *Kilauea* was back and anchored near the west entrance to the lagoon, from which the gig had departed. The steamer's commander, Captain Thomas Long, came ashore in a whaleboat. He was given three thunderous cheers by the sailors as he stepped out of the boat. While the crew stood at attention, Sicard went down to receive him. They greeted one another very cordially, then conferred soberly for a few minutes while the men, uneasy, tried not to stir in ranks. Sicard then held up his hand to command silence.

"Men, I have the great sorrow to announce to you that we have been saved at great sacrifice. Lieutenant Talbot and three of the gig's crew are dead."

He promised to give full particulars later but informed them that Captain Long wanted them to remove themselves to the *Kilauea* as fast as possible. The men needed no urging, but a low, muted sound of grief passed along the line of men as they heard of the gig crew's fate. Sicard bowed his head and others followed suit.

Captain Long asked the shipwrecked men if there was anything they wanted particularly. Tobacco was immediately asked for and a box of it sent ashore and opened on the beach before the men and equipment were embarked.

Read took the *Saginaw*'s safe and papers aboard the *Kilauea* on the first of the boats. Since Long was charged with only the rescue of the men, and not the salvaging of U. S. Government property, most of the food and equipment was collected and stored at the highest point of the island. The water supply was carefully labeled with a sign as an aid to any future castaways. After sixty-seven days on Kure or Ocean Island, the crew boarded the *Kilauea* and steamed to Honolulu.

The *Kona Packet,* a fast schooner dispatched to the succor of the shipwrecked crew by the American Minister in Honolulu, was sighted in the offing as the *Kilauea* left Ocean Island. Captain Long ran down to her and ordered her back to Honolulu. She had left seven hours after word of the crew's plight was carried to Honolulu by William Halford, but the *Kilauea,* put by the King at the service of humanity, had passed her en route to Ocean Island.

Read heard two of the *Saginaw's* men discussing the unhappy choice of sailing dates on the cruise. The traditionally unlucky Friday was the day the *Saginaw* left Midway, and the gig left Ocean Island on a Friday. The death of four of her crew was attributed to this black day of sailor superstition. One of the seamen said of his shipmate, "How Halford escaped is a mystery to me; but I guess he'll think twice before venturing on another voyage on that day of the week."

The gig had left Ocean Island on November 18th, being hauled up on the wind on the starboard tack to stand to the northward and eastward for three days, making good progress in fair weather. As they ran north, it began to get colder and the winds grew more variable. At latitude 32° the wind hauled around to the northwest and blew strong in their favor. They began to make good easting but the winds became too strong and they had to heave to.

It was Talbot's plan to run south until they reached the longitude of Kauai. However, they were off a full degree of longitude in their calculations, though they did not know it at the time.

Five days out found them without light or heat, when they lost their combination lantern-stove overboard. Though they had flint and steel, there was no tinder or dry wood aboard—

everything was wet through as a result of the leaking of the deck and the upper works—so they were without a fire until within five days of Kauai when the resourceful Halford started one, using a lens taken from an opera glass to focus the sun's rays into a hot circle in a handful of oakum and canvas.

Halford did not waste the sperm-oil fuel for the lost lantern-stove. He proposed to the other men that they use it on the potatoes. They all tried it but were so weakened that they could not keep it on their stomachs and Halford had the oil, "which helped me so much," he reported, all to himself.

While running eastward they met hard weather and had to heave to with their sea anchor out. On the second occasion that they put it to use, the line parted and they lost the sea anchor and part of the cable. They then made a drag of three oars but this also was lost. They made a third sea anchor out of two crossed oars and a square of sail which lasted them for three long turns of dirty weather before it too broke adrift and followed its fellows.

The five men suffered terribly from the wet, the cold, and from both want of food and the effects of what food they did have. The ten days' ration of food in the canvas bags they found to be mostly spoiled. The bread was a colorful, flourishing colony of mold. The two cans of beans were swollen and when opened, the tins sighed sickeningly and a fermented, odorous mess was revealed. They should have been pitched overboard but the men pinched their noses and forced the putrescent food down. They had to eat in order to live. As a result, they suffered from dysentery and perhaps botulism.

Halford later wrote, "To have continued using them would have killed us all, so we held a consultation and decided to throw them overboard and put ourselves on shorter rations."

The boiled wheat had fermented and gave them cramps and diarrhea also. The gallon of molasses leaked out into the bilge and the sugar, coffee and tea were spoiled by being wet through with salt water. Luckily, they had plenty of fresh water. The gig was ballasted with it and at the end of the trip there was still a great deal of drinking water left.

The one thing which got them through short of starvation was the supply of "dessicated potatoes," part of U.S. Navy rations at that time and sometimes called "evaporated potatoes." These great-grandfathers of the much maligned G.I. dried potatoes of World War II were in five-pound tins given them at the last minute by Paymaster Read when he discovered that the rice set aside for the gig was spoiled. The insipid mess, soaked in fresh water to swell in size, was served out in a ration of first three, and later two, teaspoons a day. It was eaten cold since they had lost their stove.

After twenty-five days, their food ran out entirely. About three days later, on the first warm day since leaving the island, Halford was at the tiller while the others lay sleeping on deck in the sun. A large booby landed on the deck and eyed the helmsman. Halford remembered, "I was afraid to rouse the others for fear of frightening the bird. I crawled along the deck and grabbed him. He didn't attempt to move. Wringing its neck, as I did not want to lose any of the blood, I just stripped off the feathers, divided it into five parts and served it up as it was. I can assure you that nothing was wasted. That was the first food we had for three days, except a drop of water, and it was the last for two days more."

Just before he sighted land, Halford was again at the tiller and the other four below. At daybreak he felt something strike against him. He grabbed it quickly and found a small flying fish about four or five inches long. A whole school came near the gig and quite a number landed on deck. Six were captured by the coxswain for breakfast, which led him to remark, "It seemed that someone was looking out for us."

One day when they were running before a gale under reefed square sail in a nasty sea, the gig struck an object with a tremendous shock. The boat was on the point of capsizing but the next sea carried her over the obstruction. Halford, standing in the afterhatch steering, looked astern to see a huge log, waterlogged and barely awash, forty or fifty feet long and about five feet in diameter.

On a bright moonlit night when the boat was making about three knots, Halford relieved Francis at the tiller and the latter crawled forward on the lee side of the deck toward one of the hatches, but slipped and fell overboard. Halford did not see him go but heard his cries for help. Fortunately, a fishing line had trailed overboard behind the gig ever since they had left Ocean Island and Francis was able to grab this. Halford hauled him aboard before the others even got on deck, Francis proving to be the only "catch" made by the fishing gear during the entire trip.

These were the only two dramatic brushes with death but a much more insidious and deadly companion was on the gig with them—illness. Muir and Andrews never got over the dysentery. Talbot recovered somewhat after seven or eight days but was very weak thereafter, though he remained cheerful. Francis was not so badly off but he did not regain his strength after he partially recovered from attacks of dysentery. It became more and more evident that the fate of all five lives rested in the still-strong hands of the coxswain, William Halford.

Luckily, Halford's rugged constitution was not badly affected by the spoiled stores and, although he was hungry, cold and at times nearly exhausted, he was able to stand his own trick at the tiller and fill in for the others when they were too weak to be of any use.

As another day broke, Halford scanned the horizon with saltsore eyes, searching for anything to break the dead, flat line of the horizon—land, a sail, a light . . . He thought he made out a dark mass astern but would not trust his eyes until the light grew. Then he saw it—Kawaihoa Point. This was the tip of

Niihau Island, the southwesternmost point in all the Hawaiian Islands.

A breakfast of raw flying fish and the sight of land cheered the sickly men immensely. (Halford recalled later how at this time "Muir, Andrews and Mr. Talbot were very weak from hunger and cold. Francis was stronger, but I could see he was failing fast this last week. I had lost considerable weight.") Muir and Andrews laboriously bailed the boat out, trying to keep ahead of a sea which crept in through the leaky upper works and the bottom's seams, opened when the gig rode over the huge log.

It was Friday morning—a lucky Friday?—December 16, 1870. They had sighted land just a week after they had expected to make Kauai. All save the coxswain at the tiller were living skeletons, "very weak from want of food and from dysentery; they were more dead than alive," but his shout of "Land ho!"— more croak than a shout—roused his moribund comrades from their lethargy and gave them new strength.

Finding that they were sixty to seventy miles southwest of what they thought their position would be, the men put the boat around on the starboard tack and stood up to northward in hopes the wind would haul around to the north so they could make a Niihau landfall on the other tack. The island was in sight, but far to windward.

"The wind kept hauling around to SW and came to blow a regular Kona, with wind, rain, thunder and lightning, but the wind was in our favor, so we made direct for the Island of Kauai and got off Black Head Sunday evening, December 19, '70," wrote Halford later.

It was a dark and dirty night. It was Halford's turn at the tiller and Lieutenant Talbot was also on deck but the other three men were below. Halford asked Talbot if he planned to remain outside or to try to run into Hanalei harbor, Kauai. Talbot was in such low spirits that Halford suggested they shorten sail and head the boat out from land until daylight. He explained that the harbor entrance was narrow, the night was darkening with clouds, and that they had stood so much for so long that one more night on the boat would not be too bad. Talbot agreed to all this so Halford shortened sail and headed her out, away from the harbor entrance. They hove to with the boat's head to the northwest.

The two men continued talking, with Halford doing his best to cheer up the lieutenant by telling him that their troubles were over and picturing what a fine time they would all have ashore in the morning. Talbot was in a pessimistic mood, however, and replied, "Halford, although we are very near the land, I don't think I will ever reach it alive."

Many years later, Halford described the incident. "I tried to laugh him out of it, for I felt very different about it. I knew that I would pull through all right no matter what happened. I got him to lie down and told him that I would stay up all night and let the others rest, for it seemed that I had more than my natural strength. The last two or three days, I could see poor Francis failing, and if he gave up it would be hard on me."

Talbot stayed below only an hour or two, then returned on deck around 1 A.M. with Andrews and Francis. The lieutenant insisted that Halford go below and get some sleep. The coxswain protested but did as he was told and, worn out, fell asleep.

After Halford went below, the boat was kept away again toward land for a short time but again hove to. At a little past 2 A.M., Talbot brought her farther in and hove to for the third time. When Halford awoke, the boat was running before the wind. He called up to ask where they were going but got no answer and fell asleep again. The motion of the boat awoke him once more and he knew that they were in shoal water. She was again off before the wind and close to the line of breakers. The boom of the surf was now close, too close.

Halford had no time to get out of the hatch. He heard Talbot sing out, "Put your helm down; haul aft your mainsheet and get out of this!" The coxswain shouted up that it was too late for that; the only thing to do was to drive her through the surf before she hit broadside. However Francis, at the tiller, obeyed his commander's orders and the "Aye, aye, sir" was hardly torn away from his lips by the wind when the gig swung into the breakers broadside and rolled over.

Halford had jumped up and awakened Muir when he heard the surf, telling the Scotsman to get on deck. The sleepy Muir remained below but Halford, starting to go on deck, was thrown out of the hatch as the gig capsized. Andrews and Francis were washed away and Halford did not see them again. The last he saw of Muir, the latter was trying to blink sleep from his eyes below deck.

Halford surfaced close to the boat, his arm becoming entangled in some of the rigging. A bight tightened around his wrist and held him fast. He pulled himself up to the boat and found that Talbot was clinging to the bilge. Halford called to him, "Get to the stern and climb up on the bottom; I will follow you."

While the lieutenant was trying to do so, the next rollers came in and turned the boat over and over. Talbot lost his hold and was washed off. Exhausted and heavily clothed, he did not have a chance in the rough surf and sank.

After the rollers had passed in their shoreward dash, Halford got up on the bottom of the gig and stripped off all his clothing, even his money belt. He kept the line fast around his wrist. Another breaker came in and crashed upon the boat. She rolled over twice but ended right side up. By now she was over the reef and inside the big breakers.

The coxswain thought he was alone on the boat until he heard a terrible groan which gave him more of a shock than the actual capsizing.

"I couldn't see anything until a flash of lightning came and showed me a dark object crawling out of one of the hatches. It didn't look like a human being. Anyway, I thought myself alone, but I roused myself and grasped it. It was only poor Muir. He had been under deck all the time, inside the boat. It must have been like a diving bell, but the poor fellow was crazy."

Halford made Muir fast to the gig with a piece of gear which was washing around and waited for the boat to drift across the mile or so of comparatively smooth water to the beach. Some instinct told him to keep to windward, so he hauled in a piece of one of the masts, which had carried away when the gig capsized, and used it as a pole to keep her head up. It was a lucky decision. He found that if he had gone only another twenty-five or thirty feet to leeward the gig would have been dashed on the rocks. He stayed on the boat until it was in about five feet of water off a beautiful, shelving, sandy beach.

Halford landed in breast-high water, taking with him the tin box of dispatches and letters which he had lashed to the after-thwart only the preceding afternoon. The other tin box had a broken cover and during the capsizing had spewed forth its contents upon the waves—Sicard's instructions to Talbot; the discharge papers of civilians Muir and Andrews; transfer papers and accounts of Francis and Halford, destined for Mare Island.

It was 3 A.M., December 19, 1870, when Halford waded ashore at Kalihiwai, five miles east of Hanalei, with the tin box fastened across his shoulders like a life preserver. It was just thirty-one days since the farewell handclasps of Ocean Island.

He then took the moaning, incoherent Muir ashore and they dropped on the beach above high-water mark where Halford tried to "rest and think." Strangely, he found himself very restless, despite his extreme fatigue. Partly because of Muir's ravings ("he gave symptoms of insanity"), the only sounds of life on the lonely beach, he plunged back into the sea where the boat was aground, full of water, between a quarter- and half-mile from shore.

Although staggering with nervous and physical exhaustion, the indomitable sailor made three more trips to the boat, wading most of the way but swimming when the breakers came in, to bring ashore the chronometer, the barometer, the opera glasses and the ship's compass. He hoped to find clothing on the gig for he was suffering from the cold, but there was none to be found. He went back toward shore for the last time and when the water was just awash his knees, he felt a pain and the stinging of salt water on his left knee. Looking down, he found a large splinter from the mast imbedded in his knee. He had not felt it until that moment. He recalled, "I pulled it out, then my head seemed to go around and I remember falling."

Utterly done-in, Halford slept where he fell until the sun was well up. When he awoke he found his body in the surf, his head just above it. He tried to rise but found that his leg "refused duty." Crawling to a piece of driftwood, he used it as a crutch and searched for Muir, who had wandered from the spot where he had left him.

He called Muir's name several times but got no answer. Shouldering the tin box, he started off toward some sheep and goats he spied grazing in the distance. He soon heard a rooster crowing and knew for sure that there were natives nearby.

As he rounded a clump of bushes, he came right upon a group of Hawaiian children playing. The children were frightened by the dirty, long-bearded, naked and wasted figure who confronted them and they ran screaming to their parents. Within a few minutes, natives gathered around Halford but none could speak English. The sailor made signs for them to carry the boat high up on the beach, which they did. He got the women and children to hunt for Muir. They found him some fifty feet from where Halford had left him, dead and black in the face. Halford sat down and promptly keeled over for the second time.

When the coxswain came to, an islander was rubbing him and speaking to him in English. The man's wife sat on a horse nearby and held the bridle of her husband's mount. The man, whose name was Peter, took off his pants and shirt and gave them to Halford. He then put him on his horse and took him to his house some distance away.

He asked who Halford was and where he came from. The coxswain explained about the gig and the wreck of the *Saginaw*. Peter gave him a fresh-water bath, a rubdown, fanned him and dressed his wounds. The sailor recalled years later that "I began to revive and then wanted to be up and doing for my shipmates who must be getting in bad shape on the island." Meanwhile, Peter took Halford over to Hanalei where Mr. and Mrs. Bindt of Plantation House treated him as though he were their own son.

Sheriff Wilcox, the coroner and Halford returned to Kalihiwai shortly for an inquest held over the bodies of Muir and Talbot, the latter having drifted ashore just before Halford left for Hanalei. Talbot's forehead was bruised and blackened; he had apparently struck the boat or wreckage before drowning. When the inquest was concluded, the two bodies were taken to Hanalei and buried the next day on a bluff overlooking the town and next to the grave of a seaman from the U.S.S. *Lackawanna*, who had died in 1867. Funeral services were conducted by Mr. Kenny, who read the Episcopalian burial service while the two daughters of the American missionary, Johnson, sang. Before Halford left Kauai, Andrews' body came ashore farther down the island and was taken to Hanalei to be buried alongside the others. Francis's body was never recovered.

Captain Dudoit of the schooner*Waiola* was in the harbor and offered to take Halford to Honolulu, but he had to go to Waimea for a load of rice first. When the sailor explained the plight of his comrades on Ocean Island, the captain agreed to start immediately. They sailed Tuesday, December 20, 1870, but it took them three days to go ninety miles and they did not reach Honolulu until 11 A.M. December 24th because of light winds.

Halford went directly to the U. S. consulate where he met the American Minister to the Kingdom of Hawaii, and told him his story of the last cruise of the *Saginaw*. Seven hours after he reported the shipwreck, the 200-ton schooner *Kona Packet* left with provisions and clothing, to be followed, two days later, by the government steamer *Kilauea* with a duplicate set of provisions. Reverend Samuel Damon gave the coxswain a Bible to comfort him while he awaited transportation home.

The mail steamer arrived in Honolulu from San Francisco on the night of the 24th and left for California again on the evening of the 26th. Halford sailed on her as a passenger and reported to Admiral J. A. Winslow. After staying the night of January 17, 1871, in San Francisco he went to Mare Island to recuperate. Here, aboard the receiving ship *Independence*, he was interviewed by San Francisco reporters.

On February 8, 1871, the other men and officers of the *Saginaw* arrived in San Francisco on the *Moses Taylor* and the last cruise of the *Saginaw* was officially ended.

The *Alta California* reporter who interviewed the coxswain while in sick bay on the *Independence* lauded the conduct of Halford, who, "triumphing over famine, and shipwreck, unmindful of himself and only intent upon saving the eighty shipmates whom he had left on the desolate island, saved the papers in case he should not live to report the wreck." The January 16, 1871 *Alta California* proposed that Halford be presented with a gold medal and a substantial purse for his valor. Contributions were to be left at the *Alta* office and the headquarters of Maurice Dore and Co. The paper stated: "We are positive the claims of few more worthy have seldom been presented to the public for approbation, and a response as generous as this man's acts are meritorious, is expected."

A San Francisco reporter wrote: "Halford, who had been 30 days and 14 hours in the boat of which he is the only survivor of the crew, came to this city on the steamer *Moses Taylor* in a pitiful condition. His body is covered with bruises and sores and his strong constitution was almost broken down."

By General Order #169, dated February 8, 1872, the courageous Halford was honored with the highest compliment his nation could pay him—the Medal of Honor. At the same time he was promoted to acting gunner.

In 1873 the *Otsego* brought to San Francisco some of the *Saginaw's* copper sheathing, her anchors and chain. The gig itself was purchased at auction in Hawaii by naval officers and brought to Mare Island. In 1882 the U.S.S. *Jamestown* carried it to the Naval Museum at the U.S. Naval Academy, Annapolis, where as a monument to the five heroes and as an inspiration to midshipmen, a tablet on the wall of the Naval Academy chapel honored the memory of Halford's lost shipmates—Talbot, Francis, Muir and Andrews. A few years ago the gig was presented to the city of Saginaw, Michigan, by the Academy.

In his official report, Sicard wrote of the coxswain and his four companions: "The men were fine specimens of seamen—cool and brave, with great endurance and excellent physical strength. They were undoubtedly, those best qualified in the whole party on Ocean Island to perform such a service." The newspapers applauded the five men who "volunteered their services, risking their lives for the remainder of the crew." George M. Robinson, Secretary of the Navy, in his Annual Report to the President, wrote: "His (Talbot's) comrades of humbler rank will not be forgotten; with him they faced the dangers of the lonely ocean and offered their lives with his to save their shipwrecked messmates, and no one can estimate how much of danger and suffering, perhaps death, was saved through

80

the courage and endurance of the sole survivor of that gallant boat's crew." But it was King Kamehameha, in an audience with Sicard and other officers of the *Saginaw*, who perhaps summed it up best when he said of the five men who took part in the gig's thirty-one day, 1,800-mile cruise: "Such examples of devotion to duty are a rich legacy to all men."

On the *Saginaw* memorial tablet at Annapolis were placed the words of the famous Biblical phrase which have never been more apropos than in reference to the action of Coxswain Halford and his companions: *Greater love hath no man than this; that a man lay down his life for his friends.*

Chapter IV

THE CASE OF BULLY WATERMAN

IT IS not surprising that the real-life model for Captain Roger Murray in Alexander Laing's historical novel *The Sea Witch* is Robert H. (Bully) Waterman. Waterman has ever been the prototype of all the tough, driving Yankee clipper masters of both history and fiction. Born in New York on March 4, 1808, Robert Waterman was only twelve years old when he first shipped out on a voyage to China. He was one of those skippers said to have climbed up to his command through the hawsehole. That is, he steadily worked his way aft from ordinary seaman to A.B., to third mate, to second, to chief mate, and finally to master.

He first won a reputation when he became mate of Captain Charles H. Marshall's *Britannia*, soon becoming the best mate . in the employ of the Black Ball Line. He kept his ship in A-1 shape but he also won notice as a strict disciplinarian, not only in the forecastle but in steerage as well.

Waterman was hard on his crews but in 1831, while on the westward passage to New York, he dove overboard to rescue one of his men who had been swept off the deck in a raging gale. The cabin passengers were so impressed with his heroism that they presented him with a testimonial. However, it must be added that Waterman, typically, gave the sailor a hammering the next day for "sojering" (malingering).

In 1833, at the age of twenty-four, Waterman was promoted to captain and given the Black Baller *South America*. He kept her for four years, then left this packet service. He made the headlines in 1837 when he took the full-pooped New Orleans packet *Natchez* to Valparaiso. In 1840 he made a good run from Coquimbo, Chile, to New York, and four years later, just ten years after assuming his first command, Waterman slammed the *Natchez* around Cape Stiff to Canton, via Valparaiso and Mazatlán, and then whipped her home in ninety-two days—and the old *Natchez*, built by Isaac Webb in 1831, had the reputation of being a slow sailer! Of course, he had added canvas to her rig and had got the most out of his crew. He was a splendid sailor who knew how to take advantage of every whisper of wind and ripple of current. Waterman had circled the globe in nine months and twenty-six days.

Wasting no time in port, he took the *Natchez* out for Valparaiso again in 1844 and made that Chilean port in jig time, then pressed on to Hong Kong. Sailing from Canton on January 15, 1845, he was off the Cape of Good Hope only a little over a month later and romped home to New York on April 3, only seventy-eight days from China. The *Natchez* had logged 13,995 miles between Macao and the Barnegat pilot. Robert Waterman strode the streets of Manhattan a hero.

The pale captain with the cold, glittering, blue-gray eyes received a great popular ovation in New York for his latest performance. People could hardly believe that he had coaxed the slow old *Natchez* (no clipper she!) into a run of only sixteen days from the Line to the Battery. Rumors flew that Captain Waterman had discovered a new, secret and shorter route home from the Orient. In 1845–1846 he made another fast out-of-season round trip to China. The delighted owners of the *Natchez*, Howland and Aspinwall, then commissioned John

Griffiths to build a masterpiece of marine architecture, the *Sea Witch*, especially for Waterman.

While the clipper was being built, Captain Waterman married Cordelia Sterling, of Bridgeport. Captain John Land took over the *Natchez* from Waterman and the latter skippered the *Rainbow* until the *Sea Witch* was ready for him. The 900-ton *Sea Witch* possessed a long, low-lying hull, painted black. With her sharply raked masts, she looked like a fleet corsair built for raiding commerce, rather than the cargo carrier she was. The black vessel with the gilded dragon figurehead was the handsomest ship sailing out of New York.

Launched December 8, 1846, from Smith and Dimon's shipyard on South Street, New York, *Sea Witch* was soon manned with a hand-picked body of men and officers, most of whom followed Waterman from the *Natchez*. Captain Waterman took her on her maiden voyage to China two days before Christmas 1846. He put to sea in a strong northeast gale but made a fine twenty-five-day run to Rio. Her New York to Hong Kong time was one hundred and four days and he made the return trip from Canton to New York, against the monsoon, in seventy-seven days, a record. Practically every leg of the voyage was in record time. Coming home, he set a mark for the Anjer to the Cape run and her Anjer–New York passage was also a new record. For ten days the *Sea Witch* averaged a splendid two hundred and forty-eight miles a day.

Waterman followed up this astounding maiden voyage with two more swift trips to China in 1847 and 1848, culminating a remarkable and unique series of ocean voyages. With a best twenty-four-hour run of three hundred and fifty-eight miles, the *Sea Witch* was the fastest thing afloat and could beat any steamer on the seas.

Stories clustered around Waterman like barnacles on a hulk, and his tough reputation was enhanced by his actions in the ports of Valparaiso and Whampoa. In the Valparaiso roadstead on his 1847–1848 trip, he invited a large party of the town's elite aboard the *Sea Witch* for a little trip "outside." Everyone had a very good time except Waterman, who lost all his money in the Spanish card game called *rocambor*. When, after some hours had passed, one of his *Chileno* guests suggested that they return to port, Waterman replied with eyebrows lifted in feigned surprise, "To port? To Valparaiso? Oh, I've squared for China. You can have a free passage and return when you like. I have lost all my money and it would incommodate me to return to Valparaiso just now." The Chileans consulted hurriedly in rapid-fire Castilian, pesos changed hands and a reimbursed captain brought the *Sea Witch* back to Chile's Vale of Paradise.

In Whampoa the *Sea Witch* found herself alongside Captain Lockwood's *Race Horse*, Captain Watkins' *Paul Jones*, and Sam Brannan's old charter, the *Brooklyn*, with Captain A. Richardson in command. A mutiny broke out on the *Brooklyn* and Richardson called an informal court-martial, composed of the American skippers, to take place aboard his ship. The mutineers were sentenced to a dozen lashes each, well laid on, and Waterman stood by to see that justice was done. The cook of the *Brooklyn* had not joined the mutiny but he was a little too loquacious and "fussy," so Waterman ordered him a dozen lashes also, "for the general joy of the company."

It was commonly known, and commented upon, that Waterman carried too much sail and that he kept padlocks on his topsail sheets and rackings to keep timorous seamen from letting go sail when it looked as if the spread of canvas might capsize the ship. Yet, in eighteen years of command, he never lost a spar or any rigging of any importance and not once did he call on the underwriters for a penny's loss or damage. Above all, he was too strict a disciplinarian even for that day and age. On sailing day he would have a bucket of water brought to him on the poop. He would then solemnly and ceremoniously wash off his "shore face" to remind his men that he expected them to obey his orders unquestioningly and on the double once they hit blue water.

On March 25, 1849, a New York lookout strained his eyes trying to identify an extreme clipper coming in. No vessels were due. The speck grew into a ship, booming home, and the lookout soon recognized her as the sleek *Sea Witch*. The Canton tea packet had made a record run—one that would never be broken by a sailing ship—seventy-four days and fourteen hours from China to New York.

The New York *Commercial Advertiser* reported: "The splendid ship *Sea Witch*, Captain Waterman, arrived here from China, having performed a voyage around the world in 194 sailing days!" Other papers joined in acclaiming Waterman, yet this record passage, the world's first permanent sailing record, was strangely forgotten in later years and Waterman's earlier (1847) and slower trip of seventy-seven days in the *Sea Witch* was listed as the record run. The clipper's best ten days' run in the true record passage, that of 1849, was 2,634 miles, averaging eleven and one-tenth knots.

Waterman's ex-mate, George Fraser, on April 13, 1850, took the *Sea Witch* to San Francisco. Fraser made the Golden Gate in ninety-seven days, smashing all California records by a fortnight. He made a point of racing swift Yankee clippers like the *Surprise, Nightingale, Race Horse,* and *Typhoon* and Britishers like the *Chrysolite, Challenger* and *Stornoway*. The *Sea Witch* did not always win under Fraser but she always ran a good race. She made her last call at San Francisco's Embarcadero in 1852.

On a trip in 1853 she was struck by lightning off Cape of Good Hope, her masts shivered and much iron work broken. She put into Valparaiso on June 25th of the following year, leaking so badly that Fraser was convinced some of the crew had bored holes in her bottom. On a passage to China in the *Sea Witch* in 1855 the driving Fraser was murdered by his chief

87

mate. The clipper put into Rio where Captain Lang took command, but the days of the hoodooed *Sea Witch* were numbered. Homeward bound from Amoy to Havana with coolies, she was wrecked on the east coast of Cuba on March 26, 1856.

Waterman had turned the *Sea Witch* over to Fraser in order to go into steam but he made just one trip, taking the *Northerner* to San Francisco, before retiring from active life. His retirement was brief, however, for a great new clipper had been built especially for him by William H. Webb at a cost of $100,-000. The largest merchantman yet built and possibly the most extreme clipper of all time, the *Challenge* measured 2,500 tons carpenter's measure, or 2,006 tons registry. By the revised tonnage laws, this meant her tonnage was 1,375. Built of white oak, live oak and pine, she was a little over two hundred and ten feet long, longer by twenty-seven feet than the 120-gun U.S.S. *Pennsylvania*, the Navy's biggest ship. The mainmast of this largest and longest merchant vessel plying the seas towered two hundred feet above the water. She was a three-decker.

Launched May 24, 1851, from Webb's Shipyard at the foot of Sixth Street before the largest crowd in New York waterfront history, she boasted a tremendous spread of canvas. She carried so much sail that it was reduced three times by captains who took over after Waterman left her. A spectator at her launching wrote: *I have seen many launches* [i.e., launchings] *including that of the U.S. ship* Ohio *but never have I witnessed such interest and excitement before as attended this launch.*

Her lower masts were painted black to match her hull, which bore a gold stripe and a gilded eagle as a figurehead. Each cathead was decorated with the representation of an eye. She was a masterpiece. The London *Times* called her the best, even if not the fastest, clipper in the world. Her owners hoped her to be the fastest as well. Duncan MacLean, the marine reporter of the Boston *Atlas* at the time, wrote:

That nothing might be wanting on the part of the owners, they obtained the services of the first of sailors to command her. Captain Robert H. Waterman, whose name is associated with the shortest passages on record from China, superintended her construction and equipment, and to his skill as a sailor, without trenching upon the province of the builder, may be attributed her completeness aloft. With a commander of such undoubted skill and daring, all that the *Challenge* can do she will be made to do.

E. A. Wheeler, who sailed on her maiden voyage as a boy, recalled her "miles of running gear" and her "spars up near Orion."

The *Challenge* was towed to the foot of Wall Street to complete her rigging. Her sails were bent, her running gear rove and cargo loaded for San Francisco. She was then hauled out into the river abreast of Governor's Island and everything made shipshape for sea. After being towed as far as Sandy Hook she lay at anchor, letting the rival *Flying Cloud* get a bigger lead on her to San Francisco, while Captain Waterman and his mate indulged in a squabble. Waterman finally sent his mate ashore. The packet *Guy Mannering* came up just as the *Challenge* was about to get underweigh again. A boat put off from the former and her first mate came aboard the new clipper. He was in trouble in New York and, afraid to go ashore, he asked Waterman for a berth. Captain Waterman signed him on as first mate and put to sea immediately.

The *Challenge* sailed on July 13, 1851, during the most unfavorable season of the year and doldrums and light northeast winds plagued her. After emerging from a series of calms, she met fine weather from 20° south to the area of the Straits of Le Maire. Cape San Diego was sighted one morning and they passed the entrance to the Straits at about 7 A.M. It looked as if they would make a speedy passage around the Horn. Off Diego Ramírez Island, however, they ran smack into a snow squall and had to shorten sail until they were under a close-reefed topsail.

For thirty-three days they struggled against the blasting westerlies before they made 50° south and reached the Pacific. The fierce cold and continual snowstorms were hard on the crew. Mate Douglass, cursing the half-frozen men for not working faster, on one occasion slacked up the lee mizzin topsail brace. This threw the sail back on the yard on the weather side and catapulted five men off. Four were lost overside and one was killed on a ventilator. The crew began to rue the day they had spoken the *Guy Mannering*.

Although the log reel showed she was doing eighteen knots many times, the *Challenge* made a tedious passage up the west coast to the Golden Gate. Only once did she log over three hundred miles in twenty-four hours. She made San Francisco on October 29th after a passage of one hundred and eight days, fair enough time but a tremendous disappointment to her owners and to Waterman. Believing her to be the fastest thing afloat, her admirers had boasted that after she was through breaking the record on her maiden voyage to California, she would offer to race any British clipper, on any terms—the winner to take both vessels. There had been every hope of breaking the record to San Francisco. Bets were offered everywhere in New York that she would beat the Boston clipper *Telegraph* as well as Grinnel, Minturn & Company's splendid *Flying Cloud*. She beat the *Telegraph* all right and logged from fourteen to eighteen knots at times, but her best twenty-four hours' run of three hundred and thirty-six miles was but small reward for the extravagant hopes placed on board her.

Waterman knew to the minute how long his spars could stand the strains of a gale. He was particularly watchful at night and, as usual, did not lose a spar, but an incompetent and mutinous crew, composed of the sweepings of Gotham's jails, thwarted his best efforts. So many A.B.'s had jumped ship in

San Francisco to go to the mines of the Mother Lode that qualified seamen were as rare as rickshaws on the New York waterfront. The few stragglers and ancients left on the beach had been snatched up by the *Telegraph, Eagle* and *Flying Cloud,* which sailed just before the *Challenge.*

Waterman had seriously considered putting back into New York early in the voyage for another crew but, knowing how expensive this would be to the owners, N. L. and G. Griswold, who had plunked down three months' advance wages to each hand, he decided to make the best of a bad bargain. The first thing Waterman did upon sailing was to call aft all eight boys and the fifty-six seamen, only a few of whom were Americans. He delivered to them a long, drawn-out harangue which lasted almost twenty minutes. He assured them of a comfortable ship and good food but demanded that they obey orders and do so quickly. During his long address the mates, carpenter, sail-maker and bosun were busy ransacking the forecastle. They opened all chests, boxes and sea bags, collecting a small arsenal of pistols, knuckle-dusters, bowie knives and slung shots. These were tossed over the side.

After the watches were chosen, Waterman had each man lay his sheath knife on the main hatch, where the carpenter broke the blade off square. Only six of his international crew of Greeks, Italians and Dutchmen could steer, so he made them quartermasters on the spot, assigning them no other duties than steering and helping to take in sail when needed. Fully one half of the crew were not sailors of any stripe but simply ruffians and blacklegs who desired a quick trip to the easy pickings in California. Their health was no better than their manners or their morals, and at one time seventeen of them were laid up with one of the more "loathsome diseases." Waterman turned the sail room into a sick bay but five died en route to San Francisco and eight were still sick in their berths when the anchor was dropped off Yerba Buena Cove.

Waterman drove his motley crew, for he had a $60,000 freight list in his cabin and a promise of a $10,000 bonus if he made San Francisco in ninety days. Even had Waterman not been after a record, the crew would have found plenty of work to do. The *Challenge* was a new ship and her rigging stretched and had to be adjusted (they had to set up the lanyards three times before they reached Cape Horn), and chafing gear had to be made. There was no watch-and-watch for the crew and they grew increasingly surly.

Waterman and his officers went armed at first but as the crew began to shape up they abandoned their side arms. The first mate, "Black" Douglass, was a 200-pound brute hated wholeheartedly by the entire crew. While searching for something in his sea chest when he first came aboard he had E. A. Wheeler, one of the ship's boys, hold a candle for him to see by. The boy did not do the job to Douglass' satisfaction so the mate slapped him so hard he saw stars. When the boy said something, Douglass made him eat the candle. Douglass seemed to delight in making the voyage unpleasant for everyone up to and including the second mate. He drove the men to work with a belaying pin and, in the words of Wheeler, "would rather have a knockdown fight with a lot of sailors than eat a good dinner."

One morning off Rio, Waterman heard shouts for help. He found his first officer with his back to the port bulwark abaft the main rigging, defending himself against the attack of four knife-wielding assailants. Backing them up was a large portion of the crew. Douglass had ordered all chests brought on deck when something was reported stolen. He examined chest after chest in front of the glowering men and the wide-eyed boys sitting atop the galley. Suddenly he was jumped by two of the crew. As soon as Waterman heard the mate's shouts for help he ran along the main deck, pulled a belaying pin from the rail and, holding it with both hands, used it as a club against Douglass' attackers. He laid out three of the mutineers, two of them

92

dead. Douglass was wounded and barely escaped with his life.

The little Englishman who had knifed the mate ran forward and disappeared. Word came aft that he had jumped overboard from the topgallant forecastle. From that time on, Waterman and his officers carried pistols at all times and the men were tapped with a belaying pin for so much as a cross word or look. Wheeler claimed that three men died as a result of this treatment before the *Challenge* rounded the Horn.

Although the facts of the mutiny were not to come out until the trial in San Francisco, the captain described the incident himself in a letter to a Boston friend:

> The truth is, when in the neighborhood of Rio, about fifty[!] of the crew fell upon the mate with the intention of killing him and afterwards me, by their own confession. I was on the poop taking observations while the mate stood forward at the gallery. They stabbed him and had beaten him shockingly before I could get to him. I struck down three of them, rescued the mate and quelled the mutiny. I flogged eight of them.

According to Wheeler, Waterman picked out thirty-six men, not eight, tied them to the rigging for a taste of the lash, the mate delivering three dozen blows to each with a piece of ratline. A month later, the mate went below for a coil of eight-inch towline and saw a man's head do a disappearing act. He grabbed the man by the hair and found it to be Birkinshaw, the little Englishman who had stabbed him and had supposedly jumped overboard to his death. For a corpse he was fat and sassy, having been smuggled food and drink by his shipmates.

The captain questioned him and ordered young Wheeler to bring a tail block and rope, which he took up to the yard where he made it fast. Douglass tied the man's arms and legs while Waterman made a hangman's noose. He slipped it around the Englishman's neck and gave it a jerk every few minutes to stimulate Birkinshaw's powers of recollection. As he blurted out the details of the mutiny, Cornelius Sterling, one of the passengers, took down his words. The rope was slipped off and the mutineer was put in irons.

Waterman spied the Farallones early on the morning of October 28, 1851, and anchored off "Bird Island" (Alcatraz) that same day. When the captain learned that the *Flying Cloud* was already in, he turned the air blue with oaths and frightened pelicans from their rookeries. He got into a quarrel with the mate, blaming the *Challenge's* poor time on Douglass and his rough treatment of the men, with their consequent unfitness for work. The captain then called the crew aft and told them that as soon as he got ashore he would see that all of those who had engaged in the mutiny were arrested. The whole crew jumped ship, of course, helped by the crimps and boarding-house runners. The *Challenge* lay at anchor for two days, unable to get to Pacific Street Wharf. No sailors or stevedores were available—she was labeled a hell ship, her officers murderers.

On the 30th the *Challenge* was finally warped up to its wharf. Boatmen and sailors collected in large numbers on the Pacific Street dock and in Whitehall boats, ready to lynch Waterman and his mate. Earlier that morning, however, the captain had gone ashore to the Customhouse and to the agents' office and was already in hiding. Boatmen collected on all sides of the clipper to prevent the escape of Waterman, whom they thought was still on board, and "Black" Douglass. The crowd on the dock increased by hundreds. There appeared to be no escape possible for the two hunted men, so many of the Whitehall boatmen rowed up to the Sansome Street dock to tie up their boats and enjoy a pipe while they walked down to Pacific Street Wharf to see the show.

As the clipper neared the crowd, Douglass scrambled over the side of the ship away from the wharf and dropped into the Whitehall boat of his friend Commodore T. H. Allen, in charge of the stevedores who were to unload the *Challenge*'s cargo. They were seen within a minute and boatmen pursued them in Whitehalls through the fleet of ships abandoned in the bay. Douglass and his friend passed Commercial Street Wharf and landed at Rincon Point where they disappeared in the brush. A mob searched the area, determined to find him and lynch him on the spot, but dusk fell with their efforts unrewarded.

The following day the maimed sailors were removed to the Marine Hospital and the mood of the crowd grew even uglier as it swelled in size. The mob marched to the office of the consignees, Alsop & Company, on California Street near Third Street. There were at least two thousand in the crowd, angered and excited by the irresponsible stories the press had picked up, willy-nilly, from the roughneck crew. The *California Courier* on November 1st carried a wild and inflammatory story probably peddled by some drunken rogue whose pepperbox or bowie knife had been thrown overboard. Waterman was described in this article as a "bloody murderer," and "a vile monster," certainly "one of the most inhuman monsters of the age."

He and "his guilty mate" were accused of wholesale murder and the paper listed nine seamen as missing. Four were noted as having been shaken from the topmast and five described as dead of wounds and ill treatment. Five more were tallied as mangled or bruised, one of whom, according to the editor, was dying that very day. To cap the hysterical yarn, the newspaper suggested that five more men were expected to die as a result of Waterman's brutality—"He is noted for his cruelty everywhere." Captain Waterman's explanation of the deaths among his crew first appeared in a letter to a Boston friend: "Off Cape Horn, three men fell from the mizzen topsail and were killed and after a few weeks, four more died of dysentery."

Right or wrong, Robert H. Waterman acquired the nickname which was to stick to him for the rest of his life—"Bully" Waterman. Whether crews really found his clippers to be "hell ships" or not, no one can say. However, knowing Waterman's loathing for "sojers," we can be sure that frauds and malingerers found hell aboard his ships. Some have claimed that Waterman always left his ship before she came to anchor in New York harbor and always boarded her off Sandy Hook to avoid the writs out for his arrest on charges of maltreatment of seamen.

The mob which gathered, bent on lynching both Waterman and Douglass, marched to the offices of the *Challenge*'s agents, Alsop & Co. They demanded that Waterman be surrendered. Charles Griswold of the firm assured them that the captain was not there and invited a committee of six of their leaders to search the office. This they did, but Waterman had been hidden first in a vault below the stairs, then shunted to the roof where he drew up the ladder behind him. He then escaped via the next-door building.

The crowd seized Captain John Land, whom they found at the office, and threatened to hang him on suspicion of having hidden Mr. Douglass. Before they could carry their threat into effect, the mob heard the tolling of the Monumental Engine Company bell. The ringing was answered by some six hundred Vigilantes who offered their services to the mayor in what was to be the last action of the Vigilantes Committee of 1851. They gathered this time not to hang someone but to prevent a lynching and to restore law and order. The Committee was particularly impatient with the mob of citizens which had organized spontaneously, in imitation of the Vigilantes themselves, to see that their peculiar concept of justice was carried out.

When Mayor Brenham, with the support of the armed Vigilantes, gave the crowd just ten minutes to disperse, they cheered the Vigilance Committee mightily, "groaned" Waterman and his mate, and broke up. Many of them reassembled on Pacific Wharf where they hashed over a proposition to burn and scut-

tle the *Challenge*. One orator separated himself from the rest
and mounted a box to preach that the fault was with the owners who had knowingly hired the tyrant, Bully Waterman: He
volunteered to be the first to set fire to the ship but he was
shouted down.

When the U. S. Marshal went aboard the *Challenge* shortly
thereafter he found that some little violence had been done
her. The doors of the cabin had been broken in with handspikes
and capstan bars. This had been done when the search for the
captain and mate was begun. Waterman had told Wheeler there
would be trouble and had given the boy the key to his cabin.
He had ordered Wheeler not to let anyone in, so the boy locked
the stateroom and hid the key. After breaking the doors in
their fruitless search, Waterman's pursuers had indulged in
some vandalism—cutting many lanyards of the standing rigging
—but had then rushed off to the consignees' office. The marshal
dispersed the crowd and told the sailors that if they had any
complaint to make they must do so formally to him. A complaint was finally made and U. S. authorities joined in the
search for Captain Waterman and Black Douglass.

Thomas Gray of the Vigilance Committee explained the
action of the Committee in defending Waterman from the
Embarcadero mob:

> We are informed that a state of feeling exists among a portion
> of the sailors who came out with Captain Waterman in the
> *Challenge* different from that which has generally supposed to
> have existed among them unanimously. A gentleman of this city
> informs us that nine of the seamen who have just arrived in her
> have waited on the consignees of this ship and informed them
> that they are willing to make a voyage to China in the *Challenge*
> with Captain Waterman as master. Five of these seamen are
> Americans and four are foreigners. The same gentleman states
> that the passengers are unanimous in justifying the course pur-
> sued by the captain on the way out.

97

The *Alta* applauded the firm action of the Committee and crowed: "Where now are those who called the Committee a mob!"

Captain Waterman dropped out of sight but Douglass was captured ten miles out of the city on the San Jose Road, hidden in a horse cart, as he fled San Francisco. It was late in the morning of November 1, 1851, when Sheriff Jack Hays brought him back to town—but not because of attempts to seize him for lynching by the fifty vengeful sailors rumored to be in pursuit of him. No, the delay was occasioned because "the prisoner insisted on taking a drink at every bar along the road."

Douglass and his companions had glowered and blustered at their captors but had made no real resistance. When apprehended, the mate did boast drunkenly, "My name is Douglass among soldiers, sailors and gentlemen. I whipped 'em and I'll whip 'em again." He added more soberly, "Well, gentlemen, if you want to hang me, here is a pretty tree. Do it like men."

Waterman's defamers were not content to label the escaped captain a brute; they had to make him out a despicable coward, to boot. Therefore, tales were invented which had him being cowed and thrashed by both his first and second officers. In some of the chapter and verse, Second Mate Alexander Coghill surpassed his superiors in brutality and raffishness. He was said to have whipped *both* Waterman and Douglass with his fists in one encounter and to have buried alive (at sea) a sailor he had kicked off the weather footropes, sewing him up in his blanket as he groaned. Small wonder that Coghill was arraigned along with Waterman and Douglass on murder charges.

The first testimony in the round robin of trials arising out of the *Challenge* case came from the blaspheming lips of George Hill, seaman. He testified that one day in a gale his watch was aloft about to take in the mizzen topsail on the second mate's orders when the chief mate sang out a command also to lay out on the yard and pick up the sail. The mate then asked "second" in rather blunt manner why he did not keep the sons of bitches on the yard. Without waiting for a reply to his more or less rhetorical question, Douglass suggested that if Second Mate Coghill did not keep the men on the yard he would come up personally and kick him off. A moment later, a man fell off the yard into the sea. Coghill cried out that they would all be knocked off if the yard were not trimmed. He then kicked a seaman named Stevens. The latter did not fall as a result of the kick but, a moment later, the sail came over the yard and carried Stevens and another man off. Both were killed.

Hill volunteered that the kick could not have caused the fall since he was between the men when it was delivered and, second, he was positive that it was the leech (the rope on the edge of the sail) which had caught Stevens and swept him off the yard. Seamen Andrew Nicholl and Thomas Johnson could add little to Hill's testimony and the court discharged the second mate from the accusation of murder but held him on bail for assault and unjustifiable treatment of the deceased.

An affidavit from Mate Douglass led to the arraignment of seamen Downey, Frederick Birkenshaw and Ralph Smith on charges of mutiny. First witness in this case was a passenger on the *Challenge* named Bradhurst. He testified that he saw Douglass being beaten by some twenty-odd sailors, one of whom was Downey, on the day of the mutiny. He did not see the knifing itself. Bradhurst stated that Waterman was going to put the mutinous men in irons below decks but they threatened to iron him and the mate if he tried to punish them. Bradhurst also witnessed the discovery of Birkenshaw, hiding in the forecastle under some coils of rope a month after the scuffle. It had been supposed that he had jumped overboard when Waterman broke up the attack on the mate. The most electrifying testimony to come from Bradhurst was the statement that Birkenshaw had told the captain that the second mate was in on the plot and had offered to supply the mutineers with irons for Waterman and Douglass. Passenger Richard Morse substantiated this testimony.

The U. S. District Court was abuzz with excitement when James Douglass himself was called to the witness stand. The burly, 200-pound bucko spoke right out, without equivocation. "I was standing on deck seeing the chests overhauled when I was seized from behind and thrown down. While I was falling, I received a wound; there were several kicking me. I rose and Smith had hold of me with both hands around my neck. I struck him twice but he still retained his hold. I called on the men for assistance and reached out and got a stick. The men ran off. The Captain came up and told Smith to let go and then seized him and broke his hold. I then started in search of Birkenshaw, learning that he was the man who first seized me. I ordered the second mate to search. He appeared very dilatory; could not find Birkenshaw. When I got aft some of the prisoners were tied. Smith said the mutiny had been in contemplation for a month."

When Coghill was called as a witness in the mutiny trial he vehemently denied that he had offered to supply irons to the plotters. Nor had he any knowledge of the mutiny until the third mate awoke him to say that there was "a row on deck." He hurried topside, where he saw men tied in the rigging on both the lee and weather sides of the ship. Douglass grabbed him by the arm and said, "Mr. Coghill, I want you to look for that man and be damned quick about it." When Coghill asked, "What man?", Douglass shouted at him, "That 'Fred' in your watch."

Coghill searched the ship but found no trace of Birkenshaw. When he reported this to Douglass, the latter commented, "This [attack] is a made-up thing among them." Pulling out a dirk, he said to the second officer, "I advise you to carry something of this kind with you." Coghill replied that he was sure he could take care of himself with just his fists. Douglass only growled, "God damn their souls, I am damned glad the row has occurred. I can lick them as much as I like and they can't do anything with me when I get to California."

On November 11th, Douglass's application for bail was refused by Commissioner Jones. The same day, James McCartney, the seaman whose affidavit had caused the chief mate's arrest and confinement, died in the Marine Hospital. Coghill was discharged from the murder accusation, but held on bail for two charges of assault and battery and eventually committed on a charge of mutiny as well.

On the 11th, Captain Waterman surrendered to the authorities, waived an examination and was committed to trial on four different warrants—three for assault and one for murder. Before he reached the stand, Coghill and Birkenshaw pleaded not guilty of mutiny. Waterman pleaded not guilty to his indictment and the difficult job of choosing a jury began. Many veniremen were excused for bias but twelve men were finally found to serve.

Birkenshaw came to the stand to tell his side of the story. When his hiding place was discovered, Mate Douglass had crowed to Waterman, "I've got the son of a bitch!" The captain then ordered the little Englishman, "Down on your knees, you son of a bitch! What did you intend doing with me?" Birkenshaw told Waterman that he knew nothing of the mutiny though the captain beat him with a stick, breaking his arm, and kept him on his knees for "six hours." (This genuflective period of time was later reduced by Birkenshaw to the more likely "twenty minutes.")

The marathon trials continued on through November, fed by a dozen indictments of Waterman, Douglass, Coghill and Birkenshaw. The testimony was amended and rehashed. Passengers W. W. Burdick and William Maston * were followed by Seaman

* Also spelled Marston and Masten in newspaper accounts.

John Leggett, who told Judge Ogden Hoffman that he saw Waterman beat Birkenshaw, while on his knees, with a stick. However, under close questioning, Leggett admitted that the death toll on the *Challenge* was not all due to brutality—"The health of the crew during the passage was bad; we had ten deaths."

A French crewman, Nisrop, was questioned through an interpreter. Then U. S. Attorneys Benham and Barbour jousted with defense counsels McLane, Hamilton and Austin. The latters' argument was that the ship was in a mutinous condition which justified the acts charged *if* committed. The judge's charge warned the jury not to pass on Waterman's general conduct but only the case in question. They retired at 11:30 A.M. and at 2 A.M. the next morning they had not reached a verdict. At 9 A.M. they came in to report no agreement or hope of one. They were discharged.

Waterman had no time for even a smile of relief. A new jury was empaneled to try him for the cruel punishment of Tons Miti alias Ions Smiti alias John Smith. Many jurors were rejected but a panel was finally organized. Andrew Nicholl and Thomas Johnson testified that they saw Waterman beat the sickly Smiti with a stick as he holystoned the deck. The district attorney hoped to question Smiti but there was no interpreter in San Francisco who could translate for him since he was a Finn. The D.A. therefore rested his case. A passenger, in testifying for the defense, stated that Smith was struck with only a small rope. The jury's verdict found Waterman guilty of assault on "John Smith."

Waterman and Douglass were next tried for beating a seaman named George Lessing but known as "The Dancing Master" because he jumped about so gingerly when flogged. George Hall had heard the captain say, "I think we'll baptize him." He saw Waterman and Douglass throw the lad into the lee scuppers, which were awash. While the boy tried to keep his head above water, the captain and the mate jumped on him. Lessing died shortly after the ducking, doubtless helped along by a massive dose of castor oil given him by the zealous but misguided passenger named Marston. Despite the "short but impressive" charge of the judge, the jury was unable to agree in nightlong deliberations.

The next case caused a stir in court as Waterman was called as a witness in the trial of Douglass for inflicting cruel and unusual punishment on Ion Smiti. The captain described the Finn. "He shipped as an ordinary seaman. He was lazy, dirty, indolent, always skulking. . . . I ordered the mate to give him a rope's end and I think he deserved it. I once ordered him to stand on the hatch and see other persons work, and asked him what he would rather do. He replied that it did not make any difference to him. The defendant [Waterman meant the plaintiff, Smiti] was not the only one who skulked; nearly the whole crew did it. I think it was the worst crew I've ever seen. I have been to sea for the last thirty years. There were not more than ten Americans in the crew. They would fight among themselves, cut, gouge, bite & kept in a continual row. . . ." He mentioned that he had seen the crew drive the malingering Finn on deck and, another time, saw them sling him on a rope. Smiti always complained of pains in his legs and other ills but, noted Waterman, "he appeared to walk well when going to the galley for his tea." Douglass was found guilty on only one of the four counts of the indictment.

The Court turned more of its attention to the mutiny as the new year began. George Smith testified the crew was beaten with belaying pins, straps, billets of wood, heavers, fists and ropes. (He had been beaten personally by Waterman with a belaying pine and a searing mallet.) Leggett, Johnson, Weldon and White had similar testimony but Charles Flanders summed it up best: "I was beat with a club myself. I did not disobey orders; the first intimation I had was a crack on the head. . . .

103

All the crews were beat except the Dagos; everybody aboard was beat except Jerry." This damaging testimony against Waterman and Douglass was weakened by that of Charles Pearson, a veteran of forty years at sea who had served on a frigate with Decatur. He had been beaten but admitted, "We had a miserable crew on board the *Challenge;* had not more than eight or ten good men; most were miserable trash." Coghill testified, putting in a good word for Birkenshaw as an obedient and efficient seaman. The jury's verdict was a surprise—Birkenshaw was not guilty of mutiny.

After Coghill was tried and convicted of brutality toward John Brown, Waterman and Douglass were brought to trial for beating Alexander Nicholl but, "the principal witness called for the prosecution being so drunk as to be unable to testify, and the U. S. District Attorney being satisfied that there was not sufficient facts to justify a prosecution of the case, entered a *nolle prosequi."* Perhaps the Court, as well as the public, was beginning to tire of the attacks on the *Challenge's* master and mate. In any case, a *nolle prosequi* was entered in the cases of assault upon Charles Pearson and Thomas Cleaver and, finally, "on the motion of the U. S. District Attorney a *nolle prosequi* was entered against both defendants for all indictments, save in the case of James Douglass for the murder of one Pawpaw. Captain Waterman was discharged on his own recognizance." Douglass was shortly released on his own recognizance and the two were free men.

The master and mate of the *Challenge* were never to tread her decks again. Captain John Land took the clipper out in 1852 after paying $200 advance money to each man who would sail on the "hell ship." He found them so mutinous he had to put into Hong Kong and get help from the Royal Marines. The *Challenge* visited San Francisco a few more times as a degraded coolie clipper, enjoyed another mutiny, and was lost on the coast of France in 1876.

Waterman, though acquitted of practically all the brutality charges made against him, was a marked man. He gave up blue-water sailing and spent his time doing salvage, buying vessels and wrecks, and serving as U. S. Inspector of Hulls for San Francisco. By 1855, E. A. Wheeler found him "about the most popular man on the city front."

Solano County folk like to remember him as one of their landed gentry, the founder of Cordelia and Fairfield, but he was always "the first of sailors." He was a tough man in a tough age. He would brook no nonsense on board his vessels, but he was no "vile monster." His friends knew that he was a complex man, tough rather than brutish, with a grain of good humor running through his hard-boiled nature. They remembered the time he had put into Valparaiso with the *Northerner*. Someone noticed that her owner, Captain Randall, was aboard and innocently asked the salty old Waterman, "What is the *Northerner* doing with two captains?" Bob Waterman's answer became a classic among yarning clipper masters: "Hell, he cleans the knives; *I* navigate the ship!"

Chapter V

LONG PIG

LIKE Cecil Rhodes or Clive of India, who seemed always to be about when Britain needed them, Ben Boyd was also a singlehanded builder of empire. Too suave and polished to be termed a "soldier of fortune," perhaps the tag "gentleman adventurer" best identifies him. One of the most colorful personalities ever to visit San Francisco, he sailed on his last voyage from Sausalito's Richardson's Bay in 1851. The exact fate of Boyd is not known to this day, the secret being locked in the heads of long-dead tribesmen of Guadalcanal.

Benjamin, the son of Edward Boyd, Esquire, was born about 1796 at Mertonhall, where the old Roman road cuts through Scotland. Although a lust for adventure and travel rivaled his natural business drive, Boyd became a London stockbroker. About 1840 he and his brother Mark floated the Royal Bank of Australia, selling debentures of the Bank to the sum of £200,000. Boyd sent a 600-ton, 250-horsepower steamer from London that same year to trade on the Australian coast and adjacent islands. The £30,000 *Seahorse,* the latest word in navigation, arrived at Port Jackson (Sydney) on June 2, 1841, and the Governor of South Australia soon used it to travel from Melbourne to Port Jackson.

Boyd sent another steamer but preferred to go Down Under

by sail, arriving at Port Phillip (Melbourne) on June 15, 1842, and at Port Jackson on July 18 in his yacht *Wanderer*. Melbourne society belle Georgiana McCrae had Boyd to dinner shortly after his arrival in Australia and on June 24, 1842, confided to her diary:

> Mr. Benjamin [Boyd] had rubbed his shoes and was still smoothing his hair when I received him. He is Rubens over again. Tells me he went to a bal masque as Rubens with his broad-leafed hat and was *comme il faut*. At the moment he has just arrived from South America in his yacht the *Wanderer* which is anchored down the bay.

As the executive agent of the Bank, Boyd held full power over the investment of Bank funds in the Australian colonies. He started in to develop the Australian economy at a rapid pace. He asked the British Government's approval of his plans for the colonization of the sub-continent and the expansion and improvement of Australian trade. He also asked that he be allowed to select five or six sites on the coast where he could erect stations for coaling his steamers and repairing their machinery. They would also serve as ports of refuge in storms.

A shrewd businessman, he asked that the Government allow him to purchase one hundred to three hundred acres at each harbor with the right of ultimate priority in purchase of further portions up to the limit fixed by the Government—five thousand acres—at each locality. He was sure the Government would even depart from established regulations in his case since he was ready to risk so much of his private fortune. He appended to his Australian plans the idea of personally visiting the South Seas in order to arrange with the natives for the formation of settlements on various islands there. He wrote of his plans on October 8, 1840, to Lord John Russell, who passed them on to Sir George Gipps.

Undersecretary Vernon Smith answered that Lord John Rus-

108

sell would offer Boyd every facility and assistance and would direct the governors of the Australian colonies to appropriate sites—to be selected by Boyd—for public wharves and landing places. On the other hand, Lord Russell would not allow the ambitious entrepreneur to drive quite as hard a bargain as he had hoped for. The Government, for instance, could not accord to an individual the right of purchase of land to the exclusion of the public-at-large nor could the Government promise to diminish duties on products Boyd would import from islands which he might settle but which were not actually British possessions.

The stubborn Boyd wrote Lord Russell again on December 11, 1840, repeated his plans for commercial intercourse, and again asked to be allowed to buy between one hundred and five hundred acres at each of five coastal sites, paying £1 per acre. Vernon Smith again answered, patiently explaining that the Government had the right to sell the land only in eighty-acre sections. Boyd kept up his sparring with the British Government for several years and soon became the greatest squatter in Australia. In 1844 it was he who signed the official protest of the Pastoral Association against the Government land policy. The statement was published in the Sydney *Morning Herald*.

Boyd paid licenses on only four stations in the Maneroo District, but the shrewd speculator actually held fourteen, occupying 231,000 acres. He paid licenses on two stations in the Port Phillip District but had four, covering 150,000 well-watered acres. He held other tracts in the Riverina District and in Queensland. Boyd always claimed that he had a freehold interest or a "fee simple" interest in the Crown lands which he had occupied, as long as he paid his £10 license fees. On his Maneroo District acreages alone he ran 10,000 cattle and 20,000 sheep. A powerful and not too scrupulous landholder, Boyd was nevertheless respected and liked. It was he who was instrumental in sending the petition to Queen Victoria which established the District of Port Phillip as a separate colony, Victoria.

Boyd pioneered not only in sheep raising but also was the first Australian whaler. At Twofold Bay he had made a settlement, Boyd Town, from which he supplied his Maneroo stations, to save the great expense of hauling overland from Sydney. He put in tallow works first, then made Twofold Bay a rendezvous for his whaling ships. On the south head of the bay he erected a lighthouse for the purpose of guiding vessels to his wharf. However, the New South Wales Government refused him permission to show a light unless he maintained it constantly. He hoped to make Boyd Town the commercial center of the area although the Government had made Eden the official township.

Boyd did not find time to plant his colonies on the South Sea islands as he had earlier planned but he did bring islanders to New South Wales as laborers, sending a steamer and five tenders to the New Hebrides to recruit young men. Rumors that the natives had been blackbirded by Boyd were investigated in 1847 and proven to be erroneous. However, this labor experiment of Boyd's was a failure although it anticipated a later, successful program of enlisting islanders for plantation work in Queensland and elsewhere. He landed several shiploads of natives at Twofold Bay and sent them to his station at Deniliquin and at Ulupna on the Murray River. They were given shepherd's duty at 6d. per week, with a new shirt and a Kilmarnock cap every year. Unfit for a pastoral life, they turned to petty thievery and other mischief and most of them drifted into Sydney where, nearly naked, they would march through the streets bearing their barbarous weapons and frightening the women and children. Boyd tried them, with hardly better results, as seamen on his whalers and many straggled back to New Hebrides. By Christmas of 1847 not more than fifty or sixty natives remained in the colony.

The "desperate enterprises" of this speculator-egoist were

held responsible for the depression in the colonies at the end of the 1840's. Shareholders in his labor-recruiting company received no return on their investment and demanded a change in the management. Arbitrators were called in and after a lot of trouble Boyd agreed to retire and resigned his claims on the company in exchange for receiving three of his whalers, his yacht *Wanderer* and two sections of land at Twofold Bay. Undaunted Boyd was ready for the next challenge. When it came, it came from California.

To garble a metaphor, "the shout heard round the world" was Sam Brannan's 1848 cry of "Gold, gold from the American River!" The New Yorkers, Sonorans, Jayhawkers, Britons, *Chilenos*, and Missouri "pewks" who dropped whatever they were doing at home to grab up blanket, dirk and gold-pan to rush for El Dorado were quickly joined by Australians. One of the first Aussies to sail for the new gold coast was Benjamin Boyd in his beautiful Royal yacht *Wanderer*.

Boyd took his fast-sailing 240-ton topsail schooner to California in 1850, with a digging party consisting mainly of Australian aborigines, sailing via Tahiti and Honolulu. He arrived at the latter port on February 21st from Lahaina, and landed twelve native seamen he had picked up from a drifting wreck. The *Wanderer* bade adieu to Honolulu on March 11th, clearing for San Francisco.

He enjoyed "seeing the Elephant" but decided to return to the Antipodes. The gold no longer lay in the streets for the picking up. Moreover, the little-known island world of the Pacific was still calling and Boyd decided to sail home to Sydney by way of Melanesia. According to his companion, John Webster, Boyd decided in California not only to make "a cruise among the islands," but also to explore the unexploited South Seas for enterprises which might attract him. Boyd had a love of adventure as well as the desire to make profits, and he still kept his early dream of founding settlements in New Guinea and the

111

Solomons. While in California his ideas had jelled into a plan for a Papuan Republic or a Papuan Confederation.

Boyd's last voyage was a true expedition. His yacht the *Wanderer* of the Royal Yachting Society was a flush-deck schooner equipped with elegant cabins. She had a heavy armament consisting of four brass deck guns (two six-pounders and two four-pounders on carriages resembling dolphins), four two-pounder rail guns, one on each side, and a traversing brass twelve-pounder, a Long Tom which had seen service at Waterloo. Boyd also had two highly ornamented signal guns, said to be from the wreck of the *Royal George* at Spithead. Each one bore a coat of arms believed to be that of Admiral Kempenfeldt.

The *Wanderer* was loaded with lots of round shot and grape for the cannons and was stocked with small arms, boarding pikes and tomahawks for the crewmen. Georgiana McCrae's son described the *Wanderer* as having the lines of an African slaver and the crew of a man-of-war. As a tender for the *Wanderer*, Boyd purchased in San Francisco the 120-ton schooner *Ariel* which, under the command of John Webster, was to carry trade goods as well as supplies for the expedition. Webster preferred to sail with his good friend Boyd, and delegated command of the *Ariel* to his sailing master, Mr. Bradley. Messers Barnes and Crawford, friends of Ben Boyd, accompanied the expedition, and the sailing master of the *Wanderer* was Mr. Ottiwell. These, with Bradley, were the only white men. The crews of both vessels were composed of islanders. In the case of the *Ariel*, the entire crew was from the New Hebrides.

After some weeks of preparation and delay, the *Wanderer* lay at Sausalito, taking on the properly famed water of that port. Webster described the Richardson's Bay anchorage:

> Saucelite [sic] is a safe anchorage inside the harbour. It is the usual resort of vessels belonging to the American Navy visiting this

port. The village of the same name is surrounded by an amphi-
theatre of hills, and contains but a few scattered cottages in the
modern style of architecture, a saw mill, and an hotel. It enjoys
an advantage over San Francisco in the salubrity of the air, in
the possession of good water, and in an absence of dust.

Webster was a great hunter, as was Boyd, and he did not fail
to note that "in the vicinity of Saucelite is found an abundance
of game, elk, deer, bears, geese, ducks &c which afford ample
recreation to the sportsmen who may be on board the vessels
lying in that vicinity."

An adverse tide and a sea breeze combined to thwart their
departure plans and they returned to their Richardson's Bay
anchorage. At daylight of June 4, 1851, they proceeded out the
Gate, followed by the *Ariel*. A light land breeze nudged them
on their way, but at the Heads the omnipresent sea breezes
made themselves felt and the *Wanderer* fought them for hours,
her "amateur crew" setting all available canvas. They passed all
the other outbound ships in the Gate easily, but once across the
bar where a high sea was running, they hove to in order to
await the *Ariel*. The tender was not in sight at sundown so they
proceeded under easy sail.

In the morning the *Ariel* was sighted astern and was allowed
to draw up on the *Wanderer*. Boyd and Bradley agreed to keep
company, and to show lights at night. They bore west for two
days to escape the ubiquitous "chilly fogs," then Boyd consulted
with Webster and the others on which land to visit first. They
decided to call at Hawaii. The men relieved the monotony of
the voyage by catching sharks and shooting at the sea fowl
which hovered in their wake.

Boyd found it difficult to teach the native crewmen to understand the points of the compass. Most exasperating of all was
a one-eyed *kanaka* from Rotuma who went by the name of
Friday. He always turned his blind eye to the compass to keep

his good one cocked at the sails. Another Rotuman, Tom, was a son of a chief and if not an A-1 sailor, he at least made an excellent cook.

A week out, Boyd sighted a large square-rigger hull down off their starboard bow, showing British colors and apparently bound for San Francisco. They clapped on all sail and ran down to her. She took the *Wanderer* for a pirate and abruptly altered her course, setting studding sails and everything else but the cook's apron to increase her speed. Boyd was willing to match the *Wanderer* against her but decided not to lose the *Ariel*. He dropped the chase by nightfall in order to rejoin his tender.

At sunset on the 25th, they sighted snow-topped Mauna Kea. The next day no land was in sight but on the 28th, the Island of Hawaii was close up. A white pilot came out in a canoe paddled by two natives and piloted the two vessels into Hilo Bay. That afternoon the Aussies paid their respects to Harbormaster Pitman and his lovely Hawaiian wife. He was a busy trader, the whalers particularly keeping him occupied. Due to the California trade boosting the price of provisions at Oahu, the whalers were going to Hilo and other ports where refreshments could be had on more reasonable terms.

The *Wanderer's* crew visited "Wai Ruka" (Wailuku) Falls and were amused by the young boys and girls who descended the cataracts in play to the basin far below. They also visited a sugar mill. Boyd and Webster were favorably impressed by the islanders, the latter writing, "The Hawaiians live under a model Government, and are making rapid strides in civilization under their King, Kamehameha III, Sovereign of all the Sandwich Islands."

Later a native called both Pomana and Sam guided Webster, Boyd and two crewmen to the crater of Kilauea while the *Ariel* and *Wanderer* took on water. On June 30th the hike to Kilauea began. After having covered about twenty miles, they camped at a village for the night. Pomana proved to be an amusing guide and fluent in English, having visited Britain thirty-one years earlier on the *Shakespeare*. He had a magnificent appetite and Webster wrote that he "attacked our provisions on every occasion with the voracity of a shark."

Crossing the smoke-hazed lava to the rim, they peered in before camping in a rude hut near the crater for the night. Their guide asked them to propitiate Pele with a wild duck they had shot but they declined and descended into the volcano next day without paying their respects to the gods. Near the bottom the two native seamen, terrified, gave up and scrambled back to the rim. Sam, or Pomana, wished to follow them but Boyd ordered him on. They viewed a small cone in violent activity, the surrounding surface quite hot. Suddenly the little cone erupted and Webster cried, "Leap for your life!" Boyd did so just as a fissure opened in the side of the cone, spewing molten lava.

They escaped unhurt and examined specimens of the matter thrown out of the cone, once the pieces had cooled. They leisurely collected volcanic samples which looked like zoophytes and other marine animals before returning to the rim. Here they followed Sam's suggestion and took a steam bath at a nearby fissure and then viewed the cherry-red abyss before going to bed. After a breakfast of wild strawberries they started back barefoot, for their shoes had burned and fallen apart on the hot lava. Stopping overnight at the village again, they breakfasted and reached the *Wanderer* after an absence of five days.

Most of the *haole* islanders visited the *Wanderer* the week after their return from Kilauea. On July 7th, Boyd, rather belatedly, fired a twenty-one-gun salute to the Hawaiian flag which was answered twenty-one times by the single gun ashore. That night they dined with Mr. and Mrs. Pitman. The following morning, Boyd was besieged by native youths who crowded the yacht, eager to join the expedition. The elders objected however and sent a *kaiko* (constable) to arrest them for "absconding

115

from their homes." The *kaiko* followed the boys below decks and ordered them ashore. Boyd tired of his presumptuousness and ordered him off the *Wanderer*. He told the constable that he would bring the boys ashore himself. The young *kanakas* were delighted as the constable was sent over the side, crestfallen.

When Boyd and the youths landed, there were several officers waiting on the beach to arrest the boys. They all marched to a judge—boys, constables, Boyd, Webster, Barnes, Crawford and Ottiwell—where a dried-up Frenchman acted as interpreter. Judge Momona adjourned the matter until the next day in order to have the boys' parents or guardians in attendance. Boyd took the boys aboard the *Wanderer* again.

Next day, all trooped back to the judge. The majority of the parents signified their willingness to allow the boys to sail on the schooner but demanded ten dollars for each boy shipped, the sum to be split between judge and schoolmaster. Boyd declined to take any of the lads under these limitations and it was necessary for the constables to lock up the boys in the calaboose to prevent their sneaking on board the yacht.

On July 10th the *Wanderer* and *Ariel* sailed from Hilo Bay in a light breeze. That night closed down dark and foggy and they lost sight of the *Ariel*. After a fruitless seach, the yacht bore away for the Kingsmill or Gilbert Group, a previously arranged rendezvous. On the 13th they spoke a Honolulu-bound schooner from Sydney which was bringing the first word of the gold strikes in Australia. This was not the only break in the monotony of the voyage, which they tried to relieve by catching fish, mainly sharks, and looking for schools of porpoises and whales, for on the 21st the cry of "Man Overboard!" went up. Timmararare was missing, as was a tub which had stood on deck.

Boyd had a boat lowered immediately and it was steered toward a spot where a flock of sea birds were circling. Sure enough, there was "Tim," holding on to the tub for dear life, a bird perched on his head. When the boat drew alongside him, he leaped aboard and broke into a chant which was followed by his slumping, unconscious, to the deck. He was revived in his hammock by a stiff glass of brandy.

When Webster asked him what the bird was doing on his head, Tim answered, "*Te manu* [bird] he speakee me, he say me no *mate* [drown]. In my country, *manu* plenty speak to man."

On the 28th they sighted a low, uncharted island almost on the line in about 176° west longtitude and on August 2nd they crossed the equator. Three days later they sighted Nukunau or Byron's Island in the Gilbert Islands. A fleet of more than one hundred canoes came out and circled the *Wanderer*. Boyd, not sure of the reception he would get from the wild Gilbert Islanders, ran out his deck guns. He relaxed, however, when he saw women and children accompanying the men in the canoes. The natives crowded on board peacefully but in such numbers that Boyd's crew had to push them over the side with the flat of their cutlasses. The Gilbert Islanders bartered coconuts, fish and shells for tobacco. "Tim" was a Gilbert Islander and he acted as interpreter to his kinsmen. Boyd and Webster learned much about the island, its customs and its seven villages from him.

The warriors carried wooden swords whose edges were armed with sharks' teeth. They also wore sea porcupine skin helmets and traveled in plank outrigger canoes fastened with sennet and calked with dried pandanus leaf. Some of the single-masted, mat-sailed canoes were fashioned of upwards of one hundred planks, and the craft ranged in length from twelve to twenty feet.

Boyd and Webster went ashore in the whaleboat but found that they could not land through the heavy surf without danger of capsizing. A native dove and anchored the boat to the bottom just outside the breakers and they transferred to canoes for the trip ashore. They arrived just in time for Boyd to save a youth, Kodoy, from strangling. He was sentenced to death for stealing coconuts. Boyd bribed the island officials with a few sticks of tobacco and saved the young islander, but, in Webster's words, "He afterwards turned out to be a bad speculation, as he was extremely lazy and cunning."

On the 8th, they reached the Island of Peru or Francis Island, but a gale prevented their landing. They ran with the wind, the islanders' canoes vainly pursuing them in hopes of obtaining a little tobacco. Next morning, Boyd fell in with Nonouti or Sydenham Island. Here they bartered with the natives of a village called Mucha but kept a wary eye on them, for these natives had attempted the capture of a whaler two years earlier but were repulsed by the crew. The *Wanderer* sailed on to Tabiteuea or Drummond's Island, giving tobacco to the natives who paddled out to greet them. The only thing they wished was tobacco. The whites commented that "clothing they do not use and they are even indifferent to knives and tomahawks."

One of the Drummond Islanders climbed aboard over the taff-rail and signified his wish to join the crew of the *Wanderer* by spitting in disgust at the men in the canoe he had just left. The canoeists departed, as well they might under such a mucousy bombardment, and the newcomer was duly installed as a crewman by being presented with a shirt. The boy's name was Bongo and next morning Friday cut off his long locks, while Kodoy watched in great amusement and satisfaction. Bongo's father came aboard to plead for the return of his son. The unfeeling youth asked, through signs, that the whites shoot his old father where he stood on deck. Boyd arranged matters to the satisfaction of all by giving the old man a file and a piece of tobacco.

They continued to Ocean Island or Paanopa, Tim's home (0° 43′ S and 169° 40′ E). The latter saluted the islanders but hid below when the king was paddled out to the yacht. Boyd

118

hustled him on deck, however, and forced the bashful Tim to greet his monarch. Next morning Boyd went ashore with Tim and was received very hospitably by the island potentate. The islanders' canoes and outriggers were well made but had no sails, and Boyd learned that the king had prohibited the use of sails to prevent his people from being tempted to go too far out to sea where they might be caught and swept away by the trade winds and mighty currents.

Tim found that his father was dead, his mother remarried, and that he had fallen heir to several hundred coconut trees. A wealthy man, he decided to leave the schooner. Boyd gave him a musket which Tim fired at intervals as he and Webster went ashore, to the astonishment of his countrymen. Tim also took his sea chest ashore, jammed with files, tobacco and tomahawks.

Ben Boyd hunted white tern on the island but carefully avoided the fish hawks, protected by royal decree. The principal chief of Paanopa was Tapuranda but it was his son, Tapu-Ki Paanopa, who had boarded the *Wanderer*. Another king lived on the northeast end of the island. Less powerful and independent than Tapuranda, he was Tapati. Webster roamed the island, and before they left, several islanders joined the crew.

On August 19th the *Wanderer* left Paanopa for Stewart's Island, Boyd leaving a letter with Tim for Bradley and the *Ariel* should they call there. At Stewart's Island, Barnes and Webster went ashore. At the end of the six-mile pull to shore Barnes' canoe capsized but no one was harmed. The two men enjoyed a fine bath on the island and stayed overnight after watching the hordes of hermit crabs scrambling about in the moonlight. Next morning they visited the larger island Sikaiana (Captain Cheyne's Sikyana). They ate delicious pork there and Webster shot a number of wild pigeons with his fowling piece and even killed a vampire bat with a four-foot six-inch wingspread, from tip to tip.

At noon of the next day they were paddled back to the *Wanderer* and Boyd went ashore after breakfast to do some exploring and shooting, as was becoming his habit during the island calls. Three unmarried islanders shipped as crewmen just before the *Wanderer* sailed. After taking aboard a stock of fresh coconuts, Boyd sailed on September 2nd and stood south for the mysterious Solomon Islands.

On the sixth they sighted San Christoval. The *Wanderer* passed to windward of Santa Ana and Santa Catalina Islands, then laid along the coast of San Christoval. The weather was squally for six days when it brightened into a warm, delightful day with flying fish rising and falling in the *Wanderer*'s track like glittering showers of blue and silver. They were cruising along only about four miles offshore with steep, heavily forested mountains looming above them.

There was no sign of inhabitants until two days later when Boyd lowered a boat so that he and Ottiwell could go ashore to ascertain if there was a good anchorage. No sooner had they begun to approach the shore than canoes appeared—beautiful boats, high-peaked at stem and stern and glittering with pearl shell. They were paddled by woolly-headed blacks who absolutely refused to come aboard the yacht.

The craft had no outriggers or sails but their crews were expert with paddles. All the men were armed, each canoe bristling with between eight and ten jagged-point spears. However, the natives made no hostile moves and Boyd was able to return to the yacht to report a splendid harbor around a point, sheltered from the prevailing winds. The *kanakas* threw on all canvas and the *Wanderer* flew around the point into the smooth and lovely harbor. Webster recalled "the scenery was as romantic as any lover of nature could desire to look upon."

A few natives were coaxed aboard and examined as carefully by their hosts as they themselves were studied by the Solomon Islanders. The latter were fairly friendly. They had low foreheads slanting up to mops of hair discolored with lime to a whitish or yellowish hue. Their teeth were stained by betel nut and they did not have the well-formed physique of the Polynesians of Boyd's crew. Unlike the Gilbert Islanders, they cared nothing for tobacco but were mad for anything made of iron—files, nails, knives or tomahawks. For iron they swapped yams, mangoes, and other fruit including the curious *vi* apple. They were intrigued by the *Wanderer*'s guns so Boyd fired a six-pounder. When it went off, the Melanesians dived over the side and, clambering into their canoes, paddled madly for shore. They could not be persuaded to return to the yacht for some time.

At sundown Boyd dismissed all the canoes and posted a strong watch on deck. He sought the natives' friendship but did not trust them in the least. Most of the crew spent the mild night sleeping on deck. The next morning, Boyd went ashore and returned early with a mess of pigeons he had shot for breakfast. After the meal, Webster went ashore for some shooting. When he returned he found numerous canoes around the *Wanderer* "but they were in no ways troublesome." It was truly a peaceful anchorage and Webster went ashore again near sundown, and later that night Boyd had a boat's crew row him up the bay in the moonlight. He returned several hours later, from seaward, having found a beautiful and landlocked harbor.

Next morning the natives helped them fill their water kegs at a stream and Webster took another hunting stroll. That evening several of the crew went ashore to investigate the village of twenty huts. Webster wrote: "By the presents of fish hooks and nails we became quite friendly with the inhabitants before we left, but we took the precaution not to separate from each other while in the village." The natives went everywhere well-armed but still showed no sign of hostility toward their visitors.

A group of strange canoes approached the *Wanderer* and a chief, Isitado, came aboard. He suggested that they visit Makira, his village. Webster noticed a paper protruding from the bag the chief wore around his neck. Isitado was eager for them to look at it. It was in French and in English. In it Captain Dutaille of H.M. Corvette *Ariadne* warned all captains of ships putting into the Bay of Leone that the natives had murdered three French missionaries in the mountains behind Makira on April 20, 1847. The paper reported that the corvette on March 2, 1848, burned the two villages of the murderers. Dutaille warned all to deal only with the natives of the village of Leone on the bay. The paper was dated March 4, 1848, Bay of Leone, San Christoval.

Webster showed the message to Boyd who agreed that they should exercise even more care and watchfulness. The natives were already beginning to steal anything loose on the schooner, especially iron, so Boyd decided to keep them off the vessel entirely. There were always ten to fifteen canoes clustered around the anchored yacht.

On one exploration, Crawford and Webster rowed into a wide bay studded with picturesque and lovely islands. On their right they passed the channel Boyd had discovered and to their left lay the great headland beyond which was Makira Bay. Landing on one of the small isles, they traded fishhooks with the natives for coconuts. Refreshed, they continued on and examined every inlet and bay, then landed again to explore the dense rain forest. When they came upon a trail the boys from the crew refused to go farther and ran back to the boat. Webster and Crawford went on, following a stream about three miles inland. Here Webster left his companion for a moment to follow a flock of pigeons he hoped to add to the ship's mess.

"When preparing to fire, I felt an indescribable sense of uneasiness—an unidentified sense of danger. Casting my eyes around, I saw at a few yards' distance the dark form of a native rise slowly from a crouching position, as if he had been in ambush. He had in his hand a formidable spear. I placed my back to the trunk of a tree. We surveyed each other in silence for some minutes."

Suddenly, the native threw his spear to the ground, assumed a friendly aspect and cried *"manu, manu!"* (bird, bird!), indicating that Webster should fire at the birds. Webster respectfully declined to empty his gun at the wild pigeons. Since he always carried nails and fishhooks in his pocket, he offered some to the savage who immediately put them in his hair, grinning hideously in satisfaction. He further indicated his pleasure by stroking Webster on the back with his hand.

Webster returned to the spot where he had left Crawford. The latter had also seen a black lurking in the bush. The two returned to the boat with the savage dogging their steps. They rested and refreshed themselves on the yacht, then went ashore again where they persuaded some of their "sable friends" to accompany them to a hilltop where, near some old deserted houses, they had good shooting. Pigeons fell right and left, and they had a full game bag when they went back to the schooner across the sunset-colored waters. The setting sun turned to a violet hue the fairy isles of Manuporo Bay.

Next day it was Ottiwell and Barnes who took the whaleboat on an exploratory circuit of the island which they now called Wanderer's Island. (They dubbed their anchorage Wanderer's Bay.) They landed on the shore but beat a hasty retreat when savages gathered in increasing numbers, all armed with spears, clubs, and bows and arrows.

With enough water aboard and the rigging and sails put back in order, Boyd prepared to leave San Christoval in search of the *Ariel*. Many canoes insisted upon remaining alongside that last night although they were frequently driven off. As the savages grew bolder, one of the canoes stole under the bow of the yacht —the point from which the vessel could be boarded most easily. Boyd fired one of the swivel guns on the rail over the heads of the Melanesians in the canoe. He heard a crash which indicated he had hit another craft hidden in the darkness behind the first. "A sudden splashing of numerous paddles indicated the presence of more canoes than we dreamed of, and at least a dozen canoes commenced a hasty retreat to shore, leaving luminous streams in their wake."

On the morning of the 16th, Boyd went ashore with Webster, two *kanakas* of the crew, and a few Makira aborigines to pay a last visit to Makira Bay while Ottiwell prepared the *Wanderer* for sailing as soon as they should return. The boat pulled out of Wanderer's Bay, they set the sail and passed Manuporo Bay, rounded the high bluff of the point and sailed almost due west along the coast with a fair wind. They found a large bay with the village of Makira at its innermost point. Sailing ten miles into the bight they reached a narrow passage which led to a spacious, hidden harbor half a mile wide and three miles long. Not till they were within half a mile of Makira were they able to sight the village.

The mountains huddled closely around the small, protected haven with its anchorage of ten to thirty fathoms. The instant Boyd and his men entered the landlocked bay they were becalmed. He ordered the sail taken in and they pulled for the village which aborigines pointed out as the residence of Isitado. Three other villages lay in sight, together with many yam clearings. The bay was the center of a well-populated area, for they found over forty houses in Makira alone. The whole village awaited them, the warriors armed with a hostile mien. But Isitado, smiling, threw his spear down on the sand and came forward to greet Boyd, who, with Webster, distributed fishhooks, nails and beads while the grim faces under woolly heads relaxed into smiles of thanks.

Boyd and Webster asked Isitado for green nuts and they soon were refreshing themselves with delicious coconut milk. They first visited the huge boathouse, a long building beside the water holding a number of canoes richly adorned with pearl shell.

Broadway wharf in the 1880s

Coal carts pass to and fro alongside the steel "Cape Horner" *Astral*

The Clipper Ship *Challenge:* as she
was launched (above); her skipper
(right); and as she appeared under
full sail (below)

The Easter Island cockleshell which
saved the crew of the *El Dorado*

The San Francisco waterfront in 1873

The Embarcadero shortly after the earthquake-fire of 1906

San Francisco Maritime Museum

Captain Ben Boyd

Sam Brannan, Frisco Filibusterer

The Ferry Building and Embarcadero as they appeared in the 1870s

The *Wild Wave* sailed to her death in the Pacific from the Embarcadero

Captain Josiah N. Knowles, Master of the *Wild Wave*

The post-Civil War Embarcadero

The ferries are gone today, but the Ferry Building—the "Queen of the Embarcadero"—still stands guard of the San Francisco waterfront, as it did in this photograph of twenty years ago

There was also wooden sculpture within the building and a fringe of human skulls decorating the rafters. Other decorations included fish skeletons, turtle heads and human rib and thigh bones. There were many war trophies in the form of broken spears and clubs and Webster noticed two large oblong wooden vessels of about fifty gallons capacity. Now he was surer than ever that their hosts were cannibals.

Hurrying to rejoin the *Wanderer* so that she could sail before sundown, Boyd presented Isitado with a tomahawk as a farewell gift. He delayed his return long enough to enter and explore one of the sea caves along the shore. Boyd saw many swallows the size of hummingbirds at the entrance and, thinking that they might build edible nests like those prized by Chinese gourmets, he ordered his tired *kanaka* oarsmen to pull into the grotto. Enormous bats flew about, screaming in the blackness of the cavern. Although they explored this cave and another (in which they found a beach on which they could land) they found no swallows' nests except upon the high roofs, far beyond reach. These were studded with them. By the time Webster had shot a specimen of the bats with a two-foot (extended) wingspread, their cave explorations had delayed them too long. They could not reach the *Wanderer* in time to sail that evening.

Since sailing was postponed until morning, Webster, Barnes and Ottiwell decided to go ashore with four crewmen to inspect the house of images which stood in another village. It was smaller than the building at Makira but fitted up in the same way, including the human skulls. The seven men hurried back to their boat when the natives began to gather in answer to a harangue by an angry elder. They were obviously in an ugly mood. When the men reached the *Wanderer,* they found from an angry Boyd that the blacks had sneaked aboard and stolen several boarding pikes, cutlasses and tomahawks in spite of the careful watch maintained on deck by the crew. All were on the alert that uneasy night but nothing untoward occurred. Next

125

morning not a canoe came out to the vessel nor could a native be seen on shore.

On the 17th of September they tripped anchor and towed the schooner out of the calm bay. Catching a breeze, they sailed along the coast in search of the tender. They saw no sign of the *Ariel* and by midnight had been caught by a gale which took their foreyard and topsail. They lay to until the next morning. The sea continued to run high and Boyd had just decided to run back into Marau or Wanderer's Bay when the sun plunged below the horizon and they were obliged to lay to in expectation of another uncomfortable night offshore. As the evening wore on a breeze which favored them came up and they stood in for Makira.

Many canoes came out to meet them and Isitado himself acted as pilot, telling them he had also boarded a ship (perhaps the *Ariel*) which had passed that way. The *Wanderer* anchored in ten fathoms and Boyd dismissed the canoes and set a watch for the night. The following day Boyd, Webster and Crawford went ashore to select a spar to replace their broken yard. Crawford set to work on it while Boyd and Webster kept the table well supplied with game.

Boyd and Webster were ashore almost every day hunting sea shells, collecting coral or shooting game. Boyd was the most cautious of the whites and he advised Webster not to get out of sight of the *Wanderer* nor to place any confidence in the blacks. He frankly regarded them as treacherous as well as thieves. They tried at every opportunity to steal Crawford's tools.

A week later, Webster went ashore alone and climbed a mountain from which he viewed the bay where the *Wanderer* lay at anchor. On the horizon he saw the "Island of Guadalcanar." (It was more commonly called Guadalcanar than Guadalcanal until World War II and it was sometimes known also as Ghila.) Suddenly, the thought occurred to him that he was on the hill above Makira, where the French missionaries had been massacred in 1847.

As he started down the five-mile trail to the beach opposite the yacht, he came across a hut. He gave nails to a native who met him there and received coconut milk in return. Continuing on down the trail, he looked back to see the aborigine following him with a spear in his hand. Webster stopped and waved him back, standing his ground. The native stopped but motioned Webster to go on. Boyd's friend refused to turn his back, however, and raised his (unloaded) gun instead. The islander ran off and disappeared in the bush. Webster went on down the trail but glanced back every few minutes to see if he was being followed. Apparently the native had been scared off and he made the boat safely.

During his absence, an aborigine had stolen two knives from the very sheaths of two *kanaka* crewmen helping Crawford shape the log into a spar. The *kanakas* chased the thief but he was soon swallowed up by the dense undergrowth. One of the boys vented his rage and contempt against the detested Melanesians by chopping a number of coconut trees with his tomahawk. The Solomon Islanders thought the affair a huge joke.

Boyd and Webster spent a day circling Makira Bay. They were very impressed with its possibilities as a harbor and Boyd decided to arrange a treaty with the natives to acquire and hold Makira and its surrounding tract of lands for a commercial future. During their tour they discovered a rocky islet piled up with two huge heaps of skeletons. They were not sure whether it was simply a casual burial place or a postprandial cannibal dumping ground, but they were inclined toward the latter supposition.

One day as Webster was making his way along the beach toward the boat which was pulling inshore to pick him up, a group of natives rushed at him with spears upraised. They had stopped and were preparing to throw when Isitado appeared among them, remonstrating. Webster jumped into the whale-boat and the *kanakas* dug in their oars, leaving the natives to their argument.

At this time Crawford discovered that his ax had been stolen. He and Ottiwell pursued the thief into the village where a woman pointed to a hut. They entered it and found the native. They grappled with him and took the ax away from him. The aborigine grabbed up a bunch of spears and hurled one with great force at Ottiwell. The latter dodged it dexterously, seized the Solomon Islander and wrenched three more spears away from him. The native fled to the bush from the redoubtable Ottiwell but soon the villagers began to gather, waving their spears.

Boyd, seeing the trouble on shore, brought the *Wanderer* close in, to command the whole village with her guns. Crawford and Ottiwell gathered up their tools and went aboard the schooner. Although Isitado remained friendly, the whites quickly noticed that all the women and children had been sent to the interior. The natives were obviously itching for a fight with these white and brown strangers.

However, Isitado was still enjoying the role of peacemaker. He came aboard to sign a document of compensation for the theft, agreeing to pay five pigs and one hundred yams. The paper contained the figure of a porker with five marks beneath it and a picture of a yam with one hundred marks. The chief went ashore and a big discussion ensued—to fight or not to fight. Boyd, Webster, Barnes, Crawford and Ottiwell kept their eyes on the crowd of milling savages. Webster later recalled, "To do them justice, they did not seem afraid of us."

The peace party won over the younger warmongers. Boyd was so pleased with peacemaker Isitado that he returned the pigs and paid for the yams delivered as indemnity. Peace reigned supreme again on San Christoval although there were still surly faces among the men when the women and children reappeared.

The next morning strange canoes were seen entering the harbor and Isitado introduced Chief Jerobo to Boyd. The chief could speak a few words of English, having been on a whaler briefly off the Solomon Islands. Boyd, using Jerobo as a translator, asked the Solomon Islanders if they would like the white men to come live with them. The answer was a hearty yes.

The spar finished, Boyd was ready to resume his leisurely cruise to the Australian gold fields. He arranged with Isitado for a farewell dance and about thirty young men gamboled on the beach. The *Wanderer's kanakas* stayed on shore to entertain the Melanesians with their wild shouts and savage yells which differed so much from the strangely pleasant melody of the woolly-headed savages' songs.

At about six in the morning they started out of the bay. Several of the village lads tried to go with them but their parents forcibly dissuaded them by pitching them off the yacht. Jerobo and his wild-looking constituents tried to persuade the whites to come ashore at another point on the San Christoval coast but Boyd made sail for Guadalcanal. They were becalmed but on the 11th they were able to stand close inshore. Here on the Guadalcanal coast the canoes did not come alongside and the natives were the wildest they had seen.

Ottiwell, Webster and a boat crew explored the shore for an anchorage as the natives followed them along the beach, brandishing spears and shouting. Webster stood up in the boat, waved his hat and in sign language tried to get them to put down their weapons. The *kanakas* rowing the whaleboat gave a shout, pulled hard on the oars and the boat shot toward the beach. Webster almost went overboard, the aborigines scattered like frightened chickens and the Polynesian oarsmen shrieked with laughter.

John Webster was the first to step out on the soil of Guadalcanal but he and the others just stretched their legs. The *Wanderer* was becalmed on the 13th and 14th of October so Boyd and Ottiwell made another whaleboat reconnaissance, finding a good anchorage in a sheltered cove. Boyd was never in better spirits than at Guadalcanal. He walked up and down the beach exclaiming, "Is this not delightful?"

The *Wanderer* lost the breeze again and had to be towed into the cove. Still, none of the natives would come alongside in their canoes, although Boyd offered knives and tomahawks to them. At sundown they fired a six-pounder to see the effect on the wild-looking Guadalcanese. The canoes retreated but seeing only smoke and hearing only noise (Boyd had fired a blank charge), they returned soon. It was a lovely night, and Boyd and Webster spent the early evening in cleaning their guns and filling their shot belts and powder flasks. The two sportsmen anticipated good hunting the next day.

A sharp watch was kept all night and Webster stood his turn. When he arose at 6 A.M., late for him, he found that Boyd was already halfway to shore. Webster hailed him and the leader of the expedition said he would be back on board for breakfast, bringing along a bag of game for dinner. With Boyd was Kapetania of Paanopa who sculled the boat. They entered a small creek, which could be seen emptying into the anchorage, and then disappeared behind a screen of vegetation at the bend of the creek. Webster had a leisurely breakfast and neither he nor the others paid any particular attention to two shots fired on shore about a quarter of an hour apart.

Few canoes were to be seen and they were only near the schooner. However, a large body of natives was seen collecting at the mouth of the creek. It was such a warm morning that all four of Boyd's white companions went into the water to enjoy a swim. The *kanaka* crewmen noticed the canoes exchanging signals and producing weapons and called the attention of Webster, Barnes, Ottiwell and Crawford to it. The four climbed on board. The savages alongside tried to get them to go ashore by crying "*laku, laku manu*" (plenty birds to shoot). They also tried to entice them ashore with women, pointing to a group of belles on the beach and shouting "*hahine, hahine.*"

Suddenly, the quiet waters of the bay began to boil with thrusting paddles and a whole fleet of canoes appeared as out of nowhere. Shrill war cries filled the air. Ottiwell expressed the worry of all when he remarked that he had heard no shots recently from shore. Webster sounded the gong for Boyd. There was no answer except the jeering of the natives.

One Melanesian went so far as to climb into the whaleboat, waving his spear. A cry from a *kanaka* up forward caught the whites' attention and they saw one of their crew running aft, his arm cut to the bone by a native weapon. At the same moment, Webster saw the Guadalcanese boarding the *Wanderer* by the bowsprit and the martingale. The unprepared Aussies and Americans armed themselves somehow in the confusion but Webster warned them not to start a fight for fear the natives would kill Mr. Boyd.

Webster still thought he could bluff these Solomon Islanders as Boyd had done at San Christoval. He did not run the deck guns out or even load them but contented himself with ordering the boarding pikes unshipped. The *kanakas* used them to keep the islanders off the ship's sides. Webster darted below and handed up to the others five or six muskets and a case of cartridges. "Keep from firing," he ordered them, "remember Mr. Boyd!"

Then suddenly, "a cry rose from the water; a cry, which heard once, could never be forgotten." War conches roared sullenly and a shower of stones, spears and arrows came whistling at the flinching crew, accompanied by a chorus of demoniacal yells. The men hid behind the bulwarks to let the first shower of missiles pass, then stood up and fired their muskets —each loaded with ten pistol balls—into the crowded canoes.

131

The effect of their firing was deadly but it did not stop the savages from boarding the *Wanderer*. Many were driven off or shot down on the aftersides of the vessel itself.

A moment of quiet was followed by another blasting of the conch shells and the natives rushed in a second attack. Boarding forward this time, they soon were driving the desperate crew aft. Their wickerwork shields held off the boarding pikes of the *kanaka* seamen, so Webster fired a double-barreled gun into their midst. Their shields had no effect against the lead balls and two fell, wounded or dying. The *kanakas* made a quick recovery, charged the Solomon Islanders and speedily cleared the deck, killing the wounded and throwing them over the side.

Webster now loaded the two-pounder swivel with grapeshot, trained it on the nearest canoe and fired. A white cloud of smoke belched from the piece and hid his view, but when it cleared away he saw the canoe upset and the water discolored with blood. The one cannon shot decided the battle; the Melanesians beat a feverish retreat.

Webster and the others had by now given up hope of seeing Boyd alive. Lulled by the beauty of the surroundings, he had gone ashore with only his fowling piece. His *kanaka* boatman was unarmed. The whites, sure of the fate of their leader, now longed to revenge him. While the *kanakas* danced and sang, Webster and his comrades ran out the deck guns and opened up on the canoes which clustered some one hundred yards away. The natives jumped from the battered canoes in wild confusion, struggled to the beach and disappeared inland, carrying their dead and wounded.

Just when Webster and the others were about to slacken their fire, they spied a native running along the beach wearing Benjamin Boyd's hat. The angered whites now brought the Long Tom into play, bombarding the village and chasing the lurking savages from their huts into the forest.

Webster left Barnes in charge of the schooner and took Otti-well, Crawford and four *kanakas* ashore to try to find some trace of Boyd and to rescue him if he were still alive. They entered the creek and left one seaman to guard the boat and to keep it afloat, ready for a quick retreat should the natives charge the small party. Scarcely one hundred yards up the stream they found Boyd's boat on the dry bank from which the tide had ebbed.

They tracked Boyd by his footprints in the sand but found that his steps circled back to the boat. Directly in front of his last footprints lay the wadding from his double-barreled gun. He had apparently fired both charges at once. Around his last steps the sand was thickly pocked with the footprints of the savages. Webster thought that the position of two deep foot-prints indicated the stance of a savage in the act of throwing a spear. He placed his feet over the marks in the sand and found himself "directly in front of Mr. Boyd's last tracks, and in the line of his last shot." Investigating further, while keeping a wary eye out for the natives, they found many more tracks of bare feet but found no further trace of Boyd or his *kanaka* companion.

The white men retraced their steps to the beach and de-stroyed the canoes which they found there. A thunderstorm came up quickly and obliged them to make a hasty retreat to the yacht as their powder was dampened and rendered useless. They were grateful that the savages did not know this.

When the weather cleared, John Webster led another search party ashore. They advanced on the village a quarter of a mile from Boyd's tracks, answering the yells of the savages with musket shots. They rushed into the village but found that all the inhabitants had fled to the hills, where they gathered in plain sight. The huts were riddled with shot from the small-arms and cannon fire, and one dead man, shot through the head, lay in a canoe. In another canoe, stranded and half-full of blood and water, they found Benjamin Boyd's sword belt and cartridge pouch.

Webster broke open the houses, which had their doorways closed and latched. There were patches and pools of blood everywhere. His hopes of finding traces of Boyd, however, were in vain. The whites searched every house, then put the village to the torch.

When they returned to the beach they found that their native crewmen had hacked up the dead savage and were apparently about to cook up the remains. With some difficulty, Webster put a stop to this barbarous gesture of defiance by the seamen. As they fired the scattered houses on the hill, the natives above rolled huge boulders down at them. The great rocks crashed down the slope, snapping branches and tearing through the brush. The men from the *Wanderer* fired at the skulking natives but their shots had little effect, so well sheltered were the Solomon Islanders.

To prevent another attack on the schooner, the whites broke up every canoe they could find. At sundown they returned to the *Wanderer* where breakfast still lay, untouched, on the cabin table awaiting Mr. Boyd's return. Webster kept half the crew on watch that night, firing guns at intervals to show the natives that they were on the alert. Dark figures could be seen on the shore, outlined by the embers of the burning huts, but no canoes came out from the beach.

As morning broke, the village site was still obscured by a light cloud of smoke. A party of eight men went ashore to once again inspect Boyd's tracks and perhaps follow them farther up the creek. They had no luck there so they turned their attention to the ruins of the village. The *kanakas* ran about as scouts, yelling and waving their cutlasses.

They pulled around the point in the whaleboat and left one man to guard it. The rest of them invaded a village. Webster detailed three of his *kanakas* to hold off a group of natives who were growing bolder. The others ransacked the houses and set them afire, and destroyed several canoes including one, with a fancy figurehead, which had led the attack on the schooner on the preceding day.

Webster recalled that a large, double-headed canoe had retreated from the engagement to another settlement farther up the coast and he decided to search that village for Boyd. On the 19th of October they stood in as close to the village as they dared—the sailing master reported no anchorage—and bombarded it with grape and round shot. The natives fled to the forest. Two miles out from shore, Webster's little army again embarked in the whaleboat, leaving the schooner to Crawford and two wounded *kanakas*. Webster had mounted one of the swivel guns in the bow of the whaleboat and he fired several shots at the huts as they approached the beach.

The shore was too rocky to land near the deserted village, so they pulled around a point and landed about a mile from the town. Three men stood guard on the boat, the others marched into the large village and searched it carefully. They found that most of the natives had removed all their possessions, but they fired the huts and destroyed the single canoe they found. Webster discovered a fresh skull which he took to be Kapetania's, because of the straight black hairs which still were attached to it in places. He gave it to one of the crew to carry but the sailor threw it away during an alarm on the mile-long march back to the whaleboat.

A black storm was brewing overhead as they neared the boat and its three-man guard. They rushed through the surf and tumbled into the boat, nearly capsizing it. Soon neither the island nor the *Wanderer* was visible; the only guide to the men crowded into the whaleboat was the wind and they prayed that it would not shift many points.

Breakers rolled in and buffeted the boat. They found it hard to keep it afloat in the successive squalls and, as night drew on, they faced the gloomy prospect of not finding the schooner or finding her driven far offshore. Crawford and the two wounded Polynesians could not manage her alone. At length, someone cried out in joy and they caught a glimpse of the schooner dead ahead of them, looming dimly through the drift. For three more hours they pulled on the oars before they could beat the storm and gain the lee side of the *Wanderer* to get safely on deck.

They found the schooner lying to, her lee guns under water. The men hurriedly squared the yards and scudded before the gale. Next morning they were far offshore, becalmed under a scorching sun and short of water. At the same time they ran out of firewood and had to burn their spare spars and the boat in which Boyd had gone ashore on Guadalcanal. Any further hope of finding Boyd seemed impossible, so Webster set a course for Australia.

On November 7th they sighted the coast and ran down to Port Macquarie. Here they ran headlong into another storm and the windlass parted as the *Wanderer* pitched heavily. She managed to hold on her anchors until daybreak when Webster fired two guns for assistance. Both masts were now sprung and her spars disabled. They could not stand to sea. A schooner captain agreed to pilot them over the bar and they lightened ship by jettisoning their iron ballast. Running before the wind, they headed in. Several times the *Wanderer* struck but the heavy seas swept her on. Suddenly, however, she struck hard. Her keel caught and she swung broadside to the rollers. Within minutes the life was crushed out of her on the rocks. The seas burst through the cabin floor, swept the decks and the *Wanderer* lay a complete wreck. One of the *kanakas* swam ashore with a light line which was fastened to a warp on the schooner and the heavy cable was soon ashore. The men all made it to the beach safely on the cable.

Crawford started immediately for Sydney to report Boyd's

disappearance and the loss of the *Wanderer*. Within a few days, the only vestige of the beautiful yacht was a scattering of timbers strewn along the high-water mark. The wanderings of the *Wanderer* were over, like her master's dream of a Papuan Confederation, but the mystery of Benjamin Boyd's fate remained.

The news of his disappearance reached San Francisco in the spring of 1852 and, according to the *Alta California*, "created a lively sensation in the public mind." In 1854 the trading cutter *Oberon*, under the command of Captain Truscott, fell in with the whaling bark *Woodlark*. Captain Field told Truscott that he had spoken the whaler *Bell*, commanded by Captain Andy, which in turn had fallen in with an unnamed American whaler off Guadalcanal. The American whaleship reported having sent boats ashore for water and had discovered in nearly all of the trees growing by the bay the name BENJAMIN BOYD cut in deep letters.

The American whaler had then sailed to San Christoval where, some three weeks earlier, a number of visiting Guadalcanese had reported that they "had in their keeping at Guadalcana a white man and a boy. . . . The man was described as being stout, very tall and having a beard."

Truscott brought the news of the carved names and the report of Boyd and Kapetania to Sydney after having a run-in with the natives of Treasury Island. Truscott, his cook, and a seaman were cut up by the savages' tomahawks without any provocation, according to the captain.

San Franciscans who had welcomed Boyd to their fair city on March 29, 1850, read an article in the *Alta California* more than four years later (October 18, 1854) which quoted the optimistic Melbourne *Argus:* "Strange as it may seem, the reasons for thinking that he is still alive are indeed so strong as to almost amount to proof." Meetings were held in Sydney and the merchants of that city approached the Government to make a rescue attempt. The Government promised to aid in the project

137

and it was hoped that the steamer *Washington* would be sent to Guadalcanal but nothing happened.

Finally, the *Oberon* was sent back by private subscription with a force of volunteers. The cutter called first at Makira, San Christoval, where the men heard reports that Boyd was definitely alive on Guadalcanal. Hardly had the *Oberon* started for the latter island, however, when some of the Guadalcanese taken aboard changed their story and said both Boyd and his *kanaka* had been killed. They explained that the story of Boyd's being alive had been invented to appease the natives of San Christoval. The Guadalcanal Islanders believed the San Christoval natives to have been great friends of the white man and they feared that they would fall upon their villages in revenge.

According to the natives' story, Kapetania had been killed upon landing but Boyd had been temporarily spared. He was later slain in revenge for the killing of five warriors by the *Wanderer's* cannonading. Finally, they reported that Boyd's skull was hanging in the canoe house of a chief called Tabula.

Truscott believed their story and offered a reward of twenty tomahawks for the skull. It was stolen, delivered to him, and the reward paid. The captain, afraid of starting a war over the skull's theft, hurried the *Oberon* away for Australia. The cutter arrived in Sydney in December 1854 where the skull was found to be that of a Papuan, not a European, and an old skull besides. Truscott had been swindled neatly of his tomahawks. The skull was placed in the Sydney Museum.

Few men doubted that Boyd and his boatman had been killed upon landing, but Captain Denham took H.M.S. *Herald* to Guadalcanal shortly after the *Oberon* left. The warship anchored off a village west of Cape Hunter on Guadalcanal on December 20, 1854. A chief came aboard who reported the sale of the skull to Truscott, adding that it had been taken from the canoe house of Chief Bosakau, the real murderer of Ben Boyd, rather than from Chief Tabula's establishment.

Large rewards for any relic of Boyd were made by Denham but they were unavailing. A canoe-load of skulls and bones was brought out but they proved to be of various Pacific races. Supe, a witness to the murder, was detained aboard the *Herald* to pilot the warship to an anchorage off Wana village. He said Benjamin Boyd had been first speared, then cut down with an ax. Denham was unable to determine whether he had been killed immediately upon landing or at some later date.

An attempt to capture Bosakau was made. One of the boats from the *Herald* pursued his swift canoe into the surf. The canoe capsized but Bosakau got ashore in spite of the fire of the men in the boat. A report later reached Denham that he had died of his wounds but this may have been for the purpose of evading further pursuit and punishment.

Denham landed a large armed party under the cover of the pinnacle and its twelve-pounder. The men made a careful search but found no trees marked with Boyd's name or initials. The boat went on to Wanderer Bay and to the site of Boyd's presumed murder on the bank of the creek. The nearby huts were searched but nothing found except a tomahawk, bearing the initials *B.B.*, which was in the possession of one of the natives. This last relic of Boyd's to be found was undoubtedly the trade tomahawk thrown by him to the natives on October 14th to attract them alongside the *Wanderer*.

No further trace of Boyd or knowledge of his fate has ever been found in the century since his death. However, little doubt remains that Benjamin Boyd and his *kanaka* comrade, Kapetania, were murdered and then eaten as "long pig" from some village cooking pot near Wanderer Bay, Guadalcanal.

Chapter VI

LETTERS OF MARQUE

LIKE many an Argonaut before him, and like more than a handful since, Asbury Harpending sailed for California to make his fortune with no more impressive prerequisites or credentials than $5 in gold coin and a Colt's revolver. A Kentuckian without a colonelcy but with a lust for adventure, he was a true soldier of fortune from the day he ran away to join William Walker's filibusters as a beardless youth. He was still in his eighteenth year when he took passage from Panama to California, whiling away the tedium of shipboard life by middle-manning five dollars' worth of bananas and oranges into a $400 bankroll.

When the steamer dumped its thousand gold-seekers on the beach at San Francisco, Harpending went directly from steerage to the Mother Lode. He found that the placers were beginning to pan out rather thin a decade after Marshall's discovery of color in the Coloma millrace, so he tried his hand at commerce. Doubtless he was reassured by his success as a banana broker on board the Panama steamer. Buying a small trading vessel, he hired a crew of Spanish-speaking seamen and took a little money and a lot of goods on a tramp-trading junket up the Gulf of California. After stopping at various pestilential and soporific

141

little ports, he put in at Mazatlán's Olas Altas Bay and decided to have another fling at mining.

His luck was good this time and he returned from the Sierra Madre Occidental to San Francisco in 1860 with jingling pockets. He might have gone up into robber-baronial company, what with his capital, energy and intelligence, but the Civil War broke and Harpending found himself a rabid rebel in a Yankee stronghold. He rallied with other Southern sympathizers in 1861 in the plot to take California out of the Union by creating a Republic of the Pacific. However, Harpending and the other conspirators of this Far West Knights of the Golden Circle were thwarted by General Albert Sidney Johnston, a Southerner commanding the Military District of the Pacific, who would have no part in the conspiracy. While Harpending was lying low, waiting for this fiasco to blow over, other Confederate partisans were busy.

San Francisco, in 1861, considered itself light-miles from the scene of hostilities when the Civil War began. Communications were slow, the Panama Canal not yet dug, and a transcontinental railroad was still eight years in the offing. "The Rock," Fort Alcatraz, had only 120 soldiers in barracks built for 600, although Johnston had ordered 10,000 muskets and ammunition to be stored there. Two companies of the 3d U. S. Artillery occupied Fort Point on the Golden Gate.

That same year, Confederate Agent John T. Pickett was operating in Mexico and issued five blank letters of marque to Don Mateo Ramírez, a government official of Sinaloa and Baja California who was "of great sagacity and prudence, and was keenly desirous of capturing a California gold ship. . . ." Pickett predicted that soon the Confederate States of America would hear of his operations in the Pacific.

Ramírez did not go privateering, but rumors of his plans and those of imaginary individuals so unnerved San Franciscans that three millions in gold was accumulated in July 1861 over and above the usual deposits because of the imagined Confederate privateers which supposedly lay in wait for the gold steamers. San Francisco became a hive of wild war rumors and the Bay City found itself, in its collective imagination at least, on the shores of what we would call a "second front" today. Plans were made for erecting batteries near Lime Point on the Marin shore of the Golden Gate, at Blunt's and Stewart's Point on Angel Island, and on Yerba Buena Island. Warships were few. The old frigate *Independence* at Mare Island had been transformed into a barracks. The new and more effective *Saginaw* was laid up for repairs. The Coast Survey ship *Active*, veteran of Puget Sound Indian wars, was rushed to San Francisco under Commander Benjamin F. Sanders and was then sent up-Bay to Mare Island where, taking on a battery of 32-pounders, she anchored to protect the powder magazine while her crew was drilled into shape on board and ashore.

The Pacific Mail Steamship Company begged the Navy Department for protection and John B. Montgomery, Flag Officer in command of the Pacific Squadron, was advised of the probable existence of C. S. N. privateers outfitting in the Pacific. He thought there was little probability of their being on the Coast, but when a privateer was reported being fitted out in a Chilean port he sent a cruiser and found the Confederate privateer to be a "ghost." However, at this time, a rudimentary convoy system for San Francisco ships was set up.

On August 11th, a private letter from Hong Kong was printed in a San Francisco paper stating that a Confederate cruiser was being readied in Shanghai for operations in the China Sea. The fact that the outfitting was to be done with United States Naval stores would seem to have compounded the crime in Regular Navy eyes. According to the rumor, two steamship captains, Allen and Lynch, and Frederick Townsend Ward, the Yankee predecessor to Chinese Gordon as commander of the "Ever Victorious" Imperial Chinese Army, were joining with an ex-United States Navy storekeeper, Judge Cleary.

The tale reached the ears of Commander James Findley Schenck of the U.S.S. *Saginaw*, which had been brought back into service and was calling at Hong Kong at the time, and he took the creaking side-wheeler to Shanghai. On August 13, 1861, he encountered the suspected vessel, the *Neva*, just outside the Wusung Bar. Schenck carefully examined the *Neva* and was convinced that the rumor was the result of the idle blabbermouthing of Storekeeper Cleary, a passenger on the vessel which he also owned. Schenck allowed the *Neva* to continue on to Kanagawa and San Francisco.

Soon, everybody with even one good eye was spying Confederate cruisers hull down on the horizon. The Honolulu *Pacific Commercial Advertiser* ran an item titled "A Privateer of the Pacific" which displayed the keen imagination, not to say courage, of Captain Edward Nickels of the clipper *Bald Eagle* on the second day of a passage out of San Francisco. Nickels was apparently a literate man and one who kept up with the papers and their privateer scares. The second day out he observed a sail on his windward quarter. He kept on course till the vessel approached close enough for him to digest the "long, low, suspicious" look of the schooner-rigged "black craft." The captain then went below, consulted his charts, comparing the course of the schooner with the wind, and concluded that the "black craft" was on a course "bound nowhere but to speak his ship." She was now close enough so that he could see that she was well-manned and no regular trader. Since Nickels had $530,000 aboard the *Bald Eagle*, he changed his course, put his clipper in her best sailing trim by setting every inch of canvas she could carry, and left the black schooner hull down astern by nightfall.

Nickels was certain the schooner was a Secesh privateer. He would not have feared an encounter with her, he made it known, since the *Bald Eagle* carried two guns and plenty of small arms, but since it was obvious that the "raider" carried guns of longer range, he crowded on all sail.

Rumors of Rebel plots bloomed as lush as May lupine in 1862. The Navy Department sent the screw sloop-of-war *Wyoming* to investigate reports of a privateer, armed with eight rifled cannon, in Chinese waters. The *Wyoming* found no Rebs but did manage to find a private war in the Straits of Shiminoseki. Here a Japanese *daimyo* brought three of his armed vessels—a steamer, a brig and a bark—into action against the *Wyoming*, together with a half-dozen land batteries mounting two to four guns each. The *Wyoming* was hulled eleven times, five crewmen were killed, and Commander David McDougall was wounded, but the rugged Scot steamed between the brig and bark (to port) and the steamer (to starboard) and, broadsiding at pistol range, exploded the Japanese steamer's boilers and holed the brig so that she settled by the stern and presumably sank. The Prince of Nagato suffered heavy damage to his war gear, troops and "face," but no decision has ever been rendered as to just who won this vest-pocket war.

The Calcutta *Englishman* in 1863 carried a story, which was snatched up by American newspapers, that the captain of the British ship *Selim* had talked to the commander of a Confederate raider cruising the Bay of Bengal who boasted he would capture, burn or destroy every vessel leaving Calcutta flying the American flag. This was again fiction or imagination at work but much closer to home—in fact, right beneath the noses of Uncle Sam's cannon—a privateer was being fitted out for the Confederacy, and by no one else but the erstwhile banana vender-miner, Asbury Harpending.

Harpending's plan, like that of many others, was to fit out a commerce raider on the Pacific Coast to prevent shipments of California gold from reaching the East. Either from high moral persuasion or apprehension as to the fate of his own skin, should

145

his plan fail, he first procured letters of marque and a commission in the Navy of the Confederate States of America to legalize his operations, although certain Southern sympathizers in California suggested he go into out-and-out piracy.

He took ship from San Francisco to Acapulco, made the journey across country safely to Vera Cruz, though he was delayed in the field by Mexican bandits, and boarded a blockade runner which skipped past the Federal warships and entered Charleston, South Carolina. In Richmond, the Confederate capital, President Jefferson Davis gave him a hearing and presented him with blank letters of marque and a packet of communications for prominent Southerners on the West Coast. He further warned Harpending of the dangers of outfitting a vessel in a Pacific port but approved of the plan to intercept California gold shipments.

Judah P. Benjamin, Confederate Secretary of State, suggested a plan which would seemingly not be an infraction of international law. He advised Harpending to outfit the privateer in a United States port but cautioned him not to commit any acts against U. S. commerce until the vessel could reach a foreign harbor where it should publicly display its letters of marque and announce its intention to prey on American shipping.

Harpending was fortunate to find a Southern financier in California—Ridgely Greathouse, a well-to-do Yreka banker. Greathouse agreed to finance the enterprise. At the same time Greathouse enlisted another soldier of fortune as a lieutenant, an Englishman named Alfred Rubery.

Rubery and Harpending tried to buy a vessel but the draft with which they attempted to make the purchase was refused for lack of funds. Agents of Greathouse in Victoria, British Columbia, were unsuccessful in finding a suitable steamer except the U. S. Revenue Cutter *Shubrick*, the capture of which they felt would be "a somewhat difficult operation, as Uncle Sam keeps a sharp lookout on things up here." So sharp that the

Shubrick's commander smelled out the plot and threw the conspirators among his crew into the Port Angeles jail. The old steamer *Oregon* was considered, but a trial trip proved her to be too slow for their purposes and she was rejected.

While the search for a speedy steamer went on, Harpending and Rubery visited lonely Cedros Island, off the Baja California coast, verifying its desirability as a rendezvous and depot location from which they could launch their attacks on Panama–San Francisco steamers.

In January 1863 Harpending returned to San Francisco and interviewed an unemployed Pacific Mail Steamship Company captain, William C. Law, at his Stockton Street roominghouse. Law swore up and down that he was a Southern sympathizer. These protestations of Mason-Dixon devotion did not impress Harpending as much as the man's undoubted competence as a navigator. In fact, Asbury was suspicious of the captain and reluctant to employ him, for he was "possessor of a sinister, villainous mug," as Harpending put it, and he looked to be capable of committing any crime.

Law may have been reptilian-looking, but he found a vessel where the conspirators had failed, and did so almost immediately. His choice was not a steamer but a 91-ton, sturdy schooner named the *J. W. Chapman.* This was the ship which stood by the U.S.S. *Vermont* for six days when she was nearly wrecked on Nantucket Shoals in February 1862. Captain A. J. Chapman had brought her into San Francisco with a cargo of beans for Hellman Bros. in a fast run of 130 days from New York, posted February 17, 1863. She was certainly speedy enough for the Confederates' purposes. Law showed Harpending the advertisement which appeared in the February 28 and March 10 numbers of the *Mercantile Gazette and Prices Current* and, after a look at the ship, the three men agreed that it was their cup of tea. Greathouse put up $6,500 for its purchase, plus a sum of money for arms and ammunition, stores, and wages for a mate and crew.

Captain Law docked the *J. W. Chapman* and hired an experienced Canadian sailor, Lorenzo L. Libby, as mate, and four sailors and a cook. Harpending hired his "marines," fifteen mercenaries, from the waterfront at the same time.

By making it known that he was planning another trading venture in Mexican waters, similar to his 1859 voyage, Harpending was able to purchase two 12-pound cannon, 200 shells, 30 kegs of powder, fuses, muskets, 150 Colt Navy revolvers, lead, 40,000 percussion caps, and uniforms. This sort of cargo was not unusual for Mexican ventures, since Mexico was in the throes of her civil war—the liberals fighting the conservatives who supported Emperor Maximilian's shaky Second Empire. Harpending carefully stowed all the cases of arms, labeled plainly OIL MILL and MACHINERY, in the hold of the *Chapman*. He then had a load of lumber sent aboard for building berths for his oversized crew, and for fitting in a lower deck and constructing a brig to hold the Yankee prisoners he expected to take when the schooner metamorphosed into a corsair.

The ringleaders agreed on the splitting of the booty. Greathouse would receive the lion's share of captured treasure because of his heavy financial stake in the enterprise. Harpending would take the next largest and Rubery, Law and Libby would divide the remainder. They did not let the crew in on their plans but allowed them to think they were signed on for Mexican coastal trading and gunrunning.

The plan was to sail from San Francisco on Sunday, March 15, 1863, for Guadalupe Island, a barren spot three hundred miles off the coast of Baja California which had replaced Cedros Island as a rendezvous point. Here Harpending and his fighting force would disembark while the *J. W. Chapman* would sail to Manzanillo to discharge cargo. Returning to Guadalupe, she would be converted into a privateer, sail again to Manzanillo where the hirelings would sign articles and have their names inserted in the blank spaces on the Richmond letter, swearing an oath of fealty to the Confederacy. The next step would be the capture and plundering of a steamer bound from San Francisco to Panama which would be used to help capture a second Panama steamer to add to their growing fleet. They then planned to seize a salvage ship engaged in recovering the gold from the steamer *Golden Gate,* shipwrecked near Manzanillo. Finally, the little Confederate flotilla would sail to Peru's Chincha Islands, burn any American guano ships there, and cross the Pacific to the China Sea and Indian Ocean to raid American commerce in those waters.

Captain Law obtained clearance papers for the *J. W. Chapman* from the Customhouse, signing and swearing to a false manifest and declaring he had a mate and a four-man crew aboard, with a cargo of quicksilver, merchandise and machinery for Manzanillo. (There actually was $38,000 of cargo aboard, including 789 flasks of mercury.)

To avoid any suspicion of the real nature of the enterprise on the waterfront, Harpending chose the very "Yankee house" of Messrs. Bunker, Greaves & Company as his shipping agent. The *J. W. Chapman* was advertised to sail on or about March 19, 1863, but the plotters prepared to slip out in the darkness of the night of March 14th, with Greathouse and Harpending promising to be on board the ship by 10 P.M.

Rubery and Harpending assembled their fighting force in the dark alley behind the American Exchange Hotel. The men broke up into three groups and strolled through the dimly lighted streets past sailors' boardinghouses and roaring saloons to East Street, the Embarcadero. As the men hurried aboard, they saw Greathouse frantically pacing the deck. Captain Law, detained in some waterfront dive, had not yet come aboard. Helpless without their navigator, Harpending and Greathouse could only nervously await his coming.

149

At 2 A.M. Harpending sent the crew below to get some sleep, the lookout being ordered to rouse them out at five. The fifteen privateersmen, with two sailors detached to see that they did not leave the ship, were bedded down in an open space left for them among the cargo directly under the main hatch.

Hour after hour they waited in vain for Captain Law. Finally, Rubery suggested that they sail without him and, at dawn, Mate Libby cast off the lines. They worked the *Chapman* away from the dock around 3 A.M. on a clear morning and reached the stream where they partially hoisted the mainsail. As if this last were a signal, two armed boats approached the schooner. Rubery insisted on hoisting the sail and making a run for it but Libby knew any escape attempt to be futile.

Carefully thought out and carried through well, the privateering plot had sprung a "leak" and word reached the ears of U. S. Revenue officials in San Francisco. They had tipped San Francisco police headquarters and detectives had been placed with Revenue officers on a night-and-day watch over the schooner. When the *J. W. Chapman* was cleared March 14th, the Government made its plans to capture her. Fearing the plotters would try to escape by night, the Government chartered the tug *Anasha* and moored it at the dock alongside the *Chapman*. Stationed aboard the tugboat were the Collector of the Port of San Francisco, Ira P. Rankin; Surveyor John T. McLean; Willard B. Farwell, a U. S. Navy officer; and Captain Isaiah W. Lees and a squad of policemen. Meanwhile, Colonel Richard C. Drumm, Adjutant General of the Department of the Pacific, ordered the commandant of Fort Alcatraz, Captain William A. Winder, to receive and hold as prisoners any persons brought to the island in the custody of revenue service officers. Since the Revenue Cutter *Shubrick* was not in the Bay, Captain Paul Shirley, commanding the U.S.S. *Cyane*, was ordered to have two boatloads of armed men ready at all hours. In the remarkable event that the Southerners should somehow evade these inner-Bay precautions, the guns of Fort Point on the Golden Gate were ready to sink her in flight.

As the ringleaders saw the boats approaching, they immediately began to tear up and burn all incriminating documents. When the sailors from the *Cyane* scrambled aboard the *J. W. Chapman*, they saw smoke from the burning documents issuing from the companionway. Some jolly tar cried out "Fire!" and Lt. Arthur R. Yates, executive officer of the *Cyane*, found his intrepid boarding party, fearful of a powder magazine afire, in full retreat back to the boats. While Yates rallied his rattled bluejackets, Harpending made good use of the respite to destroy more documents, even chewing up and swallowing some.

The boarding party, under Lt. Yates' urging, scrambled and thumped onto the schooner's decks a second time and found the privateersmen coming on deck meekly to surrender. Captain Lees had poked about below decks with a candle, shouting to Farwell, "I don't think there are more than twenty-five or thirty of the damned scoundrels in there." The privateersmen were quickly disarmed of their pistols and bowie knives.

And now, at 7:12 A.M., Captain William C. Law came aboard from a Whitehall right into the waiting arms of Navy, Revenue and San Francisco Police officers. Captain Law was not only the last to leave his ship in time of distress, he was the last even to board it.

The schooner was towed to Alcatraz Island, made fast to the wharf and all armament discharged, the ringleaders being placed in solitary confinement. They denied being privateers, asserting they were honest Yankee merchants running guns to Mexican ports for the Juarista Liberal Party. However, Captain Lees' search party not only turned up the munitions in the machinery cases but also the burned and torn scraps of paper which, when pieced together, revealed the whole plot: high seas capture of gold shipments; seizure of Benicia Arsenal, Fort Point and Fort Alcatraz; and finally, the conquest of California itself and its withdrawal from the Union. (This last was to be brought about by the efforts of an army of a thousand men, recruited at the rate of ten each from one hundred towns and camps of Northern California.)

When the news of the *Chapman* case broke, war hysteria ballooned. Newspapers ran hot and rousing editorials; the Legislature passed an Act to prevent arming and equipping piratical or privateering vessels; and the mayor and other officials of the city demanded that an energetic search be made of all Pacific Coast ports to find every other "pirates' nest." The U.S.S. *Saginaw* was ordered to Guadalupe Island and the other bleak isles off Baja California to locate the privateers' rendezvous and the supposed munitions dump. Before it could leave, however, the sheriff of Napa County revealed a Confederate plot to seize Mare Island Navy Yard, so the sailing orders of the *Saginaw* were countermanded. Volunteers from Vallejo and from among the Navy Yard employees formed two seventy-man companies and began defense drills. The commandant of Mare Island Navy Yard, Thomas Oliver Selfridge, telegraphed Secretary of the Navy Gideon Welles, requesting the purchase of two armed steamers to check privateering on the Coast. The Navy Department responded immediately and authorized the chartering and arming of two private steamers.

The lovable old salt Captain Will Law now betrayed his comrades again by turning state's evidence and revealing how Harpending had showed him the letter of marque signed by Jeff Davis. It was Law who had gone to Captain Edward Travers, the ship broker, and told him the whole plot right after he had been approached by Harpending. Travers took the story to Willard B. Farwell, Officer of the Port. Law agreed to keep Farwell posted on the scheme.

Harpending realized that Law had sold him out and called him a "cold-blooded mercenary." He never was able to get a crack at Law except once when he tried, unsuccessfully, to shoot

152

him with a hidden derringer while they were lodged in Fort Alcatraz. After the trial he never saw Law or Libby again and understood that the Government had given them passage on a China-bound ship.

The prisoners were transferred from Alcatraz Island to the Broad Street jail in San Francisco, where they cooled their heels for six months while the Government mustered legal talent and documentation to present its case. Hysterical citizens and newspapers demanded that the group be tried as pirates and one particularly jingoist journal, the *American Flag*, condemned them in a wild-eyed editorial for what it called a "capital offense."

After trying to feign insanity, even tearing out his hair by the handful and being examined by an alienist, Dr. McLean, Harpending took his medicine. The Government's first indictment was for treason, the maximum sentence for which was death. However, Congress restricted the punishment for "treason" during the Civil War—when the term meant simply giving aid to the rebellion or engaging in it—to ten years' imprisonment or a $10,000 fine. A second indictment was filed by the Government accusing the defendants of "assisting, aiding and comforting the existing rebellion against the United States."

The crew, which included two plasterers and an attorney but only one actual seaman, Alfred Humond, was released with a warning since they were judged to be free of any criminal intent. The principal defendants hoped for an acquittal since the prosecution had little evidence—little more than the scraps of paper from the deck of the *J. W. Chapman*—to back up Captain Law's statements. Then, suddenly, the case broke wide open. Greathouse, not thinking, said in front of the mate, Lorenzo Libby, "I guess we will have to go to prison for a long time, but I'll be able to buy my way out."

Lorenzo Libby was just a poor scared seaman, lucky to have a dollar in his dungarees. When he heard Greathouse's boast, he convinced himself that the others would buy their freedom and sacrifice him as scapegoat. He therefore followed Law's lead and turned state's evidence. The district attorney entered a *nolle prosequi* against Law and Libby and they became star Government witnesses.

The defense attorneys for Greathouse, Rubery and Harpending argued that the laws of war (and privateering was a legitimate mode of warfare) were outside the jurisdiction of the United States Circuit Court. Overruled, they next claimed that the schooner did not commence her cruise and, therefore, gave no actual "aid and comfort" to the enemy. District Judge Ogden Hoffman ruled, however, that "a voyage is deemed to have commenced when the vessel in readiness for sea quits her wharf or other place of mooring without intention of returning to it; it can hardly be contended that the mere postponement of actual hostilities can deprive the voyage of the character stamped upon it by its main purpose or design."

The prosecution was able to prove that the vessel was bought through a broker named Bunker; that arms and ammunition were purchased; that the *Chapman* had a false manifest; and that Rubery was a foreign adventurer. Circuit Justice Stephen J. Field charged the jury that the purchasing of the vessel and guns and the employment of the seamen were "overt acts of treason," and in doing them "the defendants were performing a part in and of the great rebellion."

An army officer testified that, in his opinion, the schooner might have destroyed a Panama steamer like the *Oregon* with her 12-pound brass boat-howitzer. Naval officers begged to differ, however. On the eighth day of the trial, after a four-minute deliberation, the twelve jurors rendered a verdict of guilty. Their decision was popular with everyone, save the defendants. Field sentenced them to the maximum ten years in prison and a $10,000 fine.

Friends began to work for the release of the trio immediately but their efforts were unnecessary. On December 18, 1863, President Lincoln proclaimed a General Amnesty Act and Greathouse and Harpending were released upon their taking the prescribed oath and posting bond for their future good behavior. Rubery, a foreigner, was pardoned by Lincoln upon the request of British statesman John Bright.

Despite their pardons, feeling ran high against the three conspirators. Harpending, hearing that orders to rearrest him had been issued, fled San Francisco for a mountain hideout in the Tehachapis. He picked a wild spot near Kernville in the middle of the Tehachapi Mountains. The wild spot was soon anything but deserted, for he discovered gold there and when word leaked out it spread like wildfire. The camp boomed and eventually became the county seat of Kern County. But Harpending was not bothered by the gold-hungry miners.

Greathouse was arrested in Yreka by army officers and brought back to San Francisco on the Sacramento River steamer. He was held in irons at the U. S. Provost Marshal's headquarters at California and Market streets, then transferred to Fort Alcatraz in the Bay. Placed on board the *Golden City* on April 13, 1864, he was sent to New York under a four-man guard. He bribed a sentry in Lafayette Prison, somehow obtained a saw, and filed his window bars. Crawling past the guards, he dived off a fifteen-foot parapet into the water. Sentinels fired at him but he swam safely to shore a mile and a quarter away. He hid for a time in New York, then took passage to England where he lived until the end of the Civil War.

Harpending returned to San Francisco after the war ended, to dabble in real estate. He went on to become a bosom friend of William C. Ralston in various mining ventures, including the great diamond hoax of the early 1870's in which even Tiffany of New York and Baron Rothschild of London were fooled by a "salted" mine.

The *J. W. Chapman* was sold by the U. S. Marshal for $7,100 in May 1863 to William R. Wadsworth, acting for U. S. Consul (Mazatlán) Robert L. Robertson. The latter intended to use the schooner as the start of a regular shipping line between San Francisco and Mazatlán. He placed Captain Charles Galacar in command of the schooner.

Captain Paul Shirley and the crew of the U.S.S. *Cyane* on October 22, 1863, claimed the vessel as a lawful prize, but Judge Hoffman dismissed their petition to have her condemned and the proceeds distributed among her *Cyane* captors. The last time the *J. W. Chapman* made the news was on February 20, 1864, when the *Alta* carried an advertisement for McRuer & Merrill, Auctioneers: THE SUPERIOR A-1 COPPERED & COPPER FASTENED CLIPPER SCHOONER *J. W. Chapman* 91 35-95 TONS REGISTER, NOW LYING OFF MARKET STREET WHARF.

Harpending's plan seems a little mad to us today, but in the light of San Francisco's Civil War unpreparedness, it could very well have opened a "second front" for the Confederacy, particularly if joint actions had been carried out with Waddell's Pacific raider, the *Shenandoah*. Soon, however, the Confederacy collapsed and the *J. W. Chapman* and the plotters who trod her decks were forgotten on San Francisco's Embarcadero.

Chapter VII

EMPEROR OF THE PORT

THE madman Joshua Norton was not the only Emperor in San Francisco's history. The first Vigilance Committee, that of 1851, was not so thoroughly organized as the 1856 Committee—which possessed a fairly complex military organization—but it did have, in addition to its police force, a "navy" under the command of "Emperor" (Captain) Edgar Wakeman.

Wakeman had joined the Vigilantes as a marshal, taking part in the arrest and execution of the Vigilantes' first victim, John Jenkins. He was quickly appointed to the command of the Water Police and his tight control of the harbor earned him the title of "Emperor of the Port." Captain Wakeman obtained copies of passenger lists of arriving vessels and detained and examined their personnel until he was satisfied as to their good character. His Water Police patrolled the Embarcadero, keeping a watchful eye on sailors, ships, storeships and warehouses; and he had a small fleet of boats on the Bay, from skiffs and Whitehall boats to the Revenue Cutter *Polk*, which was more or less placed at his orders. The Water Police were particularly on the lookout for thieves who were accustomed to slip under the stores built on pilings over San Francisco water lots. They would enter such places of business via trap doors or simply by prying up the floorboards. Men like Charles Minturn, who ran

157

the *Senator* on the Sacramento River, kept a lot of money in their offices. Sometimes the gold was held in rather flimsy strongboxes but often was kept from waterfront pirates by no more than a locked door and the thickness of the floor. Watchdogs were neither plentiful nor cheap in 1851, so the Water Police were very necessary to dockside merchants.

When the murderers and thieves of Sydney Town, as the Barbary Coast was then called, had all fled from the city, been transported, or gone underground, the Water Police disbanded and Wakeman resumed his command on the steamer *New World* on the Sacramento River run. He stuck to his job for only a year and then looked for new fields to conquer. The erstwhile "Emperor of the Port" was a born romantic, a sort of latter-day Cellini whose memoirs read like Benvenuto's plagiarized by Sir John Mandeville and edited by Baron Munchausen.

Born in Westport, Connecticut, in 1818, he was the son of the town's champion wrestler, a man who also had the distinction of possessing a double row of teeth all the way 'round, and was clearly to be feared in a rough and tumble, catch-as-catch-can fight. Young Edgar Wakeman had the sea in his blood and was only twelve and a half years old when he left home on the sloop *Mary* for New York, as a 50-cent cabin passenger. He followed the sea from that time on, signing on the *Peruvian* first, where he learned too late what sort of ship she was. One of the older crew members, planning to swim ashore while he still could, told him: "Boy, this ship is hell afloat, and I would rather die than go the voyage with those bloody officers."

As they upped anchor and made sail, the captain was busy knocking out the Negro steward. He then hauled the old cook out of his galley and, after beating and kicking him, laid him out on the deck. Where he left off, the mates picked up; and since the *Peruvian* was a leaky old tub, for the rest of the voyage the crew was busy repairing and pumping night and day, when they were not nursing their bruises.

Young Wakeman was as green as County Roscommon, of course, but the captain so planted the fear of God in him that he quickly metamorphosed from lubber to A.B., and was soon quite at home scampering up to the maintopsail yard. The captain took a liking to the lad and made him coxswain of his jolly boat, or gig, in which he was pulled ashore at Latin-American ports to smuggle goods in or gold out. The latter was often hidden in a bandage tied around Ned's waist under his clothes.

The *Peruvian* put in at Valparaiso and Callao, where no liberty was given. The mate swam ashore to escape the captain's tyranny and a United States naval lieutenant was shipped as first officer by the captain, who put on a suave, purring, gentlemanly air for the occasion. He soon dropped his hiring-hall manners, however, when the steward jumped overboard to drown himself and escape the continual cowhidings. When that unfortunate was hauled dripping on deck, he was tied to the windlass for the day. The captain then began to bully the mate, and whipped the carpenter when he fell from the mizzen mast through the skylight.

Many of the bullied, short-rationed crew died in Manila or Batavia, as the ship continued around the world, but Ned Wakeman even survived being clawed by a tiger while visiting a Malay village. There the surgeon of a Dutch man o' war grudgingly patched him up after the captain refused to allow the Hollander to cut off Wakeman's foot when the wounds mortified.

Finally, the *Peruvian* put in at Philadelphia where the lieutenant-mate quit in disgust and relief, not even waiting for his wages. The crew were paid off and waited ashore to beat up the captain. When they had their opportunity, however, they all got cold feet (after two years of abuse at the tyrant's hands) and ran for their lives. Ned was paid off at $5 a month by the wealthy captain, who favored him as much as his barnacly nature would permit.

The boy soon sailed to Liverpool as an A.B., and by his next trip out he was a second mate. He then went on one of the Liverpool packets of the Black Ball Line as chief mate, though he was not yet twenty years old. To awe the older men among the crew of Liverpool rats, Ned signed the ship's papers as a twenty-eight-year-old and grew a dark beard to hide his tender years. There were tough hands on the packets then, Liverpool Irishmen who were as eager to sheathe a knife between an officer's first and second ribs as they were loath to pass up a bottle of gin.

Life was never dull for Wakeman. He shipped in the Mediterranean and in the West Indies after leaving the packets. In Havana he killed a Cuban who attacked him with a knife, and then had to flee to Matanzas to escape the garrote. After things cooled down a bit, he returned to Havana and rejoined his ship, just in time for a mutiny. The crew attacked the second mate and nearly killed him. Then they went after Ned when he awoke. Pulling on his boots and pants, within ten minutes he had laid about so efficiently with a belaying pin that all the mutineers were on the deck in a horizontal position. He received a blow across the nose that left a black and blue mark which he carried the rest of his days. Back in port, the crew and the mates exchanged accusations before a U. S. consul and, as usual, Ned came out on top.

Thereafter, he sailed to Denmark, Russia and Norway before being wrecked on the Isle of Guernsey in December 1837. Half of his crew perished but Wakeman came ashore safely in a sealskin suit, complete with hood, to the amazement of the islanders, who thought they were seeing a sea monster striding up the beach out of the wild surf.

Making his way to New York, Wakeman was soon bound out on the brig *Forrester* for the West Indies. A segment of the *Forrester*'s crew formed a conspiracy to kill the easygoing captain and Ned, who was mate, and to run off with the brig. A Frenchman known only as Louis insulted Wakeman at St. Thomas, in the Virgin Islands, and the latter ordered him into a boat so they could go ashore to fight it out. Ned demanded that they duel with swords and had two cutlasses thrown into the boat, followed by a shovel. When French Louis asked what the mate intended to do with the shovel, Ned answered fiercely, "Dig your grave, you pirate!" Louis climbed out of the boat and fled to the forecastle, where he hid. Later, Ned found that *Forrester's* cargo had been plundered, much of it ending up in the crew's sea chests. While the captain went ashore for soldiers, Wakeman whipped a confession out of one of the sailors. French Louis turned out to be the ringleader and he and the mutineers were sent back to New York in irons.

The captain ignored Wakeman's warnings and the brigantine struck a reef on the coast of England after leaving the West Indies. She got off with the help of the cutters *Scout*, commanded by Captain Harkings (later of the *Great Western*), and the *Flying Fish*, but had to put into Harwich for repairs. Here, as everywhere, the bucko mate charmed the ladies of the port. The captain found that he could not raise enough money to pay the ship's bill so the authorities were ready to give the vessel to the carpenter for the money due him. The United States consul was making arrangements to send the crew home. Ned hurriedly stole some rigging from two Swedish schooners in the harbor and got together a crew from local fishing smacks. He invited the pilot aboard for a drop of half-and-half and then persuaded him to take them out. The cable was slipped and they ran for it.

At sea, they ran short of provisions, ate the ship's dog and the starch in the cargo—all becoming deathly ill as a result. According to Wakeman's richly embroidered memoirs, they even drew lots to see who would be the first *pièce de résistance* when they should have to resort to cannibalism. The captain drew the unlucky short straw, but a cry of "Sail ho!" saved him from the cooking pots. It was the brig *Freighter*. The *Forrester*, re-

161

victualed, made New York in a storm after which Ned hit all the pie shops in an orgy of eating. The captain, his mind affected by the privations of the voyage, "swallowed the anchor" and became a landsman.

Wakeman sailed up the Mississippi River on the second sea-going vessel to reach Vicksburg. Here he engaged in sundry duels and romances before hurrying off to the Mexican War. He served two years carrying dispatches for Commodores Perry and Kelly. He also took a prize schooner, the *Relámpago*, which he used to smuggle prisoners and gold out of Tabasco, escaping from the Mexican soldiery just in time and making for New Orleans.

In the Crescent City, the owner of the schooner put the *Relámpago* under his command, and Wakeman prepared to make her ready for San Francisco. The schooner began to leak off Havana and he had her towed to Key West. When the vessel was surveyed, it was found it would cost too much to repair her, so he abandoned the *Relámpago*. The fifty passengers, mostly cutthroats on their way to mines, spread tales that Wakeman and his crew were pirates. They even went so far as to attack the house in which he was staying, but were beaten off.

Ned turned to wrecking and repairing wrecks on Key West, making enough money in this fashion to refit the Mexican schooner and take her to New Orleans for a few trading ventures to Mexico. On one of these trips, he and his entire crew came down with yellow fever, but he managed to sail the vessel from Mexico to New Orleans with a crew consisting of himself, two sick ship's boys and a crazy passenger. He made one of the boys, Alex Childs, "captain," and taught him the rudiments of navigation and steering. Wakeman himself was too weak to stand a trick at the wheel and, as a matter of fact, was hauled off the New Orleans dock in the dead-cart when the *Relámpago* finally wallowed home. He came to, however, to the surprise of the

Negro driving the cart and, as he said, "I drank freely of quinine, until my head rang like a brass kettle."

When he arrived in New York, on the mend, he saw the spanking new steamer *New World* on the ways, ready to be launched. With his usual bluff manner, he managed to talk his way into the command of the new vessel, built for California's Sacramento River run between San Francisco and the entrepôt for the mines.

Sunday, February 10, 1850, was the day scheduled for the launching of the *New World*, the *Arctic* and the *Boston*. However, the sheriff seized the *New World* on an attachment, for the owner, William H. Brown, was unable to pay the attacher the $50,000 he owed him. Sheriff Cunningham and his squad were aboard during the launching ceremony and were visibly surprised to find that Ned's chief engineer, Billy Van Wirt, had fires under the boilers and was getting up a head of steam. When asked "How come?" Ned answered, "Well, you see, we thought it would add to the interest of the occasion if the finest steamer of the three was launched with steam up, ready to work. And besides, we want to turn the engines over to work off the rust."

Twenty thousand people jammed the quays and wharves along East River, some coming from as far afield as Boston and Augusta, Maine, cheering mightily as the *New World* revolved her paddle wheels in the air and became the first vessel to go down the ways with "steam on." At noon her trial run began. As the champagne aboard diminished, her speed increased until she hit twenty-two miles per hour. At midnight, Captain Wakeman brought her back to the dock and the crew went ashore to sleep in a hotel. Wakeman went aboard the ship again at 1 A.M., luckily, for he found a small fire in the engine room which he put out quickly.

Saturday, February 16, dawned gray and rainy. Wakeman received a note from his employer which appeared to read *You must go to sea tomorrow morning*. When he looked at it

163

again later, it appeared that the owner's scrawl really read *You must* NOT *go to sea tomorrow morning.*

As the weather cleared, Ned had the engines warmed up and shut himself in the pilothouse, after locking the crew below. He took off his hat at the pilothouse window and, at this signal, a man waiting on the wharf lifted an ax and brought it down, cutting the hawser. Two bells were rung and the spick-and-span steamer began to kick the dirty water of the East River into a white froth. As she pulled out into the river, the sheriff's men ran about the deck in wild confusion. Wakeman got a man from below to take the wheel as one of the marshals ran up.

"Who told you to take the boat from the dock? She is in our charge and we command you to take her back at once!"

Wakeman answered, "Keep cool, gentlemen. You know it rained all night and wet us through. I want to turn the machinery over a little. Sometime this vessel will undoubtedly sail for California, and I want to see that everything is in good order."

When Sheriff Dan Cunningham asked if the engines had not been turned over enough, Wakeman answered serenely that he just wanted to cruise a little to enjoy such a fine Sunday. He took the *New World* to Staten Island, and when she reached the Narrows, stopped her close inshore.

Cunningham rushed up, blowing his police whistle and crying, "I am the Sheriff of New York City and County; this vessel is in my charge, and she shall be taken back to the dock."

Wakeman responded by blowing a bosun's pipe and watching his crew answer the call of "All hands on deck!" They stormed out of the hold, clutching knives, pistols and cutlasses.

"And I am master of the good ship *New World,* afloat upon the high seas. This vessel is in my charge and let who questions it beware."

The sheriff and his men were hustled over the side into a small boat, the mate landing them where they could catch the

Staten Island ferry after wading three miles through the mud.

A high sea was running that night but was followed by clearing weather the next day. Captain Wakeman ran for Pernambuco, ignoring a British steam frigate off Rio which fired a bow gun to force the *New World* to heave to. He ran into Rio without bothering about pilots or quarantine, shrugging off the ineffectual bombardment of the forts and old hulks in the harbor. To the sputtering port authorities, he explained glibly that his vessel was sinking. He even gave orders to his crew to let water in if necessary to impress the officials of the sad condition of his new steamer. Somehow, he managed to lose the ship's papers overside in getting into his boat. Finally, exasperated by the continuing hostility of the authorities, he threatened to sink the *New World* alongside the British frigate.

He exploded when the United States consul chided him for avoiding quarantine. He shouted that the pestilence was ashore, not on the steamer, that his crew was healthy enough but "they (the *Cariocas*) were the proper party to go into quarantine, not us!" Wakeman outlasted the Brazilians in stubbornness and the Emperor ordered all quarantine flags in port to be hauled down. Now anyone could leave, but Edgar Wakeman stayed and repaired the steamer's strained hull. He shipped new hands, at a dollar a month, after yellow fever came aboard and took eighteen of his crew and officers. He could have had a double crew sailing for a plugged Cinghalese rupee each, so eager were men to quit the fever-ridden port.

Wakeman sailed from Rio's "graveyard harbor," passed through the Straits of Magellan, where he entertained a few Fuegians aboard, gave them tobacco and food, and put in again at Valparaiso. Here he was informed that the strict quarantine regulations, so similar to Rio's, were never—but *never*—relaxed. Edgar Wakeman was not going to put up with a twenty-day quarantine, even though a Chilean guard boat was posted near the *New World*. He flew his flag union down and boats from all

165

the ships in the harbor came alongside in answer to his distress signal. They paid no attention to the orders of the guard boat's crew. Wakeman said he had to have two casks of fresh water.

One American captain said, "You shall have them in an hour, if I have to kill all those Dagos in the guard boat."

Ned kept his distress signal up every day, making grievous complaints to the port officials, the American consul, and the American Minister, Bailey Peyton, in Santiago. Once again he wore everyone out and, after only eight days, the *New World* was released from quarantine.

He left Valparaiso on May 11, 1850, without a drop of fresh water on board, but in a day had plenty as they condensed more than they could use. At Callao he learned that there were two United States marshals awaiting him in Panama to arrest him on a United States bench warrant for piracy, for "stealing" the *New World*. He put in, anyway, and when one of the officers came aboard, Ned removed a cocked pistol from his coat pocket. The gentleman ran like a whippet.

He sailed from Panama on June 20th, with two hundred and seventeen passengers paying $300 each for the passage to San Francisco. With four feet of water in the hold, the steam chest cracked. He bound it with a chain and iron wedges in order to continue. The steamer ran ashore in New World Cove or Bull Bay, but got off and entered San Diego. There was no fuel there but he obtained some from a coal-laden vessel lying off San Pedro.

In a dense fog on July 11th, Ned ordered the mate to hoist all flags, since he was determined to run into anything from a half-inch auger hole on up, with the hope it might turn out to be the Golden Gate. He sighted Mile Rock and Fort Point and soon was safely in, tying the *New World* up to a ship moored off Clark's Point. He had brought her around in just one hundred and fifty days.

Wakeman plunged, as we have seen earlier, into Vigilance

Committee duties but when the Barbary Coast, or Sydney Town, as it was then called, was cleansed of its riffraff, he ran the *New World* on the Sacramento River for Marshall Hubbard and Francis Cunningham on opposite days from the *Senator's* schedule, until his license was revoked after a collision with the *Eclipse.* Captain Samuel Seymour took over the wheelhouse of the *New World* while Ned sought new worlds to conquer.

With the help of frequent brandy toddies and milk punches (notwithstanding the teetotaling claims of his widow and Mark Twain), Wakeman ventured in 1851 up into the Sierra foothills near Murphys and the Natural Bridge, where he met some of his old crew from the *New World.* He became something of a local Mother Lode legend when he baited a shark hook outside Deerhead House one night and caught a cougar with it. After poking about the gold country and having a few narrow escapes from grizzlies, he went down again to tidewater.

Back in San Francisco he used to tell the story of the visit he made, during his Sierra trip, to the owner of a large sheep ranch. As he and his host were walking across a piece of meadowland one day, they came across a fellow kneeling in a swale and in the very act of removing the skin from a fine yearling lamb he had just slaughtered.

"What's the meaning of this?" bellowed the angry rancher.

The rustler, a quick-witted fellow after Wakeman's own heart, shot back fiercely, "No sheep ever bites me and lives!"

One Friday evening Ned took a picnicking expedition out to the Farallon Islands in a large open launch of the *Sarah Sands.* Although the launch was nearly run down by the steamer *Oregon,* they reached the barren islands safely enough and landed. They fished and lunched on the islands, killed a dozen fur-bearing seals, and brought three of them back to San Francisco alive when they returned on Sunday evening.

It was not long before Ned was back in steam again, taking the *Independence* and *New Orleans* on runs to San Juan and

Panama, being blown ashore at San Juan, and meeting his future wife on the latter vessel. No trip of Wakeman's ever proved to be monotonous.

When he saw an attractive young lady asleep in an easy chair in the cabin of the *New Orleans,* he said to his companions, "Gentlemen, that is my wife. If, when she opens her eyes, she be not swivel-eyed and with all her head-nails rotted out, I shall marry that girl, if I kill eleven men before breakfast to get up an appetite."

He introduced himself, gave her three days to decide whether to marry him or not, and bade her a courteous adieu. The girl, Mary Lincoln, said yes. Before they arrived in Panama, Wakeman learned that six others had proposed unsuccessfully to her on the voyage. Their marriage was postponed while she visited in the East.

Ned shortly thereafter was honored at a testimonial dinner and, during the banquet, was presented with a diamond pin and a gold chronometer for his services to San Francisco in Vigilante days as both citizen and captain.

He took the *New Orleans* out the Gate on March 8, 1853, and steamed down to the Marquesas and Tahiti. On the latter island he claimed to have fallen over an 8,000-foot waterfall into a chasm. In Australia he and his boat crew rowed ashore to be greeted with curses and leveled muskets, much to their surprise. They were mistaken for a gang of nine convicts who were robbing farms and ships from a whaleboat they had stolen.

In forty-one days running time from the Golden Gate they reached Sydney, where Wakeman was blasted by the Sydney *Herald* for "murdering" Aussies in San Francisco as a Vigilante. A nasty-tempered crowd of Currency Lads threatened him, but he pulled out a Colt and a bowie knife and was about to whittle and puncture his way through the pressing crowd when most of them suddenly remembered engagements for which they were already tardy. This little engagement was written up by the *Herald* as a murderous assault by "the armed and ruffianly commander of the American steamer."

In going about Sydney, he wore a brace of pistols and a bowie knife belted outside his jacket despite Australian laws prohibiting the carrying of deadly weapons. Wakeman was not worried by the penalty of fifteen years' transportation. He drifted about Australia and Peru for a time and, encouraged by President Pierce, joined the new Amazon Steam Navigation Company only to receive a telegram later from Pierce ordering him to abandon the project. Wakeman believed that New York rubber interests did not want strangers steaming up the Amazon for a look-see.

After the Amazon rubber fiasco, Commodore Cornelius Vanderbilt offered him the command of the *North Star*, the finest yacht afloat and just back from her famous European voyage. Ned declined with thanks and Vanderbilt helped him slip past servers of the resuscitated piracy bench warrant and put him on the Vanderbilt Line payroll until a vacancy should occur.

Wakeman was a good seaman and he knew it. He once bragged that he "could bring a market basket around Cape Horn if he had to." His old employer, William H. Brown of the *New World*, persuaded him to bring his new steamer *Surprise* around from New York, giving him $500 a month expenses and a $10,000 interest in the vessel. Just before the *Surprise* was about to haul out into the stream, Ned was arrested for piracy and contempt of court. He went into court with his bondsman but skipped out before his case was called.

Under sail and easy steam, he took the *Surprise* to California in about four months and on Christmas Eve, 1854, married Mary Lincoln. He was cheated out of the interest in the steamer but he had received his salary and was able to start married life comfortably. He took the *Sea Bird*, the first steamer on the regular S.F.—Los Angeles run, on a trip to Honolulu; the steamer *Pacific* to Nicaragua; and captained the three-deck guano clipper *Adelaide,* of 1,800 tons, featured on a Currier and Ives print and credited in legend with having beaten the Cunard steamer *Sidon* in an 1854 transatlantic race.

Wakeman brought the *Adelaide* to San Francisco, arriving April 29, 1856, in one hundred and twenty-four days from New York. He returned with a cargo of guano in ninety-one days and came back to San Francisco on September 29, 1857. All his A.B.'s were Negroes, twenty-six of them. As the *Adelaide* was docking at San Francisco, his mate, Lewis, knocked one of the hands overboard from the topgallant forecastle. The man drowned. Lewis was arrested but cleared of any crime.

While off Elide Island, one of the crew murdered Lewis. Wakeman and the other captains in port convened as a court in the *Adelaide*'s cabin. The sailor was convicted and hanged aboard the *Adelaide.* Ned left the isle on March 28, 1858, and made New York in eighty-seven days. He went back to San Francisco one more time, then to Callao for guano, and from there sailed to Hampton Roads in sixty-five days, an excellent run. Intending to leave sail for good, he sold his share in the vessel and "went ashore" in California. It was there he built himself a cottage and raised his family. His wife always accompanied him during his four years in command of the *Adelaide.* Two children were born on the ship, the first of whom was named Adelaide Seaborn Wakeman.

In 1861 he was still "on the beach" but snapped at the offer of a job wrecking the clipper *Sea Nymph* which had run ashore on Point Reyes on May 4, 1861, one hundred and twenty days from New York. A lifeboat had capsized but the crew got a line ashore by tying it to a kite. Once one end of the line was ashore it was hauled in and a heavy hawser, tied to the other end, was secured between ship and shore. Only one man was lost in landing but the ship, with its 1,778 tons of general cargo (worth $250,000) was sold on May 9th to a Mr. Benjamin for only $9,700 dollars. Benjamin looked the situation over and, deciding he could not salvage the clipper, sold the wreck to Wakeman for a trifling sum.

For eighty-five days Wakeman lived on that fog- and windswept promontory, in charge of a crew of wreckers. Luck rode with him. The *Sea Nymph* broke up on a flood tide and everything came ashore. He recovered two schooner-loads of cargo and fixtures, making several thousand dollars clear. Had she gone to pieces on an ebb tide, he might not have made a nickel.

Captain Wakeman was chosen to command the ex-Pacific Mail steamer *John L. Stephens* which the Mexican Imperial Government contracted to run monthly between San Francisco and Mazatlán, Guaymas and La Paz, touching at Cape San Lucas, Baja California, on both the outward and return passages.

About 3 A.M. on April 6, 1866, a very dark night, Wakeman anchored off the cape and dispatched two boats ashore with loads of cargo. As usual, the whaleboat and skiff belonging to Captain Ritchie, the U. S. consular agent at Cape San Lucas, approached the steamer from the shore. Except for the captain and the watch, only a few of the crew and passengers were on deck.

Wakeman tried to make out the men in the boats which approached in the darkness. They wore Mexican sombreros and serapes and he took them for "a villainous set of adventurers," down from the mines for a fling at gambling, women and liquor.

When the watch hailed the boats, the leading steersman answered, "We are American miners bound for San Juan and want a passage on this steamer." This was reported to the first officer, who permitted them to come aboard.

As the men from the boats started to climb the Jacob's ladder on the side, Wakeman asked, "Are you Americans here?"

"Yes, sir."

"How many are there of you?"

"Eight of us for the steerage, sir."

When three of them were on deck, one came to Ned and asked, "Is this Captain Wakeman?"

"It is."

"Can I have a word with you?"

"Certainly."

The two men drew aside and the stranger said quietly, "Captain, feel of that. That is the muzzle of a pistol. Its effects are very sudden. Keep perfectly quiet or you will die before you have time to say your prayers. Be silent and your life is safe."

Two more men came up and put pistols at his temples. The leader of the boarders spoke to Wakeman again. "I am Colonel Frank F. Dana of the Mexican liberal forces. You and your crew and passengers are my prisoners. Your vessel is under arrest, according to instructions which I have received and will show you. Any resistance will be useless and may lead to unpleasant consequences."

Dana continued: "Your ship is in the hands of my soldiers. I have eighteen men now on board. [He actually had eight.] Some of them have come in by the port bow. Your officers are secured and your passengers will be disarmed. You will not be detained here long. I am looking for a passenger and for contraband of war. If you keep still and obey orders, it is well. If not," and here Dana hefted his revolver, "it is quite as well. I advise you to attempt no disturbance."

As soon as Dana came aboard, he had walked to the starboard side of the vessel (those on deck were at the port rail, looking at the land). He had taken off his rough miner's clothes, buckled on a saber and walked aft to accost Wakeman in Mexican Army uniform.

Ned was marched to the upper deck where two guards were placed over him with orders to kill him if he broke his silence. The American flag was run down and the Mexican banner raised. Dana then went through the ship, stateroom by stateroom, awakening each sleeper by putting a lantern in his face,

172

a pistol at his head, and saying, "Silence, or you are a dead man. Give up your arms and your money."

When Colonel Dana requested that Wakeman hand over the ship's papers, the captain refused. He asked, "By what authority, Colonel Dana, do you make this demand?"

The Mexican Army officer cocked his pistol and said, "By the authority of the Mexican Government, which I represent, and by the virtue of this little instrument I hold in my hand." Wakeman, more enraged than frightened, handed him the documents and Dana read them aloud.

"Cases, boxes, kegs, bales of hay . . . Humph, Captain, what *are* the contents of these various packages?"

Ned pleaded ignorance.

"Ha!" cried Dana. "Guns, powder, caps, cavalry sabers, saddles and forage for horses, boots and clothing for soldiers who are our enemies."

He examined the cargo and returned to say that he had found $40,000 worth of contraband of war and was confiscating it. He notified Wakeman formally that he was taking possession of the *John L. Stephens* as a prize of war.

Dana showed Wakeman his instructions from General Ramón Corona of the Juarista forces, "to proceed to Cape San Lucas and there to seize the steamship *John L. Stephens* and convey here to the port of Altata the captain, officers, crew and passengers to be held as prisoners of war, and the vessel and cargo to be delivered to the proper authorities."

Ned protested these proceedings in writing as illegal. Refusing to go to Altata, he said, "Colonel, you may shoot me, but you can never get this boat to Altata." He was willing to go into La Paz as a prisoner, however, so Dana ordered the steamer there while Wakeman made plans to retake his ship. He managed to get an order to his chief engineer, Hueston, to cut iron bars with which he could arm his crew of twenty-five men. It was his plan to jump the pirates when they ate; he had singled out Dana for himself.

The plot leaked out, however, and Dana's threats to kill all aboard were enough to force Wakeman to give in. When they reached La Paz, Ned tried another of his tricks. He claimed that he had so disabled the engines that Dana could not use the steamer as a privateer against French vessels at Mazatlán and Guaymas, as planned.

Mexican soldiers at La Paz took off 500 Springfield rifles, 1,000,000 boxes of percussion caps (worth up to $1 a box in Mexico), 2,700 boxes of powder, 1,150 sabers, the boots, shoes, clothing, saddles, bridles and bales of hay. All correspondence directed to the Imperial authorities in Mazatlán was seized, also, and some private property from the cargo, mainly wine, found its way ashore or into Dana's waiting schooner.

Colonel Dana tried to get Wakeman to bond the vessel for $100,000. Wakeman always claimed that he refused to sign anything but gave Dana $500 for a promise from Dana that he would not harm the ship, crew or passengers and that he would return, unharmed, the three passengers he had sworn to hang. One of Dana's group later claimed that Wakeman and Ritchie did bond the ship for $100,000.

The three captives were released after the mail agent, Navarrete, paid $500, Ogoer, a Guaymas merchant, paid $200, and Chavon, a Frenchman, was "bled to the tune of $2,500."

As Dana was leaving the ship he said, "Wakeman, you must not take me for a coward or for a fool, but I have actually given up to you this fine steamer and most of her valuable cargo, which I would not have given to any other living man. I beg you will accept this pistol as a token of respect for a brave and determined man."

When Dana had gone, some of the citizens of La Paz determined to seize the steamer. They were led by the Collector of the Port. Wakeman, left in charge of the ship by Dana with

174

orders not to allow her to sail until late afternoon, broke out two cases of Henry rifles the colonel had overlooked and fired one of the vessel's two rifled cannon. The collector ran away and his makeshift army disintegrated while Wakeman sailed for Guaymas.

Much to Wakeman's disgust, his employer held him liable for the $500 he said he had given to Dana (or, as the Sacramento *Union* reported the incident, for the "$500 down and a bond for $1,500 more"). Wakeman left his employ in a rage and traveled back to New York as a passenger, taking the shipboard leisure time to invent—as he modestly and characteristically put it— "the best detaching gear to let go a boat from the davits that has ever been invented."

He next took command of the steamer *America,* broke a shaft and put into Acapulco where port authorities, the United States consul and the Pacific Mail Steamship Company agent badgered him unmercifully, trying to persuade him to let the *America* be towed to San Francisco. He snorted, steamed out and made it to Frisco on one paddle wheel.

Contracting a fever during a visit to Panama in 1868, he "went ashore" again to recoup his health. He went to Camp Scott, Paradise Valley, Nevada, to recuperate as guest of Colonel Karge, a Polish veteran of Russian wars, a linguist and a scholar, who craved stimulating company at his isolated cavalry post.

Once more Ned went to sea when he sailed the steamer *D. C. Haskins* out of New York for San Francisco and ran right into the middle of a Caribbean hurricane. The steamer began to settle and her crew took to the small boats. At midnight, November 7, 1869, she sank. Of the entire crew only some of the men in Wakeman's overcrowded boat survived, eight out of the eleven, in addition to himself. They pulled north until they were rescued by the schooner *Grasmere,* commanded by Captain Augustus Kellin.

Back in New York, Wakeman visited his old friend Commodore Vanderbilt and then returned to California where he tried his hand at farming. The pull of the sea was too strong and he fitted out Webb Line steamers for the run Down Under. He shipped on one liner which blew out its boilers but he insisted that they go on to Hawaii, in spite of an incipient mutiny by the crew when they heard the news. Not only did the old sea dog make Honolulu safely on one boiler plus the sails, but, en route, he rescued a ship's captain from his waterlogged derelict.

In Honolulu he enjoyed himself hugely with two other old skippers, Captain James Blethen, later San Francisco's Harbormaster, and the old sealer, Captain Thomas Long. After a visit to Samoa, where he surveyed harbors for W. H. Webb and issued a report that received rather wide notice, he sailed for San Francisco as captain of the *Mohongo*. On his second return trip from Honolulu to San Francisco on the *Mohongo*, he had a stroke on July 9, 1872, just five and one-half days out, and was paralyzed on his right side. The attack was probably the result of the time spent in the *D. C. Haskins'* open boat, where exposure undermined his health.

Ned Wakeman spent his declining years in travel, just as he had spent his active, quarter-deck years. He went to New Zealand and to Magdalena Bay to see the orchilla factory, and to the Colorado River via the Gulf of California. Then he dropped out of the public eye for a period.

On December 3, 1872, Samuel Langhorne Clemens sat down at his desk in Hartford, Connecticut, and wrote to the *Daily Alta California*:

> Certain gentlemen here in the East have done me the honor to make me their mouthpiece in a matter which should command the interest and the sympathy of many Californians. They represent that the veteran Captain, Ned Wakeman, is lying paralyzed and helpless at his home in your city and they beg that his old friends on the Pacific Coast will do towards him as they would

gladly do themselves if they were back now in San Francisco—that is, take the old mariner's case in hand and assist him and his family to the pecuniary aid they stand so sore in need of. His house is mortgaged for $5,000 and he will be sold out, unless this is done. I have made voyages with the old man when fortune was a friend to him, and am aware that he gave with a generous heart and willing hand to all the needy that came in his way and now that twenty years of rough toil on the watery highways of the Far West find him wrecked and in distress, I am sure that the splendid generosity which has made the name of California to be honored in all lands, will come to him in such a shape that he shall confess that the seeds that he sowed in better days did not fall upon unfruitful soil.

Will not some of the old friends of Captain Wakeman in your city take this matter in hand, and do by him as he would surely have done by them were their cases reversed?

MARK TWAIN

The letter appeared on the first page of the *Daily Alta* on December 14, 1872. It reappeared in the *Weekly Alta* on December 21st and was accompanied by another local letter praising Wakeman and stating that a subscription book was being passed, with donations to be left at the *Alta* office.

That same year he began his memoirs which were practically complete when he died on May 8, 1875, on a Saturday evening in East Oakland at the age of fifty-seven.

Chapter VIII

A PHILOSOPHER AND A FILIBUSTERER

STUDENTS of California history are warned in their appren-
ticeship to handle H. H. Bancroft with care, for the mass-
production historian rode his biases as a trooper rides his steed.
The guileless are sometimes taken in by the pseudo-objectivity
of sections of his work as much as by the sheer, awe-inspiring
magnitude of his output. He produced some thirty-nine volumes
of Western American history.

Curiously, Bancroft had no use for Sam Brannan, the Argo-
nautic Mormon, and yet he grudgingly wrote of him, "He probably did more for San Francisco . . . than was effected by the
combined efforts of scores of others." And Bancroft was right.
He could have torn Brannan's reputation to shreds, or dismissed
him entirely, but he was honest enough to recognize the value
and importance of this man he disliked.

Sam Brannan wore a coat of many colors. He was printer,
pioneer, privateer, millionaire, "Saint," apostate, entrepreneur,
bigamist and drunk. Twice he captained marine expeditions,
although he was never master of a vessel as was his brother
John. Sam did sail once from New York to New Orleans as a
fuzzy-cheeked forecastle hand but had a bellyful of merchant
marine bullying on the one month's passage and returned to
tramp printing.

179

The expeditions which he led were unusual experiences, to
say the least. His first one saw him arriving, disgusted, at Yerba
Buena on July 31, 1846, with the 372-ton *Brooklyn* (Captain A.
Richardson in command) loaded with disgruntled Mormon
colonists. His Latter Day Saints' followers were angry with their
shepherd for his shipboard tyranny and particularly for his ex-
communication of four lusty fellows of the company for "wicked
and licentious conduct." Brannan himself was enraged for quite
a different reason. He tore his hat from his head and stamped
on it when he found the American flag flying above Portsmouth
Square. He had expected to find Mexican California a haven
for the exiles of Nauvoo and Carthage, fleeing Yankee persecu-
tion. His first words on viewing the lovely hills and coves of
Yerba Buena were, "There's that damned flag again!" (Sometimes reported as, "There's that damned *rag* again!")

He had chartered the *Brooklyn* for $1,200 a month, assuming
all risks and paying all port charges plus the costs of converting
the hull to handle the two hundred and thirty-eight Saints who
crowded in with a $16,000 cargo of seeds, books, tools, sawmills,
food, cows, a printing press, pigs, and chickens. Brannan had
had to postpone her sailing date once, but on February 4, 1846—
the same day that Brigham Young and his contingent crossed the
Mississippi River on the ice—the *Brooklyn* hauled her anchor
and put to sea. The adult Saints had paid a fare of $50 a head
plus $25 for food for the privilege of going to Zion by boat.
Juvenile Saints went for half fare.

In five and a half months he brought his quarrelsome colony
from New York to California via the Horn. He stopped in Honolulu long enough to obtain one hundred and fifty muskets and
on the passage from Hawaii he drilled his Mormon Battalion
for possible duty against Mexican troops in war-torn California.
Brannan found that Captain John B. Montgomery and the U.S.S.
Portsmouth had not only thwarted his Mexican Zion plans by
planting the Stars and Stripes in the plaza of Yerba Buena but

had the peace and security of the port quite in hand. The only times Sam Brannan's unit went into action was during the locally famed Coffee Pot Cannonade and in the nocturnal engagement which might have been called Yerba Buena's Whisky Rebellion.

The first of these farcical engagements took place shortly after a Captain King arrived from the Sandwich Islands and put up in John Henry Brown's hotel. Every day his *kanaka* steward made coffee in a newly patented pot which seems to have been a sort of paleolithic pressure-cooker. The device was a one and a half gallon pot, surmounted with a large iron wheel hidden under a cover with a screw on the outside.

One particular day the *kanaka* had work to do at coffee time so he left the contrivance in the care of the second cook with instructions to turn the screw tighter if too much steam escaped. The second cook decided to do the thing up right and ran the screw down hard so *no* steam could escape. He escaped with minor burns and bruises as the pot exploded, "blowing him 20 yards from the kitchen," as one eyewitness extravagantly put it.

Captain Joseph B. Hull, the fussbudget characterized by Philosopher Pickett as "a brainless biped," and most certainly an excitable granny, ran to the barracks in the Customhouse upon hearing the explosion and ordered the drummer to beat the long roll, as he was sure that the Mexicans had come to retake the city. He then ran about ordering citizens to form up as auxiliaries, sent out U. S. Marines as scouts and signaled the ships in the bay to be ready with landing parties. Brannan's Mormon Battalion came on the double and received a welcome worthy of conquering heroes. William S. Clark ran all the way from Clark's Point to the plaza, sure that "the greasers" were coming. When the cook's burns had been buttered and the remains of the coffeepot autopsied, the militiamen disbanded to the snickers of onlookers and the growls of red-faced Hull.

Brannan's men turned out in one more such emergency before going into permanent retirement. Again the battle site was

181

Brown's Portsmouth Hotel. This time it was a dark night when Lieutenant Harry B. Watson, a bottle-battling marine of some years' standing, crept up to Brown's window to give the accustomed signal which would result in the innkeeper's filling his emptied flask. This particular night, Brown was especially tired from being up late the two preceding evenings with five whaling captains and the officers of the *Portsmouth*. Sleeping more soundly than usual, he did not hear the impatient raps on his window shutter. Finally, the lieutenant, who was already deep in his cups, fired his pistol and bellowed the whisky-winning password at the top of his voice: "THE SPANIARDS ARE IN THE BRUSH!"

Brown jumped out of bed and hurried to fill Watson's flask, but the damage was done. Again the long roll sounded at the old adobe Customhouse and U. S. Marines and Brannan's volunteers turned out, armed to the teeth. They rushed to their stations and a brief but lively battle ensued, with the Saints winging several "Mexicans" (scrub oaks) on the dark hillsides.

The *Brooklyn* had hardly dropped her hook into the rich mud of the bay bottom when Sam Brannan was deep in the heart of city affairs. Within two weeks of wading ashore, he had preached the first *non*Roman-Catholic sermon in Yerba Buena. This was no small news item in a town which boasted a permanent population of only some sixty-odd inhabitants until the total was swelled by the arrival of the U. S. Navy and Sam's two hundred and thirty-eight Saints.

Horseplay and practical jokes were leaned upon heavily by the citizens, together with gambling, in amusement-poor and women-poor Yerba Buena of 1846. Some of the local boys initiated Sam into San Francisco citizenship by blindfolding him in the middle of Portsmouth Plaza, turning him around several times and placing bets on just what course he would take. Sam staggered off and, sure enough, followed the line of least resistance into a slimy pool of water where adobe bricks had been puddled behind a building on the corner of Kearney and Clay streets. He hesitated, and was lost. Plunging on ahead he was soon down in the filthy pond, up to his neck, suitably initiated and christened with Yerba Buena's ubiquitous mud.

Brannan would have had scarcely better luck had he chosen almost any other point on the compass, for nascent San Francisco was wallowing in a sea of mud and sand. At one busy corner the famed sign was posted: THIS STREET IMPASSABLE, NOT EVEN JACKASSABLE. General William Tecumseh Sherman wrote:

> Montgomery Street had been filled with brush and clay and I always dreaded to ride on horseback along it, because the mud was so deep a horse's legs would become entangled in the bushes below, and the rider was likely to be thrown and drowned in the mud. I have seen mules stumble in the street and drown in the liquid mud.

It was said three men suffocated in the Montgomery Street muck one night and, both night and day, drunks would be found mired to their waists in the street. The old story that San Francisco had a sidewalk made of pianos grew out of the true condition of Montgomery Street between Clay and Jackson. The sidewalk for this block was made up largely of abandoned cookstoves but in one spot, where a stove had sunk from sight, a damaged piano was inserted in the breach, and so the tall tale evolved.

Sam Brannan decided that he would make his future in the swampy little town at the break in the Coast Range. Here he was honored with the first jury trial in American California when charges were brought against him for allegedly mishandling funds on the *Brooklyn*. A hung jury led to dismissal of the case, and he rushed East to persuade Brigham Young to abandon Utah for California.

Young was adamant in his refusal and his obduracy before all of Sam's arguments was probably the straw that broke the Lat-

ter Day Saints elder's back and sent him skidding down the
road to apostasy. He had sided with young Joseph Smith, son
of the prophet and founder, against Brigham Young at the time
of the great schism. As a result of this second clash with Young,
Sam drifted rapidly away from Mormonism, like a bottle on an
ebb tide responding to an offshore breeze. He made capital of
his experience in printing and publishing the New York L. D. S.
Church *Messenger,* by bringing out San Francisco's first newspaper, the *California Star.* He set up stores at Sutter's Coloma
millsite and at Natoma, his own millsite, where he dealt with
whites and Indians somewhat in the manner of the squawman-
trader Jim Savage.

At Sutter's Fort and Coloma he ran into one of California's
great characters, Charles Edward (Philosopher) Pickett, who
was also having a fling at storekeeping. He was California's
legislative-political gadfly, a muckraker and partisan pam-
phleteer. Had he not been of such a crusty and eccentric nature,
he might have been dubbed a do-gooder. He was a fighter for
what he considered to be right and square. In Philosopher
Pickett, Sam Brannan met his match in rugged individualism.

A cousin of the Confederate general who won fame, but lost
the battle, at Gettysburg, Pickett had first come west to Oregon,
where he got along well with Father de Smet and the Catholic
nuns but clashed immediately with the Protestant missionaries.
One of the latter described him as a man of "abusive and hog-
gish manner and ungentlemanly conduct, bearing the character
of a sponge and a loafer and, above all, a debaucher with Indian
women."

The Philosopher's quarrels with the Methodists were not over
morals or theology but concerned land possession. The Oregon
missionaries did not neglect this world in preparing for the next,
and acquired that most solid of all wealth, land. Pickett claimed
that the men of the cloth went so far as to incite the Indians to
murder him to get rid of him and his homestead. Like Brannan,

he turned to publishing, issuing the first newspaper in Oregon Territory, a little manuscript bulletin called *The Flumgudgeon Gazette and Bumble Bee Budget* and used an editorial pseudonym, "The Curltail Coon."

When he came south to California he passed through Sutter's Fort where he was pressed into service as a guard over General Mariano Vallejo, imprisoned by the Bear Flag rebels. His sympathy and kindness won Vallejo's lifelong friendship. Going down to Yerba Buena, he impressed Captain John B. Montgomery of the *Portsmouth* enough to be offered the position of alcalde of the town, an office just vacated by José Jesús Noé.

Pickett declined the offer and, finding another close friend in Kanaka Bill Davis, moved in with him. His impetuosity and impertinence soon found him an enemy in Captain Hull of the sloop-of-war *Warren* and with martial law in effect in Yerba Buena, that irascible commander placed him under house arrest for a trivial offense and threatened to throw him into the *Warren's* brig if he left the vicinity of Davis's store.

Philosopher Pickett kept close to home but continued his amateurish but muscular muckraking, calling Alcalde Washington A. Bartlett to account for mismanagement of municipal funds and describing him as an "unprincipled villain." He dabbled in law but considered himself a journalist and philosopher and actually listed his occupations thus in the San Francisco City Directory. He sailed to Hawaii with William Heath Davis, into the maw of a southeaster, on March 13, 1847. Davis's old tub, the *Euphemia*, lurched and shuddered its way through a drenching rainstorm and heavy sea with a cargo of furs, tallow, shingles, Mexican dollars and one very seasick philosopher.

Pickett found the islands disillusioning. Fresh from reading Melville's *Typee*, he expected a primitive and unspoiled society. To his intense disgust, he found his old bêtes noires—missionaries—riding high and dictating the life of the islanders.

185

The cranky Philosopher found the natives little more to his liking than the missionaries. He wrote to friends in Oregon:

> God help the Christianized nations, for the missionaries here can't or rather they have not done it, as they [the Hawaiians] are now worse in character and condition than before these holy modern apostles came amongst them. . . . I don't believe there is a single Kanaka in the Pacific Ocean who believes in the doctrines they teach. . . . The character of the native population may be summed up in two words. They are all whores and rogues. Not an honest man or a virtuous woman amongst them, from the King and Queen down.

As may be expected, Pickett won no friends in the Sandwich Islands. However, William Heath Davis, part-Hawaiian himself, accepted the Philosopher's prejudice as simply one of his many eccentricities and preserved their warm friendship. Before he left the Waimea Valley, Pickett wrote to Davis in Honolulu, "The damned missionaries prohibit traveling on Sunday, and I was told that had I started directly for Hilo tomorrow instead of the volcano as I do, that my servant with my baggage would be stopped and have to pay a dollar fine to go on. Can this indeed be the law?"

Pickett is remembered, when he is recalled at all, for founding the California sheep industry. He never forgot a visit to a Scot's sheep ranch in the Puget Sound country and, while in Hawaii, he bought five young, nearly pure-strain merinos, two rams and three ewes. He got them to Honolulu with much difficulty and stood guard over them in the yard of his hotel for a month, "for occasionally they played truant in the streets."

Late in August 1847 he took his merinos aboard the American schooner *Providence* and, nursing them dutifully on the long, thirty-five-day passage, finally landed them on the beach at Yerba Buena. He hired a launch on the waterfront and shipped his sheep across San Francisco Bay and up Sonoma

186

Creek to the town of Sonoma, remaining in San Francisco himself in hopes of raising capital for his sheepherding venture.

About this time Sam Brannan brought the first news of gold
to San Francisco by dashing into Portsmouth Square waving a
flask of dust and shouting, "Gold! Gold! Gold from the American River!" Pickett, like everyone else in town, packed up and
went to Sutter's Fort. He went as a merchant, however, and not
as a miner, preferring to dig the gold from pokes and pockets
rather than seams and riffles.

It was here he met Sam Brannan, then on his way to becoming the Golden State's first millionaire. White Horse Alderman,
a badman fresh from Oregon with the blood of two victims on
his hands, had got into an altercation with Pickett and he and
his ax came off second best to the redoubtable Philosopher and
his double-barreled shotgun. The result of this fight was the
first trial at Sutter's Fort. This time Sam Brannan, defendant in
the first American trial in San Francisco, sat in the chair as
alcalde because the first alcalde, Bates, was a friend of the bad
character just demised and had resigned in fear he might follow
him to Hell if he crossed the angry Philosopher. The second
alcalde, Fowler, quit his office in a nervous sweat, too.

The historian Bancroft wrote this colorful account of the trial
in his *California Inter Pocula*:

> One alcalde, however, was deemed sufficient, and Brannan was
> chosen for the position. A prosecuting attorney was likewise re-
> quired, but not one seemed to relish the office, as each person
> nominated immediately declined and proposed another. Finally
> Brannan was obliged to accept that office also. A sheriff was then
> elected, the offender arrested, a jury empanelled, and the trial
> begun.
>
> On being brought into court, which was held in a room on the
> western side of the fort, Pickett was requested to lay his arms on
> the table, which he did. On the same table stood a plentiful sup-
> ply of brandy and a pitcher of water, of which judge, jury,

prisoner, and spectators partook at pleasure during the trial; the brandy, from its rapid disappearance, being evidently more to their taste than the water.

Then the questions seriously arose whether in a criminal court, where a man was on trial for his life, smoking was proper. Appetite presses a strong argument; precedent was found in the California women who smoked at bull-fights, executions, and funerals, and if ladies indulged in the practice, tobacco could not be out of place anywhere.

The trial proceeded; equity in its broadest forms alone was sought, but still there must be the form. At length, the judge rose and began a plea for the prosecution.

"Hold on, Brannan," said Pickett, "you are the judge."

"I know it," Brannan replied, "and I am prosecuting attorney too."

Brannan the pleader then addressed Brannan the judge in conjunction with the jury; after which Pickett arose, tossed off a glass of brandy, and made a telling speech, for he was an able man. As soon as it was over, the night being well advanced, the jury scattered, more intent on finding their beds than a verdict.

Then the question arose: What shall be done with the prisoner? "Place him in confinement," said the judge.

"There is no prison," replied the sheriff.

"Put him in irons."

"Got none," said the officer of the law.

Making a virtue of necessity the judge then called the ayes and noes, whether the prisoner should be admitted to bail. The ayes had it. The prisoner took from the table his revolver and bowie knife, and marched off.

Next day the jury were drummed together, held a conference, and disagreed. A new trial was ordered and the prisoner acquitted.

Pickett quarreled with John Sutter, Jr., but seemed to hit it off fairly well with Brannan at Sutter's Fort. He found he was making no money in competition with Brannan and others, however, so he returned to the bay city and there resumed his attacks on Tammany politicos, big business—particularly the banks—and Frémont. He leveled both editorial barrels at California's whiskered knight-errant, calling him a bastard and a political tool among other things.

Pickett was violent, strident and abusive in his attacks but he did denounce chicanery and double-dealing in both business and government. Bancroft wrote of him:

> San Francisco, as well as Athens, had its Diogenes. Philosopher Pickett was his name. Between Philosopher and his Athenian prototype there existed certain differences incident in some measure to differences in age and country. For example, instead of rolling in hot sand and clasping snow-clad statues, the California philosopher sunned himself on the piazza of his hotel, and drank iced juleps. His tub stood in the lobby of the legislature, where he practiced the profession of commanding men.
>
> He once told an aspirant to a legislative clerkship, eager for his influence, that "surely you must know that an honest man stands no more chance before a California legislature than a cat in Hades without claws. If you want office, cheat at poker, brawl o' nights, murder a man or two, show your breadth at bribery—anything rather than display such weak imperfections as honor, honesty and good character. Our legislators will none of these."

Pickett always felt that much study was necessary in order to master the "art of soft soaping and backside licking to get California offices."

Perhaps the high-water mark in Pickett's career was reached years later when he turned his editorial armament on Judge J. B. Crockett, claiming that the California Supreme Court Justice's term had expired August 6, 1874. Unsuccessful in his attempts to arouse public pressure on the judge, Pickett tried a frontal attack. As the judges filed into the courtroom to take their chairs one day, Pickett stepped out from a crowd of lawyers and, pushing ahead of Crockett, plunked himself down in the justice's seat.

189

An astounded Chief Justice Wallace called for the bailiff but he was not at hand. He thereupon laid a dignified hand on the Philosopher, who gripped the arms of the chair, refused to budge, and cried out, "Crockett is a bogus justice! I have as much right to this seat as he!" He then grabbed the Chief Justice, determined to fight for the chair.

After a brief scuffle, Pickett was overpowered by the clerk of the court and the crier. Sent to jail and assessed a $1,000 fine for contempt of court, he stayed there, unable to raise that amount. He gave his address in the 1875 San Francisco City Directory as *Branch County Jail, S.W. Corner Francisco and Stockton* (streets). He soon won over his jailers and was given a small sentry room as a private suite which came to be called "The Philosopher's Fort."

When released he was chastened not a whit, but immediately turned on the State Supreme Court, suing the justices for $100,-000 for false imprisonment. He next pamphleteered against the Big Four (Hopkins, Huntington, Crocker and Stanford—particularly the latter) and proposed a plan for a California resources exhibit for the French Exposition of 1878. The State Assembly took his proposal as a joke and suggested that Pickett be made a commissioner along with Emperor Norton and another San Francisco street character, the Gutter Snipe.

He continued to expose "plundercrats" with his pamphlets until he died in 1882 in the mining town of Mariposa, on his way home from a visit to Yosemite. One obituary described him as "noted for his eccentricity" and "unquestionably a man of great ability [but] who lacked a purpose in life." This is wrong. Pickett had all kinds of purposes in life, mainly the exposing of the shoddy, the phony, and the corrupt in public office.

After Sam Brannan's trial of Philosopher Pickett, their trails parted. Brannan gave up his brief executive-judicial position and returned to the pursuit of plenty. His stores prospered and his land purchases skyrocketed in value. He soon owned one-fourth of Sutter's embarcadero, the river frontage which grew to be Sacramento, and he founded the towns of New Hope (now a ghost town) on Mormon Island and the lasting, well-to-do Yuba City.

At Mormon Island he collected and pocketed the regular tithes of the Latter Day Saint miners. When Brigham Young heard of this, he is said to have sent "Destroying Angels" to collect from Sam, whom he had excommunicated. Sam met these gunmen with his own hardcases and they never got through the Sierra to bother him. After five years of ineffective effort, Brigham gave up and let the matter drop.

Brannan, at this stage in his career, had the Midas touch. He did a little China tea trading and "coined" money as a result. He speculated in San Francisco real estate and soon owned one-third of the city. As early as 1850 he was one of the city's half-dozen outstanding civic leaders. He was chosen to lead the citizens' posse against the rough Bowery Boys discharged from Colonel J. D. Stevenson's regiment, who, with other drifters, formed a gang of hoodlums styled the Regulators but better known by their other, more truly descriptive name, the Hounds.

These were American toughs, inspired by the xenophobia of the Know Nothing Party, and they used their patriotic bigotry as a shield to hide all kinds of thievery, assault, rape, arson and murder. Their favorite targets were the *Chilenos* of San Francisco, Chilean miners who had drifted down from the Sierra to eke out a marginal existence in urban squalor.

The thirty-year-old Brannan perhaps liked the brief tastes of authority and leadership offered him in the Church, on the *Brooklyn* and during Pickett's trial, for as the leader of the party of two hundred and thirty deputies, he plunged right ahead when he found Alcalde T. M. Leavenworth was afraid to make a move against the rough element. Nine of the Hounds were convicted by Brannan's force and banished from San Francisco; others were sentenced to terms up to ten years on the prison brig *Euphemia,* the same old vessel that had carried Philosopher Pickett to Hawaii.

Unfortunately, none of the sentences pronounced was actually carried out. When Brannan left the continuation of his efforts to others, he found that they let him down. However, the scare which he had thrown into the Hounds was such that they laid low until they threw in with the Sydney Ducks in 1851 in a critical bid for control of San Francisco by the underworld.

Though filibustering was frowned upon in high places and in the pages of *Harper's Monthly* a hundred years ago, in the eyes of the common man filibustering was as praiseworthy as the profession of bootlegging during Prohibition. Horace Bell stated that it was as unpopular in many areas to oppose filibustering in the ante bellum decade as it was to oppose slavery in many quarters. California was one such area, poised as it was on the brink of Manifest Destiny's empire, with Hawaii an attractive target 2,000 miles to windward, a rich, ripe fruit dangling before the eyes of these imperialistically inclined Americans who smelled so strongly of gunpowder. The Sandwich Islands just waited to be plucked away from a king who was often so dead drunk that he would accommodatingly sign away his sovereignty in a generous stupor.

California pioneer Antonio María Osío wrote to the canny Scottish foreign minister in King Kamehameha's service, Robert Crichton Wyllie, to warn him of the filibustering plans under way in the very shadow of Telegraph Hill. Wyllie thanked him for the warning but wrote that he already knew of the machinations.

The most concrete rumor which Wyllie picked up was that about one hundred filibusterers planned to leave San Francisco on November 1, 1851, to "pass the winter" in Honolulu. This was Sam Brannan's *Game Cock* expedition, a combination picnic, yachting trip and filibustering expedition which came on the heels of, and probably emerged from, James S. Estell's plan

192

to seize the Sandwich Islands and make them a U. S. possession.

Brannan led a group of sporting gentleman friends, including A. A. Selover, the man who heaved Jay Gould out of his way by the seat of his finely tailored pants, and Captain William F. Swasey, author of *Early Days and Men of California.* George Frank Lemon and Major Edward S. Riggs joined the gay group and two "bhoys" who later sailed with William Walker's filibustering expedition, Joe Riddick and Chris Lilly, were along.

Everyone said it was a filibustering expedition but Sam Brannan claimed it was just a yachting trip on a grandiose scale. It is very probable that Sam's expedition was more lark than anything else, as he claimed. Sam was no "Gray-Eyed Man of Destiny." He did know the value of money and that real estate, insular or continental, was the soundest of investments. It is very likely that his major interest was speculation and not annexation.

The rumors had placed the company aboard Bully Waterman's smart clipper the *Sea Witch* and the San Francisco *Daily Evening Picayune* of October 15, 1851 reported that "a party of restless young bloods numbering about one hundred and sixty-nine are about sailing from this port for the Sandwich Islands for the purpose, it is said, of revolutionizing the government of his Kanaka majesty." The party actually numbered twenty-five, not one hundred and sixty-nine persons, and they were on a clipper ship but it was not Bully Waterman's *Sea Witch.*

Earlier in the month Sam and his cronies had chartered the *Game Cock,* a first-rate extreme clipper of 1,392 tons. She had been built by Samuel Hale, of East Boston, for a very successful merchant and ex-sea captain, Daniel C. Bacon. Launched December 21, 1850, she soon showed why everything in her design had been sacrificed for speed. Though she never quite realized the world-beating expectations of her owners, she hung up some remarkably fine passages in her long, thirty-year career. Definitely one of the fastest clippers afloat, she led all others in fleetness going to windward.

The one lasting record she hung up was on her maiden voyage under Captain Lewis G. Hollis, when she carried the Brannan "yachting party" to Honolulu. She made three hundred and twenty-five miles in one day, the best day's run of her life. The sixteen-day passage from the Golden Gate to Diamond Head was not super-fast time but she lay off port for only twelve hours and then made Hong Kong in just a few hours under twenty days, a record passage for the San Francisco–Hong Kong run.

The *Game Cock* was in and out of San Francisco for years afterward, while Brannan's other "command," the old *Brooklyn* —a ribby skeleton—lay rotting on the filthy beach at Aspinwall. In 1880 the *Game Cock*, aged and infirm, was finally condemned at the Cape of Good Hope.

Brannan and his party boarded the *Game Cock* on November 2nd and sailed out through the Golden Gate. The sleek clipper was fitted out for faro, rouge et noire, monte and roulette 'tween-decks to keep the "bhoys" amused during their two weeks' trip at sea.

The *California Daily Courier* (October 29, 1851) warned that the men were "well armed and of that peculiar temperament that prefers a row of any kind." While Brannan and his merry men were en route, Wyllie took further defense measures in Honolulu. Pikemen and cavalry were mustered and a paper army of more than 5,000 men established.

On November 15th, Sam Brannan—"the First Forty-Niner," as he was called—landed in Hawaii. (Actually, he had been a Forty-Sixer in both California and in Hawaii on the *Brooklyn*.) He carried an armload of documents providing for the cession of lands in the islands and they lacked only the necessary seals and Kamehameha's signature. When Sam debarked at Honolulu, the King was taking his ease at Lahaina on the Island of

Maui. Brannan sent a three-man committee on the yacht *Maria* to call upon His Majesty but William Cooper Parke, Marshal of the Hawaiian Islands, got to sea first with letters from high officials urging the King to call out his *hulumanu* guards. When the filibustering trio arrived, one of them exclaimed, "That damned marshal has been to Lahaina and prevented our seeing the King."

Kamehameha, however, paid no heed to the pleas of Parke and Wyllie to rally his people in defense of their fatherland and the marshal reported to Wyllie that local authorities were poorly equipped to handle even a "peaceful invasion." He was convinced that Brannan planned to press for a quick resignation from the King, already badgered and harassed by his missionary advisers and presumably not unwilling to retire to a life of peace and quiet. Parke thought Brannan would make himself Governor General and then distribute to his faithful poker partners such positions as Collector of the Port, Commander of Troops, and so forth.

Trouble for Sam arose when word was circulated that he had had a part in the destruction of Hawaii-bound mail on the *Game Cock*. A broadside appeared on the streets of Honolulu accusing him and two of his companions of stealing and destroying letters on the clipper. The press picked up the story from the broadside. A friend of Sam's named Hanna brought libel proceedings against James H. Tanner, the author of the broadside, but the case was dismissed by the Hawaiian court.

The mail sacks had been broken into on the *Game Cock*, but not by Sam Brannan. A man named Petrovits confessed seizing and destroying five letters: one addressed to the Catholic bishop; three to Prince Alexander of Hawaii; and one to British Consul General William Miller. (The first thing this ex-general in Bolívar's army had done when Brannan came ashore was to fire a letter home to his government, making crystal clear to London his disapproval of the San Francisco expedition.)

195

The papers reflected, and incited, enough public opinion in Hawaii to arouse the whalers in port to an ugly state of mind. Hungry for letters from home, they were in a mood to ally themselves with Wyllie's pikemen against Brannan's "renegades" until the affair cooled down.

Luther Severance, U. S. Commissioner in Honolulu, was no happier with the presence of Brannan than was General Miller. He wrote Washington that "The Hawaiians now look to us as their friends, but if harassed by marauding expeditions from the American coast they will look elsewhere for friends and bring the English more into favor, especially if the American Government is not prompt to suppress such invasions." When the French Minister in Washington also complained, Daniel Webster informed him that the California authorities had been ordered to prevent the organization of any filibustering expeditions.

Brannan bought Hawaiian property during his stay, including a Scotsman's sugar plantation on Kauai and a coral bungalow on Richard Street, Honolulu, from a Mr. Bolster and Theodore Shillaber. To this $60,000 bungalow King Kamehameha III, a jolly good fellow, used to come to be initiated into the mysteries of monte and draw poker.

It was claimed by members of the *Game Cock* expedition later that Kamehameha became so captivated by Brannan and his group that he offered to hand over the Kingdom for an annual guaranteed income of only $25,000, and to sail to California with his new-found friends. Brannan was ready to close the bargain by paying the first installment and getting the papers of cession in order. However, the King's ministers, Judd and Wyllie, finally got his ear and talked some sense into His Majesty.

Kamehameha did draw up a treaty of annexation to the United States, with the advice of Wyllie and in consultation with U. S. Commissioner David L. Gregg. This was to forestall any filibustering coup The final signing was delayed until the threat poised by the *Game Cock* expedition was over, and the death of Kamehameha III ended the plan.

Sam Brannan apparently lost his shirt in his Hawaiian real estate operations, sinking $125,000 in it and retrieving only some $45,000 when he sold out. However, he was ready to leave. He had forgotten his troubles (the Hounds had burned his house down and he had had a spat with his nagging wife), and was eager to go home. His friends were also tiring of exotic but provincial Honolulu and yearned for the boom-metropolis on the Golden Gate. Satiated at last with the pleasures of Oahu, they returned to San Francisco on New Year's Day 1852, empty-handed as far as annexed territories were concerned but with twenty-two barrels of whale oil in the hold and each man with a hatful of happy memories.

Sam Brannan had connections with San Francisco waterfront activities other than filibustering. He joined Henry Mellus, William Howard and James Ward to build the port's first modern wharf, a $200,000 structure running 2,000 feet out into the bay from Leidesdorff Street. He drifted away from the waterfront and even from San Francisco itself in his later declining years.

Brannan was back in the news again briefly in the fall of 1860 when he got into a fist-fight with Captain Farnham of the slaver *Wanderer* in New York. Pistols were drawn but Officer Mingary of the city's 8th Precinct dashed into the St. Nicholas Hotel to stop the fight before blood was shed. He arrested Sam and a friend and let the slaver go.

Brannan's fortunes skidded crazily downhill from the Civil War on and San Francisco's first millionaire found himself forced to sleep in two-bit flophouses when he returned to the city in 1887. He died in Escondido, in Southern California, on May 6, 1889, tended only by a Mexican woman. He was stony broke and completely forgotten, and was buried in the potter's field.

197

Chapter IX

CLIPPER SKIPPERS

IT was not Britannia but Brother Jonathan (or, if you prefer, Uncle Sam) who ruled the waves during the years of 1850–1860 as far as maritime commerce was concerned. The British had nothing to compare with the sleek and sharp clippers which slid down the marine ways of New York, Boston and Baltimore in the last of the ante bellum decades. Their heyday was brief, for already their doom was sealed by paddle wheels, walking beams and boilers, but they faced up to steam proudly and made the most of their day of glory.

Yankee clippers with bones in their teeth, sailing under vast clouds of canvas, made it around the Horn to San Francisco in as little as three months. Speed was what shippers wanted and speed was what they got from the *Challenge, Flying Cloud, Northern Light* and their fair sisters of sail.

Freight rates soared in the clipper ship era to four times the old figures, yet merchants and shippers fought one another for the limited space in the holds. Sometimes even passengers' cabins were pressed into service for carrying cargo and the *Samuel Russell,* when she loaded for San Francisco in January 1850, had the sails taken out of her forepeak and shifted to her cabin to make more room for cargo below decks.

Clipper captains would clap on full sail when they were hardly across the bar, for fast passages meant extra bonus money and they were not content until they had cut the time to booming San Francisco by a third. If they did not show their sternposts to the best steamers of the day they hung their heads in mortification. Clippers in New York and Boston harbors flew pennants reading EIGHTY DAYS TO THE GOLDEN GATE. Except for the *Northern Light*'s west-to-east record trip, they never attained that goal, but no one in his right mind can say that they did not try.

John S. Hittell, the San Francisco historian of the 1870's, wrote, "Sailors saw them at first with amazement and have not yet lost their admiration of the clippers." Owners saw their bank accounts grow as freight receipts from *one* voyage paid for the entire cost of a vessel and, in some cases, doubled the figure of the building costs.

Shippers paid a dollar a cubic foot to place cargo in the hold of the *Stag Hound,* one of Donald McKay's masterpieces of marine design. The underwriter, Walter Jones, said to Captain Josiah Richardson before he sailed for San Francisco, "I should think you would be somewhat nervous in going on so long a voyage in so sharp a ship, so heavily sparred."

"No, Mr. Jones. I would not go in the ship at all if I thought for a minute she would be my coffin."

On February 15, 1851, she sailed and made a 112-day passage that was uneventful except for the rescue of the shipwrecked crew of the Russian brigantine *La Sylphide* off the Brazilian coast. A little on the stuffy side for a clipper captain, Richardson wrote of the Pacific port shortly after he arrived, "San Francisco must reform, break off from its iniquities, or God's curses will follow it." He brought the *Stag Hound* back to New York ten months and twenty-three days after he had left. Her single around-the-world voyage paid for her construction costs and left a net profit of $80,000! Richardson returned to the sink of depravity by the Golden Gate in 1852 on the *Staffordshire,* whipping the *Shooting Star* and the famed *Flying Cloud*. With a 101-day passage on his record, the puritanical captain was briefly cock-of-the-walk on the San Francisco waterfront.

The racing of clippers around Cape Stiff to San Francisco became something approaching a national sport and captains who could hit the magic one-hundred-day mark were the heroes of the times. Most of these clipper captains were extroverts and men of a more flashy pattern than Richardson, but there were some safe and sane plodders on clipper poops. However, the headlines belonged to the reckless "drivers" of the game, men like Judah P. Baker who slammed the new *Flying Dragon* around the Horn in 1853, lost her jibboom, sprung her bowsprit, and so overtaxed himself that he died before he reached the Golden Gate, aged only forty-six years.

Another driver was Captain Sumner Pierce, of Barnstable, who wore a clean boiled shirt every day, sometimes bringing back seven hundred of them to be laundered after a voyage. He commanded the clippers *Lightfoot* and *Sunshine* and was poisoned by the mutinous crew of the latter ship.

Swiftest of all the greyhounds of the deep was Captain Freeman Hatch's *Northern Light*. A Boston merchant in San Francisco offered Hatch a new suit of clothes if he would beat the *Trade Wind* back east. Another clipper ready to sail was the *Contest*, lighter and faster, and victory in the three-sided race was already conceded to her. The *Trade Wind* got away March 10, 1853; two days later the *Contest* sailed, and on the 13th the *Northern Light* bade adieu to San Francisco Bay.

Long before he reached home, Captain Hatch had won his new suit. He passed the *Trade Wind* easily and took off after the swift *Contest*. South of the Horn he caught her amid wild seas and shouted to Captain Brewster, "Sorry not to stop, but I can't hold my horses."

However, Hatch found passing the *Contest* a more difficult chore than catching her, and after traveling in company for a

201

day or so, the *Northern Light* began to fall behind. By using all his skill as a seaman, Hatch put together a forty-mile edge on his rival at the Equator, secured the windward position about one hundred and forty miles east of the *Contest* and made the run home to Boston in seventy-six days and eight hours from San Francisco, a record never equaled. It was two and a half days later that the whipped *Contest* reached New York.

Captain Hatch went ashore from the *Northern Light* before the chain had hardly ceased rattling through the hawse pipe. He hired a hack and drove like a madman to the home of the ship's owner, James Huckins, shouting from outside the house, "Here I am with the *Northern Light*, but I've strained her dreadfully getting here."

"Did you beat the *Contest?*" asked Huckins.

"Yes."

"Then I don't care a damn how much you strained her!"

The *Northern Light* went on to some great passages before she was sunk in a collision with a Frenchman in 1862 but her fame rests on her record passage of 1853 from San Francisco to Boston. Hatch is remembered even in death for his record run. On his tombstone in the Eastham, Massachusetts, cemetery is carved: FREEMAN HATCH, 1820–1889. *He became famous making the astonishing passage in clipper ship* Northern Light, *from San Francisco to Boston, in 76 days, 6* [sic] *hours—an achievement won by no mortal before or since.*

On the east-to-west run, Donald McKay's *Flying Cloud* took the palm, eighty-nine days and eight hours, anchor to anchor, from New York to San Francisco via Cape Horn. The last entry in her log for the record passage was: "At 6 A.M. made South Farallone. NE 2 degrees, E six miles, at 7 took a pilot, at 11 hour 30 miles came to anchor in five fathoms of water off North Head, San Francisco Harbor."

Only a few clippers could set records from port to port and more than a few of the "greyhounds" were never reported by the Marine Exchange lookout in San Francisco. Some disappeared without a trace while others piled up on lonely coasts or on bleak guano islands of the Pacific. A few died on San Francisco's very doorstep in the years before George Davidson charted the coast and paved the way for lighthouses and other navigational aids.

The *San Francisco,* with Captain Isaac Sitzer in command, beat four other clippers and a full-rigged ship to the Heads in 1854 on her maiden voyage and the captain wrote in his log, ". . . Farallon Islands being distant about half a mile, took pilot, which ends our voyage of 105 days." Her voyage was ended, unfortunately, with her life. On February 8th the pilot brought the clipper into the watery gash in the Coast Range that is the Golden Gate. She missed stays and went on the rocks of Rialto Cove, just inside Point Bonita, the North Head of the harbor entrance.

A horde of looters took to their small boats, crossed from San Francisco to the Marin County shore and began to strip the clipper of her $400,000 cargo, although representatives of the owner and agent tried to drive them away. Soldiers came from the Presidio to join the plunderers. In poetic justice, a storm came up and many of the small craft, heavily laden with stolen cargo, were swamped. Twelve of the hijackers were drowned in the Golden Gate. The ship was sold, as she lay, to Captain Robert H. (Bully) Waterman for $12,000. He managed to get $20,000 worth of cargo out of her before the swells broke up the hulk of the once-proud clipper.

New Year's Day 1863 saw the clipper *Noonday* approaching San Francisco after a slow but safe passage of 139 days out of Boston. The weather was clear and the bow wave curled back from a smooth sea although there was a long swell on. The *Noonday* was making ten knots under all sail, to main-skysail and topgallant studdingsails, when she struck a submerged rock about eight miles west of North Farallon Island. Her speed ran her clear and the shock was not strong enough to carry away any of her spars or rigging, but she began to fill. Captain Henry discovered her bottom had been badly stove and he and his crew were able to save only a few personal effects before she went down in forty fathoms.

The pilot boat *Relief*, two miles distant at the time of the accident, picked up all hands. The rock, covered with eighteen feet of water, had been known to the pilots as Fanny Rock, but never placed on the charts. In a locking-the-barn-door-after-the-horse-has-escaped maneuver, the rock was not only charted and buoyed subsequent to the wreck, but was named Noonday Rock. Captain Rodgers of the Coast Survey found it a large rock with two sharp pinnacles eighteen feet under water.

This should have closed the books on Noonday Rock but in 1879 the ship *Alaska* gave the buoy a wide berth only to run onto a rock. She limped into port and reported her discovery of a new rock, but it was found that the *Alaska* had run on the one and only Noonday Rock. The buoy had drifted a mile away from its anchorage. Thirty-five thousand dollars was appropriated to blow it up and remove it as a menace. One of its pinnacles was blown off but to the amazement of all when soundings were made, it was found that only fourteen feet of water covered it where there had earlier been eighteen.

When one considers the ferocity of the wishfully named Pacific at certain seasons—the gray threat of coastal fog in summer, the uncharted rocks offshore, and the total lack of lighthouses a century ago—it is surprising that more vessels did not dig their graves on the California tidemark. One clipper whose bones do lie on the beach about fifty miles south of San Francisco is the *Carrier Pigeon*. She went ashore June 6, 1853. All of Captain Azariah Doane's hands were saved but the ship—worth $54,000 alone—and its 1,300 tons of cargo were sold, as was, for $1,500. Her case was similar to that of the *Noonday*. The point on which she crashed was named Pigeon Point in her honor and the Government constructed a lighthouse and fog-signal station there later to prevent other wrecks.

Another fine clipper, the *Flying Dragon*, came running up from Newcastle, New South Wales, with 1,000 tons of coal and entered the port on the night of January 29, 1862. She met thicker weather inside than out, with heavy rain falling. Suddenly she was struck by a fierce squall. Captain Horace H. Watson let go both anchors but a defective windlass thwarted his maneuver. Before enough chain could be put out, she was driven on the reef footing Arch Rock and held there by the surging flood tide. A tug was sent to haul her off and a squad of soldiers from Fort Alcatraz to help pump her out, but all efforts were useless. Next morning she fell over on her side and disappeared. The conduct of the pilot in charge was examined but he was fully exonerated of any responsibility for the mishap.

The *Flying Dragon*, a veteran of five San Francisco–Australia passages, was an unlucky ship. When she had left Baker's Island the preceding February with a load of guano, she was found to be leaking sixty inches an hour. Captain Watson was forced to jettison four hundred of her 1,225 tons of cargo. The crew mutinied and tried to make him abandon ship but he forced them at pistol point to man the pumps. Still, he would have foundered had not the King of Tongatabu sent a relief force of natives to help at the pumps. Almost all of the remaining cargo was discharged and finally the leak was stopped. When she arrived at Sydney she was docked and repaired before proceeding to her tragic appointment with Arch Rock.

The *Euterpe*, 118 days from New York, arrived off San Francisco on June 25, 1860, took on a pilot, and started in. She grounded in a fog off Fort Point but, after lightening one hundred and forty tons of cargo, she got off with four feet of water in the hold, and an ultimate repair bill of $24,000, a reminder that the "finest natural harbor in the world" can be a treacherous one at times, as well.

Less often, vessels were disabled or wrecked when outbound, much to the embarrassment of the bar pilots in command. In 1857 the clipper *Flying Fish*, bound out for Manila, crossed the bar only to find she had lost her rudder. She was blown ninety miles offshore while a temporary one was rigged and then beat back to the Gate in the teeth of the northerly winds. Towed safely into port, she was a lucky ship. She had cheated the hungry shores of the Golden Gate of a sure wreck.

Narrow escapes were common. Ten years later, the *Elizabeth Kimball* went ashore on Black Point while beating out of the Bay, but no serious damage was done. The *John Stuart*, a medium clipper, missed stays in tacking just outside Fort Point in June 1853 and nearly went on the rocks, but she let go sixty fathoms of chain and was brought up safely. A similar incident occurred in January 1865 when the Peruvian coolie clipper *R. Protolongo*, formerly the *Starlight*, was ready for sea in ballast but with $80,000 of treasure aboard. She was caught in a terrific blow and had to slip both anchors to prevent her going ashore. The only thing which saved her from piling up on a San Francisco beach was a favorable shift in the wind.

Some clippers made a target of Mile Rocks in their dash for the open sea. Captain Charles H. Salter's extreme clipper *Typhoon* struck Mile Rocks while outbound on June 27, 1853, and stove in her bottom. She had ten and a half feet of water in her hold by the time she reached Rincon Point in her retreat from the sea. The *Syren* in April 1861 followed her lead and while beating out the Gate under a pilot's charge, and tacking off Mile Rocks, gathered sternway and smashed into one of the huge rocks. She shivered her bowsprit and opened up the wood ends. She struck a second time but came off and was headed back for her wharf with four feet of water in her hold. She could not make it and, nearly sinking under her crew, had to be beached by them on the mud flats. Her cargo was discharged and she was taken to Mare Island for dry-docking and $15,000 of repairs.

Other clippers were not so lucky as these. The *Golden Fleece* cleared for Manila in April 1854 but, while proceeding to sea, missed stays. Caught in an eddy, she drifted helplessly onto the rocks just outside Fort Point. The tugs *Resolute* and *Hercules* tried to get her off but she had gone on broadside and soon bilged. The next day being Sunday, the beaches and headlands were crowded with sightseers watching her death throes. Many of the curious visited the wreck itself. She lost her mizzen mast and fore and main topmasts over the side when she stranded but it was not until October 23rd that her tough hull broke up under the continuous pounding of the heavy surf. The pilot placed the blame for her loss on the crew's "letting go the main brace before the order was given." Captain Freeman's beautiful clipper, less than two years old, was sold as junk. The hulk brought $2,600, the sails and rigging $500.

Her owners built a second *Golden Fleece* in 1855 which had a little tiff with the Golden Gate herself. She was entering the harbor on June 21, 1857, with a pilot in charge when she struck Four Fathom Bank in the area of reefs off Point Bonita called the Potato Patch. The crew worked hard at the pumps but when the water in the hold got up to fourteen feet she had to be run on the mud flats to save her. She was soon repaired and back in service again.

Another luckless vessel was the *Winged Racer,* under Captain Cummings. Having cleared for Liverpool with 30,244 bags of wheat, three cases of books, and eighty-five bags and ten boxes of sugar, she was doing down the bay on October 3, 1861, under full sail with a pilot in command. Suddenly the tide set her on a sunken rock between Arch Rock and Alcatraz Island. She swung off the rock but it had knocked a hole in her bottom and, leaking badly, she was taken to North Point Wharf with eight feet of water in her hold. Her cargo was discharged and she was sent to dry dock at Mare Island for new planking, calking and coppering, plus a replacement of part of her keel. After adding some $42,000 to the money in circulation in the San Francisco Bay area, she continued on her way, falling prey to the Confederate raider *Alabama* in the Straits of Sunda two years later.

Another clipper to bite the rich mud of San Francisco's shoals was the *Sierra Nevada*, commanded by Captain Horton. Beating out of the Gate for Callao on April 29, 1862, she missed stays and went ashore on Fort Point. Despite a dense fog, the revenue cutter *Shubrick* was able to get a line aboard her and pull her off. She was docked at Mare Island for repairs, then went merrily down-bay and promptly dragged her anchor in midstream and collided with the clipper *Phantom*, running up another heavy repair bill for damages to spars and rigging.

Captain George Henry Wilson had the doubtful honor of being shipwrecked in San Francisco Bay twice. He was in the ship *Tonquin* when she stranded and was lost on Whaleman's Spit (afterwards called Tonquin Shoal) just inside the Golden Gate in November 1849 and, on December 1, 1852, he lost his ship *Samoset* at Fort Point as she entered the harbor.

Reefs and gales were not the only California bêtes noires of clipper captains. Dense curtains of fog poured through the Golden Gate each summer, filling the narrow passage tightly from Point Cavallo to Lands End, climbing up over Angel Island's Blunt Point and blanketing a stretch of mid-bay waters all the way to the Berkeley shore.

Many wrecks were due to the blinding fog and many fast passages were undone at the very gates of San Francisco because of it. In January 1853 the *Raduga* was detained for nine days outside the Gate by dense fogs, and in August of the same years the *Snow Squall* rolled inside Point Reyes in a pea-souper for four days before she could feel her way into port.

We are accustomed by prints and descriptions to view the clipper ship of old as always heeled over and racing along with a bow wave curling back from a speeding stem. But there were times when San Francisco's distinctive mists—described as early as 1579 by Sir Francis Drake's chaplain as "vile, stinkeing fogs"—turned the sleekest clippers into rolling hulks, helpless as dis-masted hay scows.

San Francisco's fog, even when it did not mean "breakers ahead!" was hated by clipper masters. When Tully Crosby raced his *Kingfisher* through the Gate within hailing distance of Captain Caldwell's *Bald Eagle* in October 1853 it was only because he had blown a full five-day lead over the *Bald Eagle*. The time had been spent rolling in a thick fog off the Heads. Crosby was just one of a long line of masters who plastered the Albion-like cliffs of northern California's coast with invective.

Fogs and reefs, wrecks and near-wrecks, all these failed to throw any fear into the hearts of the clipper captains. Sometimes they sailed from Atlantic dock to Pacific wharf without benefit of warping, pilots, or tugs. On July 1, 1852, the San Francisco *Alta California* bubbled enthusiastically:

> One of the most beautiful harbor sights that has occurred for some time came off yesterday. The magnificent clipper *Hoogly,* which has been lying at the end of Broadway Wharf, loosed her sails about noon, cast off her lines, swept away majestically from the end of the wharf and put directly to sea. This is an occurrence which has only happened in San Francisco two or three times before and was very creditable to all concerned. She carries a crew of 25 men; they were all aboard at the appointed hour; the jib, foretopsail, and main-topmast staysail were loosed; the bow line cast off. The ship leaned over and shot swiftly away without accident. A large number of spectators were on Broadway, Pacific, Commercial, and Market Street Wharves, viewing the scene.

A little more than a month later the crack *Hoogly* stranded going upriver to Shanghai and was a total loss.

Captain Charles Porter Low supplied waterfront habitués

with conversation for a fortnight in August 1851 when he brought the *N. B. Palmer* right up to her berth without any assistance from towboats or anything else, except Divine Providence, perhaps.

The pilot had anchored her in the stream three miles from the wharf and refused to bring her up to the wharf until the next day. Low took all responsibility and hove up the anchor, set all sails including skysails, and with a light beam wind made his way in on the ebb tide until he was close to the wharf. He knew that sails would stop a ship as well as carry her ahead. He had the mainyard backed and the ship was brought alongside the wharf without a jar. This was the finest piece of seamanship ever seen in San Francisco, even if the *N. B. Palmer*'s flying jibboom did lift two planks off the wheelbox of the *Senator*, lying alongside the next wharf. The crowd cheered Low mightily and the agent cried "Well done!"

Clipper captains were proud of more than speed records. A feat like Captain Low's or a trim and spotless ship meant something in the last days of sail. When Captain Eben H. Linnell brought the *Flying Mist* to San Francisco in November 1856 he set no speed records but he did make his mark as the skipper of a taut ship. He wrote a friend, "The Port Warden, in making his report, states that the *Flying Mist* is the only ship that ever came into this port entirely free of sweat or dampness; also the least broken packages." Linnell had a life that was as exciting as it was brief. He rescued a yacht in distress off the Chilean coast after he sailed from California, took the *Mist* to lonely Baker's Island for guano, lost her on the New Zealand coast and, while bringing the *Eagle Wing* back to Frisco in 1864, was caught in a bight of the spanker-boom vang when the sail jibed in a squall. Thrown hard against the spokes of the wheel, he was killed.

One of the most efficiently worked of all clippers was the *Messenger*, which set a record for dispatch in cargo unloading in 1854. She arrived off the Heads on July 17th, entered at San Francisco's Customhouse at 10 A.M. of July 18th. She discharged a full cargo of assorted merchandise in twenty-six hours from three hatches, with double teams of horses hoisting the nets. The speedy work was done so carefully that the bill for damages was only $10. She cleared on Wednesday afternoon and took on four hundred and fifty tons of ballast, swept her decks and was ready for sea. From crossing the bar inward until she was at sea, China-bound under full sail, only ninety-seven hours had elapsed and thirty-five of these were idle hours because she arrived too late to enter at the Customhouse her first day and because the towboat was not free to take her to sea on Thursday afternoon.

The clippers were staunch ships, tough as Brazil nuts, and could take just about anything served out to them by Old Mother Nature. A typical report was Captain Freeman's of 1854, when he brought the *Witchcraft* to California. "I have met with no accident on the passage, not so much as parted a rope yarn; did not close reef topsails once. I am at a loss to explain how I like the *Witchcraft;* we never know when the weather is bad."

Captain Johnson of the *Invincible* was caught in a typhoon on a passage from San Francisco to Hong Kong in July 1852. He reported: "Just as I got the royal yards down, it came buzzing enough to blow one's hair off; relieving tackles were hooked on and let down to the main deck to keep the men on their feet. The sea was tremendous but it was beautiful to see her behave; not a shiver or shake, no water on board, and lying to without a rag of sail. While many others would be dismasted, our good ship did not do $5 damage and on the 8th came out in fine weather like a new pin."

The clippers all had their bad moments, of course, and these were of varying duration and severity. Captain Milton P. Hedge, in a sorry 146-day passage to San Francisco in the *Web-*

211

foot, spent a solid month off Cape Horn, losing his hatches and chunks of his bulwarks to the angry sea. Caleb Sprague, in the *Neptune's Car* in 1861, made it around Cape Stiff three times only to be blown back again. She lost spars, upper masts and rigging. Then the tired clipper's seams opened, at which point the crew mutinied and refused to man the pumps. Captain Sprague threw the leader in irons and managed to make Callao, where he kicked off the malcontents and replaced them with a new crew. Finally after an endless, 186 days from New York he reached San Francisco.

"This is the hardest passage I ever made," sighed Captain Elijah Crocker of the *Conqueror* on his bad-luck voyage of 1876. Two weeks out of New York storms carried away all the iron work on the lower main topsail yards. Gale winds, often dead ahead, split his sails and forced him to run one hundred miles out of his course to save his spars while the *Conqueror* leaked eight inches an hour. On Independence Day, the pumps' engine failed and they had to be worked by hand. By August 1st the crew was worn out from pumping and the clipper was taking fifteen inches of sea water an hour. He kept her under easy sail to prevent her foundering, repaired the pumps somehow and battled the inpour, now measuring sixteen inches an hour. For the last three weeks of the passage pumping never stopped.

On the night of August 22nd both pumps gave out completely. The *Conqueror* was in sight of the Heads of the Golden Gate, however, and though she made three feet of water in the hold in half an hour, she crawled into port safely. The San Francisco *Daily News* of August 24, 1876, suggested to the underwriters that Crocker be rewarded:

> Here is a man who not only carried on his shoulders all the responsibility inseparable from such an occasion, but who also navigated the ship, stood his watch, worked the pumps, ran the engine and encouraged his men by his presence and example.

Some clippers did lose their sticks, despite the skill of their masters, and had to limp into San Francisco. Captain George Cumming was bringing the *Young America* to California in 1868 with a load of railroad iron when, off the Rio de la Plata, she was hit by a whirlwind. The *Young America* became unmanageable and was soon lying on her beam ends. Cumming ordered stays and shrouds cut, but before his command could be obeyed the gale shifted and carried away the main-topgallant and fore-royal mast and cut the mizzen down to the lower masthead. The *Young America* had added a lot of water to her already heavy cargo and was laboring heavily, but passengers joined the crew at the pumps and freed the hold of the water she had taken in. The gale subsided into an ugly cross-sea but the standing rigging kept the wreckage alongside.

Five days after the dismasting, a jury mizzenmast had been stepped. Ten days after the whirlwind the topgallant and main-top sails were sent up and Captain Cumming resumed his passage. He brought the clipper into the Golden Gate in only 117 days from New York, under the neatest jury rig ever seen in San Francisco. Looking like a yacht, with all standing rigging in apple-pie order and everything about the vessel taut and shipshape, the *Young America* and Captain Cumming became the talk of the Embarcadero. Praise was heaped upon Cumming and the underwriters presented him with a purse of $1,000 in gold. Had he put into Rio to step a new mast, he would have had to discharge his cargo and this would have amounted to virtual confiscation. The *Young America* was repaired at San Francisco and sailed until 1886, when she left the Delaware Breakwater never to be heard from again.

Sometimes clippers encountered legal and political reefs in San Francisco Bay as well as physical obstructions to navigation. When the *Telegraph* arrived September 5, 1861, from Liverpool, much battered by storms, she had no time to lick her wounds but was immediately seized by the U. S. authorities because she was owned by a Confederate. While anchored in the bay she was fouled by the ship *Inspector* to the tune of one thousand Yankee dollars in repairs and then sat for a year until the U. S. Marshal sold her to a San Francisco company.

Desertion presented another constant problem to clipper masters, as well as to the skippers of the barks, ships, brigs and schooners which called at "the Naples of the West." In a port like San Francisco, with the gold fields at its back, desertion was as common as crimping. The adventure of young John Higgins of the *Albatross* was an interesting if not typical case of wanderlust. He jumped ship in San Francisco in 1850 and hurried to the gold fields with the rest of the crew. Thinking he would do better Down Under, he shipped for Sydney on the steamer *Monumental City*, was wrecked and crawled ashore on the Australian coast. Still not satisfied with his luck, he shipped as second officer on a local trading brig, was wrecked in the Carolines and adopted by a chief. He married the latter's daughter and became a sort of "King of the Cannibal Isles" until he was killed in a war with other natives.

When Captain Wood's *Polynesia* was anchored in San Francisco harbor ready to sail for Hong Kong, her crew deserted for the Cariboo mines of British Columbia but were rounded up by San Francisco police before they had got very far. They were loaded back aboard. This crew was not so easily whipped in its ambitions, however, and at 1 A.M. of March 3, 1862, Wood found his clipper suddenly on fire. He clapped on hatches, leaving only enough room for lines of hoses to enter the hold, and welcomed the assistance of fifty men with portable pumps from the U.S.S. *St. Mary's*. The fire kept gaining, in spite of all their efforts, and the captain decided to scuttle the *Polynesia* before she set fire to the other vessels which surrounded her in the fairway. This plan was quashed by the Harbor Master, who did not want the stream littered with scuttled hulks.

Finally the anchor chain was cut through with a collection of chisels, saws and files and she was taken in tow—blazing cheerfully now— and beached on the mud flats of the South End. She was a total loss and her hulk was sold for breaking up. The Cariboo placers did not see her firebug crew, however. They were clapped in irons by Captain Wood and sent ashore to meditate upon their errors in the San Francisco jail.

When Joshua Sears took the *Wild Hunter* into San Francisco in 1857, his crew deserted *en masse* for the mines of the Mother Lode. He wrote home: "It is the custom here for everybody to leave their ship and they don't want to be behind the times." After two months in port he managed to muster a crew and he sailed in ballast. In the forecastle he had "two half-way sailors, white; eight boys; one shoemaker; four Manila men; three Malays and three Kanakas."

Sears dodged a typhoon and beat the clipper *Mameluke* to Singapore, but later the *Wild Hunter* was a disappointment in terms of speed. The captain wrote: "We have painted the ship all over, outside and in . . . and she shines like a nigger's eye [but] we had four or five vessels in company last week and they all sail as fast as we do, and some of them outsail us. I don't know what is the matter with the old ship. One ugly looking Portuguese brig kept us company three days, the darnedest looking dugout I ever saw." Sears next sailed for San Francisco with a cargo of Chinese coolies and opium on board the *Wild Hunter*. The clipper was in a dirty business and she got her just deserts for degrading herself. The sea dished out such storms that the *Wild Hunter* staggered into San Francisco Bay on February 28, 1860, with Sears reporting losses of sails, spars and men.

Although some skippers and owners would not soil their hands on the coolie trade—just a shade this side of blackbirding —they were the exceptions to the rule. The action of the owners of Captain Josiah Gorham's *Kit Carson,* in giving him orders in 1859 *not* to load coolies no matter how dull the freight market in China might be, was quite atypical. With the California gold boom tapering off, more and more clipper skippers went into the dirty business of guano or the dirtier businesses of running coolies or opium.

Captain Luther Hurd brought a bunch of coolies from Swatow to the Chinchas in the *Winged Racer* in 1856. Before they sailed, sixty were flogged in one morning for disciplinary purposes. San Francisco, as well as the Peruvian guano islands, was a market for cheap coolie labor. For example, Captain Shungar Slade landed seven hundred Chinese from the *Wizard* at the Lombard Street Dock on June 28, 1857, and Captain Charles Low brought four hundred (at $75 a head) into port on the *N. B. Palmer* in October 1861.

A clipper ship sailor traditionally would joke about anything, including weevils in his biscuit and stripes on his back. There was nothing funny about the guano trade. It was a dirty business. Yet sailors told yarns about guano and the Guano Islands (Chinchas) just as they did about everything else. One such tale was picked up by the San Francisco newspaper, the *Wide West*, in its June 7, 1857, number. Titled simply "A Sailor's Yarn About Guano," it reads like this:

> An old salt of our acquaintance says that when he was in the guano trade he sailed in a brig which might have been a tender to Noah's Ark. On a return trip with a load of guano, the hatches were left open one night, and a tremendous shower wet the guano in the hold, and produced the most surprising effects.
>
> The timbers of the vessel grew and sprouted in all directions; between the decks was a complete bower. The forecastle became an impenetrable thicket, and the cabin a beautiful arbor. The rudder post being made of white oak, grew into a "live oak" tree, which afforded a grateful shade to the man at the helm, though he was sometimes annoyed by the acorns rattling upon his tarpaulin hat. The masts became very imposing with their evergreen foliage and, strange to relate, the foretopmast, which

216

had been carried away in a gale, grew out again, and the altitude of all the masts was so much increased as to render the brig extremely crank.

The vessel had boughs on her stern and the figure head (speaking figuratively) was as full of boughs as a dancing master. They were obliged to prune the bowsprit and some of the other spars twice a week. The quarter deck was covered with shrubbery, and the cook's cabin-house resembled a rustic summer house.

Crab apples grew on the pump handle and a cherry table in the cabin bore fruit. Perhaps the most remarkable circumstances occasioned by the stimulating and fertilizing power of the guano was that the cockroaches on board became so large that they could get up the anchor and make sail on the brig.

One of the owners facetiously remarked that she went out a full-rigged brig and came back half *bark*. There is nothing like guano to make things grow and for strict truth and veracity, give us an old sailor when he lays himself out on a long yarn.

There was very little to laugh at in the Chinchas. They were three miserable islets, none more than a mile across, lying about fourteen miles offshore and about ninety miles from Callao. The steep-sided, jagged islands were volcanic in origin but their porphyritic rock was buried deep under thousands of tons of bird droppings. In the center of the island the guano was two hundred feet thick. Where it had been dug away there appeared to be deep railroad cuts through light ochre hills. Scattered here and there were the wretched cane shanties of the Chinese coolies and their overseers.

During the boom days of the fifties and sixties, the principal station was on North Island. Here a deputy commandant was stationed, a few soldiers and their women, some Negro drivers and hangers-on. The guano blew into all the huts, leaving a heavily ammoniated yellow dust on everything. Nothing seemed to be able to live in it except fleas, lizards and the coolies.

On Middle Island at the time of the guano clippers there

217

were fewer laborers and hovels and none on South Island. The Middle Island chief overseer was a Hungarian who called himself Kossuth and claimed to be the great Magyar liberal's brother. (A claim no one in his right senses honored with the slightest shred of belief.) Whoever he was, he had come to New York in 1850, drifted to San Francisco and then down to the Chinchas to make money. And there was good money in the dirty business. Kossuth received a good salary and the masters of the clippers anchored off the filthy islets were not there on pleasure cruises. It was said that Kossuth favored the Americans over the British. It is certain he favored himself over all.

The guano was dug from the hills and conveyed in wheelbarrows to the *mangueras,* as the Peruvians called their depots on the edge of the cliffs. On North Island the coolies were reinforced by two steam paddies, which cut the guano, and cars on rails which carted it away. The depots were great enclosures of cane, with openings at the bottom connected to canvas pipes or chutes which emptied either into launches or directly into the ships themselves, lying at the base of the cliff.

An American eyewitness described the scene in Littell's *Living Age* and his report was picked up by *The New York Times* and eventually, March 19, 1854, by San Francisco's *Wide West.*

> When a ship or launch is loading she is in a complete smother, as if ashes were poured into her from a hundred and fifty feet overhead. With their yards cock-billed, and rolling their royal masts almost against the face of the rock, all covered with guano, you would hardly recognize some of the finest clippers, that before they left New York or Boston, were praised in the papers, visited by ladies, and, instead of guano, had their cabins perfumed by champagne. But the dust is easily washed off; the sea birds smooth their plumage when they commence their homeward flight.

218

Awaiting their cargoes of fertilizer on just one day in the fall of 1853 were the *Albus,* the *Storm King,* the *Dacotah,* the *Witchcraft,* the *Empress of the Seas,* the *Governor Morton,* the *New York,* the *Danube,* and many others.

In 1853 the coolies were still being brought mostly in British bottoms but the Yankees got a bite of this trade shortly. The coolies were promised a Peruvian *real* a day when they signed their five-year contract under the misapprehension that they were sailing to California to labor in the gold mines. The poor Chinese really were sold into absolute slavery, whether the Peruvian Government adhered to the five-year contract or not. There were more than eight hundred coolies on the islands in 1853 and "G. W. P." on the *Albus* observed that "as fast as death thins them out, the number is increased by new importations." Those on the Middle Island were given a daily stint of five tons of guano each per day, encouraged in their endeavors by the Negro guards with their heavy leather whips.

This coolie slaving, like South Sea blackbirding and the Guinea slave trade, was "an outrage to humanity" in the eyes of nineteenth-century observers, but it was too lucrative a business to protest too much. "G. W. P.," a little early for full American participation in the coolie end of the business though just in time for the Yankee monopoly on the guano hauling, claimed that "the worst slavery that exists among the civilized nations of the earth is maintained by the British subjects who transport coolies to the Chincha Islands."

The clipper *Falcon* was sold in San Francisco in 1864 for $28,000 in gold to Canavero and Company of Lima, whose agent was Nicholas Larco of San Francisco. She became perhaps the most notorious coolie clipper of all time when, renamed the *Napoleon Canavero,* she was bringing laborers from China to the Chinchas in 1866. During the passage the coolies rebelled but were driven below decks by force of arms. The hatches were put on and secured. The coolies thereupon set fire to the ship, and the crew, unable to extinguish the flames, abandoned the ex-*Falcon* without removing the Chinese trapped below. All of the six hundred and forty unfortunates perished on the burning vessel while the crew were picked up by a passing vessel.

From the very first, there were agents of the coolie trade in San Francisco. Many Chinese left California for the Chinchas beguiled by the glittering misrepresentations of the guano company agents. In the early months of 1850, for example, of some eight hundred Chinese in California, about three hundred sailed from San Francisco to work on the Chincha Islands.

Eventually, San Francisco got fed up with this mixture of coolies and guano. When a ship left port on August 2, 1856, bound for the Chinchas with a large number of Chinese aboard, the U. S. Marshal sent the *Martin White* steaming out the Gate with orders to detain the slaver and to serve her captain with writs of habeas corpus for the coolies. The coolies were still enticed or bullied into going to the Chinchas, both from China and from California, but the brutality of the trade was not so blatantly flaunted as in the earlier years.

While mutiny was less a problem to clipper captains than was desertion, it was by no means confined to the sporadic outbursts of coolies confined below decks with their dead and dying. Mutiny was definitely a problem to the driving skippers and brutal bucko mates of a century ago. There is even one authenticated case of a ship's officer leading a mutiny against the captain. Captain James Jenkins of the *Chilo,* in the 1860's, put down a revolt led by the second officer.

A more usual case was that of the *Memnon,* when Captain Joseph R. Gordon—with "all hands refusing duty"—had to put into Montevideo in a welter of flying belaying pins. Another mutiny occurred right in San Francisco's own back yard when Captain Samuel Very, Jr., of the *Hurricane,* anchored in Quarantine, had his mutinous crew taken off by officers of the revenue brig *Washington*. The mutineers were taken to the latter ship and clapped in irons.

Most famous of all mutinies, as far as San Francisco was concerned, was the *White Swallow* case. In 1865 the *White Swallow* sailed from New York for San Francisco under Captain Elijah E. Knowles. Her rigging was in poor shape and the captain forced the crew to do hard work by beating them with brass knuckles and belaying pins. While making ten knots and rolling and pitching in a bad sea, Knowles had men over the side working on stagings. Two of the men were lost. The crew finally had a bellyful and took matters into their own hands. They seized the captain and two mates but did not harm them, only confiscating their weapons and keeping them in irons for three days. They allowed the captain to take the deck to direct the managing of the ship and to take observations.

Knowles signed a written statement drawn up by the sailors which absolved the men of all blame or intention to do harm or damage. In doing so he also signed a promise to give them good treatment, no unnecessary or extra-dangerous work, and watch-and-watch whenever possible. Under these conditions, the crew brought the *White Swallow* into San Francisco where Knowles promptly reneged on his word and had the six ringleaders arrested for mutiny.

The case attracted a lot of attention on the Coast during its week-long trial, for mutiny was absolutely taboo. It turned out to be a milestone on the long trek of American seamen toward the promised land of guaranteed human rights. The decision of the jury was in accordance with the charge of the judge, for the case was decided in favor of the crew and against the captain and his officers. The admissions of the mates plus the testimony of the passengers decided the case. The American sailor had won one of his first victories in the battle for civil rights and for years the *White Swallow* was a major topic of discussion, not only in San Francisco but in all seafaring towns of the world.

On a dark night in July 1852, Captain Charles P. Low of the *N. B. Palmer,* whom we have met before, heard one of his men whisper, "Call the Captain." This was answered by another voice whispering, "Give me a pistol and I'll shoot him." Mr. Haines, the mate, met Captain Low and gave him a musket but warned him not to go on deck because one of the mutineers had a revolver and had just shot him in the leg. Low disregarded the warning and went on deck, taking his mates with him. He persuaded the mutineers to surrender and then marched all hands to the poop and searched them. Two were put in irons and a short while later a sailor named Lemons surrendered himself as the one who had shot the first mate. He was put in irons and the others released.

Low's troubles were not yet over, however. Dublin Jack, a forecastle tough, knocked down not one but both the second and and third mates. He used a handspike on them for ironing his friend Lemons. He also dared to step across a rope which Low had stretched across the ship with a warning that he would shoot any man who crossed it. Low was not ready to shoot his crewmen but he was not going to have his authority challenged again, so he seized Dublin Jack by the throat, dragged him forty feet to the quarter-deck. He ironed him, called all hands to witness punishment and gave both Lemons and Dublin Jack four dozen lashes. The two culprits were then thrown into the booby hatch, still in irons, where they stayed until the ship reached Valparaiso. There they were sent home to be tried for fomenting and attempting a mutiny and murder on the high seas.

Most commanders and mates of clippers had to be slightly on the tough side themselves to handle the hard cases, drunks and malcontents who shipped as crewmen, not to mention the chiseling crimps in port. They ran to the order of men like Mate Daniel Willis Howes who quelled a mutiny in the China Sea by holding a red-hot poker to the touch hole of the ship's cannon which was leveled at the mutinous crew. Then there was

Captain Rodney Baxter of the *Flying Scud* who triced men up at the first whisper of mutiny, ready and willing to flog the truth out of them. If there were too many skulls for Baxter to crack personally, he had two mates to whom he could delegate the disciplining, his first, Mr. Campbell, and his second, Mr. Faunce. The latter had proved his mettle by once beating off fifteen mutineers all by himself.

More common than either problem of mutiny and desertion was the problem of incapacity for duty because of drunkenness. Sailors, dry as a bone (internally) from months in a forecastle, would do a homing act for San Francisco's saloons once they touched port. When the crimps dragged them out of the gin-mills and into the waiting Whitehall boats, the shanghaied seamen were usually too drunk, or doped, to know whether they were bound for Petaluma or the Paracels. Captain Linas Windsor wrote as his first entry in the log as he took the *Viking* out past the Farallons in 1854, "First day out, all hands— nearly—drunk." This entry was repeated, or could have been, in half the vessels that cleared San Francisco in the nineteenth century.

Not all clipper skippers were hornyhanded, hard-swearing drivers. Occasionally, even the hand that rocked the cradle held the wheel as well. Captain William H. Burgess took his wife along on his voyages in *Whirlwind* and *Challenger* and his good spouse cured the old man of the profanity habit, among other things. Burgess took the latter clipper out of San Francisco in 1855 with orders to pick up a load of guano at the Chinchas for delivery to Le Havre. The captain was taken seriously ill at the Chincha Islands and was confined to his bed with the nearest doctor twenty-two days away at Valparaiso. Mate Henry Winsor was able to shoot the sun but could not work out the ship's position from his observations. Mrs. Burgess stepped into her husband's place, made the necessary calculations and, together, she and the mate navigated the clipper to Valparaiso. Captain Burgess lived only forty-eight hours after their arrival.

Mrs. Burgess accompanied her husband's body home to West Sandwich (now Sagamore), Massachusetts, on the *Harriet Irving*. First, however, she gave her Bible to the captain's mulatto steward for his devotion to her husband, especially during his last days. The steward treasured the Bible and kept it with him, but lost it in May 1862 when his ship *Ringleader*, under Captain Otis White, bound from Hong Kong to San Francisco, was wrecked on Formosa and looted by Chinese pirates. A few days later a Mr. Dennison visited the wreck, found the Bible with Mrs. Burgess's inscription in it and sent it on to her by Richard Henry Dana.

More famous than Mrs. Burgess was Mrs. Patten, the nineteen-year-old wife of Captain Joshua A. Patten of the clipper *Neptune's Car*. She sailed with her husband from New York for San Francisco in June 1856 and before the *Car* reached Cape Horn, Captain Patten had to put his chief officer under arrest for incompetence and neglect of duty. The weather was cold and stormy and Patten, doing the work of both master and mate, fell ill. His sickness developed into what was then called "brain fever" and he went completely deaf and blind.

The second mate was a good seaman but was illiterate and knew absolutely nothing of navigation. Therefore Mrs. Patten, with the wisdom of her less-than-twenty years and the experience of a previous round-the-world voyage with her husband, took command. She did a bang-up job as master and mate, bringing the *Neptune's Car* into San Francisco on November 15, 1856, in just 136 days from New York and 52 days after assuming command. She acted as nurse and doctor to her husband in addition to her navigational duties. When the chief mate asked to be returned to duty, she turned him down and put her trust in herself and in the faithful second mate.

Captain Patten never got his health back and died in Boston

on July 26, 1857, at the age of thirty-six years. During the funeral, the colors of all the shipping in Boston harbor flew at half-staff. Mrs. Patten was briefly lionized and adopted noisily by the women's suffrage movement. She was dubbed "The Florence Nightingale of the Ocean" and $1,399 was raised and presented to her a year after her return to New England. Mrs. Patten stuck to her knitting, however, and never did go to sea again.

Probably the most famous of all clipper captains was the hard-driving trio of Josiah Perkins Cressy, Philip Dumaresq, and Robert H. (Bully) Waterman. Cressy got command of McKay's spanking-new *Flying Cloud* because of his reputation for fast China passages in the *Oneida*. On the *Flying Cloud's* maiden voyage Cressy made San Francisco on August 31, 1851, eighty-nine days and twenty-one hours, anchor to anchor, from New York. This was the second-best time ever made. She beat this time, and set a world's record for sail which still stands, on her fourth voyage.

On this world-shaking fourth voyage she left New York on January 21, 1854, at twelve noon, civil time, in tow of the tug *Achilles* from the foot of Maiden Lane. She arrived in San Francisco Bay on April 20th, having logged 15,091 nautical miles, anchor to anchor, in the fabulous time of eighty-nine days and eight hours. Her poorest day was a 26-mile run in the North Pacific with her best one-day run some 360 miles in the South Atlantic. Some partisans of the *Andrew Jackson* claim that that clipper beat the *Flying Cloud's* record, but her run was eighty-nine days and twenty hours, pilot to pilot, and ninety days and twelve hours, anchor to anchor.

After setting this record, Cressy continued on to Hong Kong, ran on a reef a few days out of Whampoa but got off and made New York with the pumps throbbing all the way home. For saving his ship and cargo, valued conservatively at $1,000,000,

Captain Cressy received a silver service and a commendation from the owners and underwriters.

Cressy took a vacation while Captain Reynard brought the clipper around to San Francisco. Cressy returned to San Francisco to resume command and took her out, for the last time, on January 4, 1857, for New York. She went into the lumber trade, broke her back when she went ashore after leaving St. Johns, and was burned for her copper. The name of her captain at the time of her death has been lost to history but his nickname, surprisingly, is a matter of record—he was called the "Wild Goose."

Acting Volunteer Lieutenant Cressy took command of the extreme clipper *Ino* during the Civil War. The Government put eight thirty-two pounders aboard and a twenty-pound Parrott rifle, and manned her with a crew of one hundred and forty-four men. She was rated as a ship of war, fourth class. Cressy took her in search of the Confederate raider *Sumter*. Things started well when he made a record run to Cádiz of twelve days in spite of heavy weather. However, Commander Craven of the U.S.S. *Tuscarora* begged to differ with Cressy over some point and, of course, the Regular Navy won. Cressy and the *Ino* were ordered home and the ex-clipper captain replaced.

Cressy, who had started sailing as a boy in a thirteen-foot dory with a leg-of-mutton sail, got the bad taste of navy brass out of his mouth by going back into the clipper trade with the *Archer*. San Francisco did not forget Cressy for a long time. Merchants honored him for his record voyage, and he was praised in all corners of the city for having "eclipsed the finest and most costly merchant ship in the world" (Bully Waterman's *Challenge*). He died in Salem in 1871.

Phil Dumaresq, of Channel Island stock, was another driver. He was called the "Prince of Captains," and made a great name for himself on China passages before sailing to California. He brought the old *Great Britain*, a twenty-six-year-old Liverpool packet, anything but a clipper, home to New York from Java Head in just eighty-four days in '49. Sample entries from Dumaresq's logbook reveal why "Prince Philip" was able to show his heels to every other captain on the high seas:

> Squally, under double reefed topsails, passed a ship lying-to under a close-reefed maintopsail. . . . Jan. 24th, a southwest gale, close reefed topsails, split courses; before doing this we were going seven and one half knots close hauled, within six points of the wind under double-reefed topsails and courses. January 25th, split all three topsails and had to heave to; Jan. 27th, seven vessels in sight and we outsail all of them. . . . Feb. 1st, fresh trades, passed a ship under double reefs, we with our royals and studding-sails set. . . .

Dumaresq was born at Swan Island on the Kennebec River, near Richmond, Maine, in 1804. Unlike most of his quarter-deck comrades, he had no desire to follow the sea when he was a boy. However, when he was sixteen he was sent by the family physician on an ocean voyage to China to better his health. He grew robust on the voyage, fell in love with the sea, and by the time he was twenty-two years old had his own command. It was said of his opium clipper *Antelope* that she was the only square-rigged vessel able to beat through Formosa Channel against the northeast monsoon. Dumaresq used her speed not only to beat the tides, monsoons and currents of the China Sea, but also to outrun Chinese pirates. He later took the *Akbar* on some fast New York–China passages.

After the *Great Britain*, the *Antelope*, the *Akbar* and the *Houqua*, Dumaresq was given the command of the 190-foot clipper *Surprise*. The New York *Herald* described her as the handsomest vessel in port. She was manned by thirty A.B.'s, six ordinary seamen, four boys, two bosuns, a carpenter, a sail-maker, two cooks, a steward and four mates. The *Surprise* was the second clipper into San Francisco in 1851 and Dumaresq's time of ninety-six days and fifteen hours to Clark's Point from Sandy Hook was the fastest time yet hung up, beating Bully Waterman's record of ninety-seven days in the *Sea Witch.*

A San Francisco merchant rode out to North Beach on March 19, 1851—the ninety-sixth day—to see if he could spot her off the port. The weather was thick and he saw nothing, and he turned his nag back toward the city, downcast. He had hardly arrived downtown when Dumaresq brought her smartly through the Gate and, by noon, was ashore receiving congratulations and slaps on the back. Captain Dumaresq had a cargo manifest for this trip which was twenty-five feet long and which represented $78,000 of freight in the hold. He had really let her run all-out, reefing the topsails only twice in the 16,308 miles from Sandy Hook.

When he brought the extreme clipper *Bald Eagle* up to Market Street Wharf in 1853, he whipped the *Jacob Bell,* a clipper racing against him, by fifteen days. In the *Romance of the Seas,* on her maiden voyage in 1854, he thrashed Captain George Brewster's *David Brown,* also on her maiden voyage in another race to San Francisco. He followed this up with a tight victory over Brewster on the next leg of a round-the-world voyage, winning over him by only one hour on the forty-five-day passage to Hong Kong. Dumaresq set the *Romance of the Seas'* skysail and three royal studding sails before he sighted the Farallons and did not take them in until she entered Hong Kong harbor.

Dumaresq had retired from the sea when his wife and daughter died unexpectedly. To occupy his mind, he superintended the construction of the *Florence.* He fell for the trim clipper and when it was launched February 23, 1856, he took command of her. Often so fully loaded that she stowed double her tonnage, he drove her to some fast passages, clipping by ships under double reefs while the *Florence* sped along under topgallants and perhaps even a main royal. Incredibly, even grotesquely, the Prince of Captains died by falling off a steamer, the *Empire State,* in June 1861 and drowning.

Captain Joseph Hamilton of the *Eclipse* was never much of a record maker or breaker, but he is remembered because of a toast given him in the old hulk that was the famous Niantic Hotel on San Francisco's waterfront. The *Niantic* was an English ship which had sailed from Liverpool to Valparaiso where she was bought by a Chilean merchant firm, Moorhead, Whitehead and Waddington. They refitted her and sent her to Panama under Captain Cleveland. She reached port in April 1849 and took on two hundred and forty-eight passengers and a load of tropical produce for San Francisco, arriving July 5, 1849. Within a week all hands had deserted and she was left abandoned in the stream. Her consignee, Cook, Baker and Co., hauled her close inshore and used her as a storeship.

Contrary to popular legend, she was not a rotten old tub but was an ex-tea carrier on her maiden voyage as a sperm whaler when diverted to Panama by the two hundred and forty-eight passengers at $150 a head. She was clean, whitewashed, and had a seven-foot clearance between decks. During her two-month voyage from Panama to San Francisco, she had no trouble and not a pump was ever manned.

As a storeship at Sansome and Clay streets, she rented for $20,000 a month. She was hauled well inshore and piles and some of her own spars were driven in around her. A pump-log was used for one pile and, to the amazement of spectators, struck a stream of water which flowed for many days. She did yeoman duty as warehouse, hotel, saloon, gambling hulk, fandango hall, and a sailor's boardinghouse which welcomed runaways one night and shanghaied them out the next morning.

The great fire of '51 razed her down to her copper sheathing so a few redwood logs were upended around her and the Niantic Building perched on top. This, the first San Francisco seaside hostelry, was run by L. H. Roby and boasted a sign which read:

REST FOR THE WEARY AND STORAGE FOR TRUNKS. A guest was accused of stealing large sums of money and was sent to San Quentin. A laborious search was made of the old hulk's timbers (the "basement" of the hotel) but no loot was found. The Niantic Hotel passed through many hands before being torn down in 1872 when thirty-five baskets of Jacque et Fils brand champagne were found in the ship's hull, stored for Van Brunt & Verplanck and forgotten. It was of "very fair flavor" when uncorked, having been so completely covered that little air had gotten in to deteriorate it while it lay in storage for twenty-one years.

Hamilton had just brought the *Eclipse* in with a cargo consigned to Beck and Elam and was being entertained shortly after his arrival in the Niantic Hotel. A gentleman staggered to his feet and made a toast:

"Gentlemen, I give you the shipper clips ... the clippy sh ... the ... Gentlemen! I give you the slipper ..." He paused, gripped the table edge until his knuckles showed white, and went on slowly and doggedly. "Gentlemen ... I ... give ... you ... the ... ship ... E ... clipse, ... and her gallantcaptain-Hamilton."

Chapter X

GENTLEMEN OF JAPAN

THE latest chapter in the long, but little-known, history of trans-Pacific junk navigation has only recently been written. On August 9, 1955, a bearded young American from Fresno, California, stretched the kinks out of his sea legs after tying up the junk *Free China* to Pier 43 of the Embarcadero, just astern the old windjammer *Balclutha*. Calvin Mehlert, U. S. vice-consul at Taipei, Formosa, and his five Chinese companions—members of Chiang Kai-shek's Provincial Fisheries Administration—had just completed a journey of 4,500 miles from Yokosuka to San Francisco in fifty-four days.

The *Free China* was the first junk to visit America since Robert Ripley's *Mon Lei* made an eighty-six-day crossing in 1942. It was also one of possibly hundreds of junks and sampans which have made the crossing all the way or part-way, either voluntarily or accidentally. The best-known voyage of all is the highly publicized failure of Richard Halliburton to reach the World's Fair on Treasure Island in San Francisco Bay in 1939. He sailed in the *Sea Dragon* from China but the junk was caught in a mid-Pacific typhoon and all hands perished.

In 1908 the *Whang Ho* made the crossing from China to Sydney and thence to San Francisco. Her captain, Mark Allen Graham, was a San Francisco character who planned to take

231

her east either via the Straits of Magellan or around Cape Horn. Graham sailed out the Gate and his backer, Abe Bekins of the *Whang Ho* Company, thought he was well on his way to Tierra del Fuego. Then disturbing rumors began to pop up to the effect that Graham and his junk were idling around in the South Seas. Finally, Bekins learned the real story. Captain Graham had stuck to his junk only until she got abreast Point Bonita, then had jumped ship and signed on the steam schooner *W. G. Murphy* as mate.

When the *Murphy* called at San Francisco again, Bekins had an Irish cop waiting on the dock with a warrant for Graham's arrest on a charge of embezzlement. The policeman searched the *W. G. Murphy* from keel to crow's-nest without finding Graham. The latter, as agile physically as he was mentally, had jumped from the *Murphy* onto the *Robert Dollar* as the steam schooners passed one another.

A three-hour search of the *Robert Dollar* turned up the elusive ex-captain cuddled up in a coal bunker. He was convicted on the felony charge but placed on probation—he had a loving wife and small baby—when he promised to pay back to Bekins the $390 he had buncoed out of him for, of all things, Straits of Magellan pilotage fees!

In 1847–48 the junk *Keying* visited New York, Boston and other eastern ports before sailing to England and then home via the Cape of Good Hope. She was pictured on one of Currier & Ives' prints. Another junk was in San Francisco harbor during the same general period. Albert Lyman, a young Argonaut who came around the Horn in the schooner *General Morgan*, reported in his diary on August 28, 1849, that "a Chinese junk came into port yesterday and anchored a little ahead of us. Her sails are made of matting, and altogether she is a singular and queer-looking craft. Her China men seem to be quite active sailors."

There are at least two apocryphal voyages of Chinese junks

to California which must be mentioned here before turning to the larger Japanese phase of the junk story. Historian Charles E. Chapman allowed himself to be persuaded, mainly by a Chinese encyclopedia, that a Buddhist priest, Hui Shen, had visited California in A.D. 499. Hui Shen did not actually claim the discoverer's title to Fusang, as California was then called, but lobbed the honor back to five anonymous mendicant Buddhists from Kabul. They made the trip to Carmel, or thereabouts, in A.D. 458 according to Hui Shen. Various people, including San Francisco historian Charles Caldwell Dobie and a German professor named Schlegel, have knocked holes in the yarn but some still hold the story to be history rather than the fuzziest of legends.

A Reverend Dr. Shaw stole the discovery honors away from the five begging Afghans when he discovered, he said, a rare old manuscript in a Chinese city on the upper Whang Ho River in 1890. The New York *Tribune* story had it from Shaw that a coastal trader, Hee Li, actually discovered California—and concomitantly America—in 217 B.C., just 1,673 years before Christopher Columbus's voice had even changed.

For those who like to adopt historic "legends," we might caution that the reverend intended that Hee Li's patronymic be pronounced "lie" and that the good doctor named another, pensive member of the crew Hi Thinc. The story is a good one. Hee Li was blown out to sea by a great gale. When the wind died and the seas quieted, he consulted his compass and set a course to westward. He kept on this course for three and a half months before he sighted land. It was not Kwangtung or Fukien but the pine-clad shores of Monterey Bay! The mystery of such a strange landfall was not cleared up until a crewman, industriously polishing up the compass, discovered a dead *yang-si* bug on its back in the instrument, wedged under the compass needle. When the cockroach was removed and thrown over the side, the needle swung back to magnetic north and Hee Li discovered that he had sailed 180° off course.

The wrong-way Celestial stayed on the California coast for about three months, exploring some fifty miles southward and some one hundred miles to the north. He discovered a huge cut in the coast line which he named, rather unimaginatively for a clever Chinese, Hong-Tsi or Great Bay. This was, of course, San Francisco Bay.

We do not know why Hee Li tired of San Francisco; he may have caught poison oak or found the fog bad for his sinuses, but, in any case, he sailed back to China and oblivion.

Douglas S. Watson performed a skillful historical autopsy on the legend and, among other things, pointed out that the Chinese compass pointed south and was not used in marine navigation by the Chinese until the sixth century A.D. He did not quarrel over the *yang-si* and it seems safe to assume that the Chinese did indeed have roaches by 217 B.C.

Leaving legend and returning to history, we find that the first Chinese to arrive in San Francisco came not in a junk but in the galley of the Yankee brig *Bolivar* in 1838. This unnamed cabin boy stayed hardly long enough to throw a shadow, however, and it was nine years later that a merchant, Chum Ming, came to San Francisco to settle. In February 1848 the brig *Eagle* brought two Chinese men and a woman from Hong Kong and a year later there were fifty-three Chinamen and one Chinese woman in California. By January 1850 this number had swelled to seven hundred and eighty-nine men and women, among whom were probably some of the crewmen of the junk seen by Albert Lyman in the bay.

Strangely enough, all of the junks which have sailed directly and deliberately to California from the Orient have been Chinese. Conversely, all the junks in the historical record which have drifted into Pacific Coast waters have been Nipponese—none Chinese. Hubert H. Bancroft stated that forty-one Japanese junks had drifted to the Pacific Coast of America between the years 1782 and 1875. Another student of the subject, Arthur Woolacott, F.R.G.S., claimed in the maritime history journal *Sea Lore* that more than a hundred have been wrecked on our West Coast. The list made up by Charles W. Brooks for the California Academy of Sciences falls in between these two estimates.

It has long been the popular belief in this country that Japan was a closed book until pried open by the haughty Commodore Matthew Calbraith Perry in 1853. Like so many generalizations and popular ideas, this one is erroneous. Far from being *terra incognita*, the bashful Empire was known to Americans long before the Treaty of Kanagawa, and contacts between Japan and western America—though involuntary for the most part— were both numerous and continuous. As early as 1500, of course, the Portuguese and Spanish were opening up trade with Japan. However, the zeal of their missionaries, among other things, so angered the Japanese that in 1624 they banished all foreigners save the English and Dutch.

The Shoguns and Mikados deliberately adopted a policy of xenophobia, absolutely forbidding their citizens to visit foreign countries or vessels. In their determination to keep all contact with the foreign devils limited to the muddy little island of Deshima, where the Dutch were tolerated, an imperial decree of 1637 forbade all Japanese who left "Nihon" to return. Death was proclaimed the penalty for travel abroad or the study of a foreign language.

A decree of the Shogun Iyemitsu (1639) forbade the construction of vessels upon European models or of larger size or differing design from the traditional junk. Junks were ordered to be built with open sterns and large, square rudders, making them unfit for long sea voyages. As a consequence of these edicts, when fishing or trading junks were forced out to sea they quickly lost their clumsy rudders. Wallowing in the troughs of the waves, they then rolled their masts out and were left at the mercy of the deadly Japan Current which swept them eastward in a great arc that deposited their crews, dead or alive, on the coasts of Washington or California. This oceanic river, also called Kuroshiro or Black Current, is the same stream which shows its other, benign face to America, warming California's shores and bringing to San Francisco its delightful modified-Mediterranean climate.

The first recorded rescue of Japanese seamen by Europeans or Americans occurred in 1613 when Captain John Saris of the British ship *Clovis* arrived at Nagasaki with a Japanese picked up on Bantam Island. In 1685 the Portuguese tried to regain the favor of the Japanese, and thereby re-establish their lost trade, by sending back a number of native seamen whom they had rescued from a drifting vessel. The Japanese did not bother them but neither did they allow them to land.

Even earlier, in 1617, a junk from Mogami was wrecked on the Mexican coast near Acapulco and at about the same time the Russians picked up a junk in the Aleutians. They tried to land the castaways at Hakodate but were not allowed to do so and had to take them on to Siberia. In 1694 a junk from Osaka stranded on the Kamchatka coast at the mouth of the Opala River. The sole survivor of the wreck was taken to Moscow after joining Atlassow's expedition to Yakutsk. There were several other cases reported by the Russians, including a junk stranded in April 1710 in Kaligirian Bay, Kamchatka. Ten crewmen landed only to find themselves in the hands of the wild Kamchadals who killed four of them and took the other six prisoner. Four of the Nipponese eventually were rescued by the Russians and one, named Sanima, was taken to St. Petersburg in 1714.

Another Kamchatka Peninsula stranding occurred on July 8, 1729, when the junk *Wakashima* of Satsuma, bound for Osaka, was beached in Avatcha Bay after having been at sea in distress for six months. A Cossack petty officer, Andreas Schtinnikov, was given presents by the junk's captain which only served to excite his greed. He took his Cossacks off in an apparently peaceful departure but hid and ordered the Kamchadal tribes-men to fall upon the Japanese by surprise. They did so, mur-dering seventeen out of the nineteen men.

The two survivors, an old man named Sosa and an eleven-year-old boy, Gonsa, who was the son of the Japanese pilot, were taken by Schtinnikov to the Upper Kamchatka Ostrog after he plundered the junk of its cargo of cotton, silk stuffs, rice and paper. Schtinnikov's superiors got word of his high-handed dealings and hanged him, according to one version. Another account had him tried and sentenced to the punish-ment of the knout. In any case, Sosa and Gonsa were taken to Yakutsk in 1731, thence to Tobolsk, and finally to St. Petersburg in 1732. In this city the two Japanese, baptized Casmas and Damian, taught the Russians the Japanese language until they died, respectively, in 1736 and 1739.

The Aleutian Island chain claimed more castaways in 1782 when a junk was wrecked there after drifting aimlessly in the Kuro Siwo (Kuroshiro) Current. The survivors were taken in a Russian-American Company vessel to Okhotsk and from there to Irkutsk. In 1792 the Governor General of Siberia ordered them repatriated on the transport *Catherine,* then at Okhotsk. She wintered on the north shore of Yezo (Hokkaido) and then sailed to Hakodate where Japanese officials politely, but no less firmly, refused them permission to land the Japanese sailors.

Yankee skippers got a peek at Japan when the Dutch, during the Napoleonic Wars, allowed neutral American vessels to make the annual call at Deshima, since they feared that their own ships might fall prey to British cruisers in the Pacific. Eight American vessels were hired in the years 1797–1809, the first being the *Eliza* of Boston, under the command of Captain W. R. Stewart.

The *Eliza* and the American ships which followed her to

Japan had to sail under the Dutch flag, of course, to satisfy the Japanese. In 1803, however, Stewart brazenly sailed into Nagasaki, the Stars and Stripes whipping in the breeze. He asked permission to trade and to take on water and whale oil. He was turned down on trading, but given his water and oil and ordered to leave. Later, another American ship, the *Eclipse*, called at Nagasaki, ostensibly to obtain provisions but really to trade. She was ordered out like the *Eliza* after having her wants supplied. Except for whaleships which cruised over the Japan Grounds and put in now and then for repairs or supplies, Americans after the close of the Napoleonic Wars temporarily respected Japan's desire to be left alone. Contacts were limited to the rescue of drifting junks.

Japonski Island, Alaska, was named for the crew of a junk wrecked on the coast near Sitka in 1805. The Russians quartered the seamen on the island until they could be taken to Yezo the following year. Six years later, Captain Ricord of the Russian sloop-of-war *Diana* took seven Japanese shipwrecked seamen from Kamchatka to Japan to exchange them for Captain Vasili Mikhailovich Golovnin and six other Russians held prisoner there. Ricord was unable to land, however, and returned to Kamchatka on October 12, 1812. The *Diana* made a second attempt at landing the sailors at Kunashiri Bay, on the southernmost of the Kuril Islands, October 16, 1813. This attempt was successful and Captain Golovnin and his men were liberated.

In 1813 Captain John Jennings of the brig *Forrester* rescued the captain of a dismasted junk drifting just off Vancouver Island. Two seamen were also saved; the thirty-two others had died of hunger since the junk had sailed from Yedo for "Niphon" eighteen months earlier. Jennings turned the three over to the Russians, who promised to undertake their return to Japan. The second report of a Japanese junk in California waters was made on March 24, 1815, and involved the *Forrester* again. Captain

Alexander Adams, a Honolulu pilot serving as sailing master on the vessel under Captain Piggott, sighted a junk at sunrise off the Santa Barbara coast. Although it was blowing a gale, he managed to board her and found fourteen bodies in the hold but the captain, the carpenter and one seaman were alive. They had been on a trip from Osaka to Yedo (Tokyo) five months earlier when they had lost their masts after their rudder was torn away.

In 1833 a junk was wrecked on Cape Flattery in Washington, with many of the crew already dead and sealed in firkins ready for burial. The Hudson's Bay Company ship *Lama*, under Captain McNeal, rescued the survivors, two men and a boy, from the Indians and took them to England, touching at Honolulu en route. In 1836 they sailed to Canton where they stayed with the German missionary Karl Gutzlaff, who learned their language and intended to accompany them back to Japan. The three Japanese left Macao in 1837 on the American brig *Morrison*, dispatched by Clarence A. King for Yedo Bay, in company with four other Japanese picked up from a junk stranded on the east coast of one of the Philippine Islands. This expedition was the first American attempt to get a foot in the Japanese trade door since the Napoleonic Wars, and the shipwrecked seamen were used as a pry. It was Olyphant & Co. of Canton, an American firm, which decided that such a humanitarian act might thaw the obstinate Japanese Government. They chose Captain David Ingersoll to command the *Morrison*, loading her with presents "illustrative of American civilization" and a small cargo of cloth for trade. Her guns had been removed in order to emphasize to the Mikado the peaceful nature of her cruise.

Proceeding to Yedo Bay, the *Morrison* was fired upon by shore batteries and allowed no communication with the government at Yedo (Tokyo). At Kagoshima Bay she received exactly the same treatment. By now the smell of gunpowder had entirely cured the shipwreckees of their homesickness and the

239

mission was abandoned. The *Morrison* returned the Japanese and two observers who were aboard, Samuel Williams and Dr. Peter Parker, to Canton and Macao.

Captain Cathcart of the American whaleship *James Loper* reported the next junk. He found one floating halfway between Hawaii and Japan on June 6, 1839, and set fire to it after taking three of the seven survivors to Lahaina and putting the other four on Captain Ray's *Obed Mitchell* and other whaleships which stood by. Cathcart had his trio for four and a half months, treating them very well and taking care of all their wants. When he landed them, they had all the movable property from the junk, including money—gold and silver "in parallelograms"—which the captain had kept in safety for them. He asked no recompense.

Reverend Dwight Baldwin interviewed them in Lahaina, having quite a bit of difficulty since they had picked up very little English in spite of their long stay on the *James Loper*. The Hawaiian language was tried on them with even poorer results than English. Finally a Chinese was called in, since the written languages of China and Japan were known to be nearly alike. Questions were written down, puzzled over, figured out, and the answers written down in turn.

The oldest of the Orientals was Heshero, a small and spare man of about fifty years of age. He had attended school and was the most skilled with brush and India ink. He liked to make himself useful and was described as a model of industry. He was the most devout of the survivors, having an idol in the form of a gilded human figure on a velvetlike cloth to which he was most devoted. It was rolled up with a string of beads and enclosed in a wooden box when not being venerated.

He was well-to-do, had a wife and five children in Japan, and was the owner of the disabled junk plus one or two more in Japan. When he and his crewmen were taken aboard the whaleship, he first paid his men what was due them. Captain Cathcart was called in as a judge to decide whether they should be paid only up until the junk was disabled or until they finally left it.

Ijero, another survivor, was about twenty-five or thirty years of age, of only middling stature but "exceeding muscular." More than once in the islands he took up a barrel of flour from the beach, carried it to a building and set it down steadily on the floor. He was believed to have been the clerk on the junk and was fairly well versed in writing. Like many "white-collar men," he was in many ways more intelligent than his wealthy employer, picking up both the English and Hawaiian languages much more quickly than Heshero, for example.

Kinisiu was a boy of sixteen or seventeen years, silent and sedate. He was "seemingly disposed to do nothing but to spend his time in idleness." The three lived at first with a Chinese but became dissatisfied with this arrangement after a day or so and came to Baldwin's house with their effects, including lots of clothing, several basket trunks, an iron-bound box or two, and a bag of Heshero's money which they entrusted to the minister. During the first few weeks of their stay, their great hope was to get a ship to Oahu and from there to get passage to Canton and, somehow, make their way home. Whenever a ship anchored in the roads they would come running to Mr. Baldwin. They finally got a vessel to take them to Honolulu but Heshero died suddenly and was buried there.

There were no ships in port bound for China, so Ijero returned to Baldwin's house, bringing three more castaways who had been landed at Honolulu. They were named, or at least called, Roqf (six); Shetz (seven); and Hach (eight). Their junk was the *Choja Maru* from Iko or Iko No Kinye on the island of Nippon (Honshu), the largest of the Japanese Islands. They described Iko as being slightly northwest of the capital and about a hundred miles distant or a ten-day walk. They also

241

told of the island of Sodo, rich in gold and silver, which lay only a day's sail, about seventy miles, from Iko.

The *Choja Maru* was in the coasting trade, carrying rice, sake and dried fish. They had passed through the straits between Honshu and Matsmai or Yezo (Hokkaido) when a westerly gale drove them out of sight of land and dismasted them about January 1, 1839. Luckily, the junk's hull was still sound. They contrived a jury mast to try to beat back to Japan, using Heshero's compass. Winds and currents thwarted them, however, and took them east.

On June 6th they fell in with the *James Loper*, shortly after their water supply failed. They had hoped and prayed for rain, and put pieces of silver in their mouths to cool their parched tongues. After six days without any water, they caught a little rain in their hands and in containers and even had a little left when they abandoned the junk. The rice was all gone but some fish remained. Three of them died during the waterless period and none could stand when they were rescued. Even husky Ijero could only crawl.

Baldwin learned about Japanese diet and customs from the three men and was astonished and shocked by their nation's intemperance . . . "they do business in the forenoon and lie drunk the rest of the day." He also learned about their religion and their system of numbers and ran an article on the same in *The Polynesian*, before the six left Oahu. Ijero had been taught that Christians were very bad people and was agreeably surprised at the kindness of the people from America, the land the Japanese called "Augusto," according to Baldwin.

H. A. Peirce & Company offered the Japanese a passage to Kamchatka, though Baldwin thought there was little chance they would receive a friendly welcome in Japan after the treatment meted out to the *Morrison*. The little group sailed on the British brig *Harlequin*, in command of Captain Cheine, who had taken thirteen Japanese castaways from Honolulu to Petropavlovsk in 1834, from which town they were repatriated by the Russians.

That same year of 1840, Nathaniel Savory, of Boston, reported a Japanese junk of forty tons as having entered Port Lloyd, Bonin Islands, with a cargo of dried fish. It is not clear whether this landfall was deliberate or a result of misadventure, but the junk was repaired during the winter of that year and returned to Japan the following spring. In 1841 Captain W. H. Whitfield of the American whaler *John Howland* rescued survivors of a Japanese shipwreck from an uninhabited Pacific island where they had spent one hundred and eighty days living on sea fowl. He brought them to Honolulu where two of them, Denzo and Goeman, remained while the third man, Nakahama Manjiro, sailed to the United States to be educated by Captain Whitfield.

On April first of 1846, Captain Mercator Cooper of Sag Harbor, commanding the whaleship *Manhattan*, rescued eleven Japanese from St. Peter's Island, a few degrees southeast of Japan, and took them to Yedo Bay, picking up eleven more en route from a floating wreck. When he arrived on the Japanese coast he sent messengers to the Emperor and, surprisingly, the latter allowed him to land and visit the capital. After treating the Americans kindly and giving them presents, the Emperor ordered them to leave and forbade them to return to Japan.

Year after year the scattered contacts continued and by 1846 the United States Government was interested enough in Japan to send Commodore James Biddle with the *Columbus* and the *Vincennes* to Yedo Bay, where they anchored July 19th. After ten days of dickering, America's trade advances were scorned and Biddle withdrew. In 1848 Captain Cox of New London rescued fifteen survivors of a twenty-man crew from their junk, landing them at Lahaina in the Hawaiian Islands. In 1849 James Glynn took the sixteen-gun sloop *Preble* to Nagasaki to demand the release of American and *kanaka* sailors held prisoner in

Japan. After many parleys, thirteen deserters from the whale-ship *Lagoda* were delivered to him with Ranald McDonald of the American whaler *Plymouth*. McDonald had voluntarily set himself adrift off the Japanese coast in a small boat in order to visit the Empire but had been jailed, like the deserting whale-men, in Nagasaki.

The walls of exclusion finally came tumbling down in 1853, when Commodore Perry's powerful squadron pried open Japan's closed door. *Punch* took the opportunity to point out that Perry was determined to open the Japanese ports if he had to open his own (gun) ports first. Meanwhile, however, more unofficial Japanese-American contacts were being made via the rescue of shipwrecked seamen. Nakahama Manjiro, who had been res-cued from a desert island in 1841, returned from America to Hawaii after attending school and learning the cooper's trade. He was commonly called John Mung and in succeeding years he sailed on whaling voyages and tried his luck in California's gold regions before deciding to return to his homeland from Hawaii. He had no sooner arrived in Hawaii in 1850, from San Francisco, than he was called upon to act as an interpreter for a new group of Japanese brought to Oahu.

Captain George H. Clark of the whaleship *Henry Kneeland* found the junk *"Teenzumolly"* (*Tenju Maru*) on April 22, 1850, drifting helplessly. Friedrich Gerstaecker, the wandering Teu-ton, wrote of the report of this junk by Mr. Damon: "If Mr. Damon had not a Rev. before his name, I should suspect that *Teenzumolly* was not quite original." The junk's captain was Kusuke and Kekuzero was mate.

The *Tenju Maru* had taken a cargo of rice to Yedo and dis-charged same, receiving silver and paper money in exchange, and had then started on the three-day homeward passage. Ad-verse winds caught them and drove them ashore. At the end of sixteen days, their water supply was exhausted and, after twenty-six days, their rice was gone. They lived on refuse, fish scales and what little rainwater they could capture from occasional showers and snow flurries. After sixty-six days, their rudderless, dismasted junk was found by Clark. He delivered six of the men to the Russians at Petropavlovsk under the promise that they would return them to Japan. Two more were taken by W. H. Sherman, captain of the *Nimrod,* and two by Captain Zebedee A. Devoll of the *Marengo.*

Kekuzero assured Damon that there was no truth to the story that returned Japanese were put to death. Through interpreter Nakahama Manjiro he went on to declare that "should any vessel take them back to their native village, the inhabitants would rejoice to hail the vessel and would put on board a supply of fresh provisions without charge."

As more Japanese castaways arrived in Honolulu, picked up by the whaleship *Copa,* Manjiro laid plans for his return to Dai Nippon. It was his ambition to "command a junk and navigate her with compass and quadrant, and show his Japanese countrymen that the 'outside barbarians' understand navigation." Manjiro deposited $75 with Samuel Damon, who obtained $100 more from Honolulu residents, and the Oriental was able to buy a whaleboat. Damon was also behind the advertisement in the *Polynesian* entitled EXPEDITION TO JAPAN, which asked for donations of clothing, shoes, a compass and a nautical almanac for 1850, and a fowling piece.

The American consul, Elisha H. Allen, gave Manjiro a letter stating that he and his companions, Denzo and Gouemon, were rescued Japanese castaways; that Manjiro had been on whaling voyages; had studied farming and the cooper's trade in America; and had gone to California during the Gold Rush. The letter asked that the three returnees be treated kindly, and ended with a testimonial by the consul: "I am informed by the chaplain of the Seamen's Friend Society that John Manjiro has sustained a good character and has improved in knowledge. He will tell his countrymen of Japan how happy the Americans would be to

245

make their acquaintance and visit them in their ships and give gold and silver for their goods."

Consul Allen gave Manjiro a certified document of American citizenship, well sequinned with official seals, and the three men boarded the *Sarah Boyd*. Captain Whitmore planned to put the whaleboat, which Manjiro named the *Adventure,* over the side while off the Loo Choo (Ryukyu) Islands. Manjiro was confident that he could navigate the boat to Japan from there.

After the *Sarah Boyd* sailed, nothing was heard of the three Japanese. Friends in Honolulu tried to find out their fate but even Commodore Perry's expedition could throw no light on the *Adventure*'s fate. Two years after they sailed, Friedrich Gerstaecker fell in with a Dutchman in Batavia who had just returned from Japan on the annual Dutch trading vessel. The Hollander's report to the German was the first word of Manjiro and his companions.

He told Gerstaecker: "A year ago, or better, a whaleboat with three men, provided with everything necessary for navigation, but only a small quantity of provisions, had reached the Japan coast, where the Japanese government immediately took possession of it. One of the men spoke the language very well, another decently, and the third indifferently. They had some money with them, gold and silver, and related that they had been wrecked several years before on a certain part of the coast and saved by an American vessel which took them with her to America. But there they became homesick, and determined at last on risking everything only to see their birthplace again; they had therefore fitted out this whaleboat and came with it all the way from America, throwing themselves at the feet and mercy of the Emperor of Japan."

There was no further word of Manjiro until St. Patrick's Day 1860, when the steam corvette *Kanriu Maru* waddled into San Francisco Bay with an admiral's flag whipping against the top of the mizzen mast and the Rising Sun ensign curling and uncurling at the main. All San Francisco wanted to see the *Kanriu Maru*, one-third of the Japanese Imperial Navy. She was a ten-gun, 290-ton corvette. With a complement of sixty-nine officers, midshipmen and men, she was forty days from Yedo (Tokyo) via Kanagawa. She had used sail most of the way, depending on her engines only for auxiliary power. Embarrassingly, her admiral, captain and many of her crew had been seasick on the crossing. They found the assistance of Lt. John M. Brooke and his crew from the shipwrecked *Fenimore Cooper* very welcome. Brooke had agreed to pilot the vessel to San Francisco.

The press had a difficult time spelling the name of the corvette, calling it at various times *Candinmarruh, Kandinmarrah* and *Kandmi Marru*, and most of them did not even attempt the admiral's name, Kiemora Saitono Leami, or that of Captain Katslintarro. The former spoke no English but broke out in smiles as he presented the departing *Fenimore Cooper* sailors with gold pieces as souvenirs of their stay aboard the *Kanriu Maru*. With a crew that was green in more ways than one, a lot of the responsibility for the success of the cruise of the *Kanriu Maru* fell upon the acting captain and sailing master. He was identified as "Mangeroo" at first, until he was recognized as none other than Nakahama Manjiro. The humble ex-castaway, once known as John Mung, had returned to California on the quarter-deck of a warship, wearing the two swords of a *samurai*.

Manjiro told his story to friends in San Francisco and, later, in Hawaii. Captain Whitmore had launched the *Adventure* from the deck of the *Sarah Boyd* in January 1851 off Grand Loo Choo Island in a fresh northwest wind, chilled with hail. The three men rowed hard but it took them ten hours to make the shore, which lay only five miles away. They anchored for the night and next morning Manjiro sent Denzo ashore.

Denzo returned with tears in his eyes. He explained that he had forgotten his native tongue and could not communicate with his countrymen. All three then went ashore, Manjiro car-

247

rying a loaded pistol as a precaution against a hostile reception. He made signs to the people for water and they were conducted to a pond where they boiled their coffee (they were American-ized *Issei,* already, in 1851!) and ate beef and pork in "American fashion." The people gave them sweet potatoes and rice to round out their meal. Since they could not converse with the Ryukyuans, they allowed the latter to lead them to a govern-ment office a mile away where they were offered rice again, to see if they knew how to eat it. Manjiro recalled later, "We showed them that we knew how to handle chopsticks and this exploit settled the question of our nationality, for we were pro-nounced *Japanese!*"

A messenger was sent the ten miles to the city where, after some bantering and threats, the American-Japanese were taken under the care of the King of Loo Choo, who treated them very kindly. They spent six months with him and were then con-veyed in the annual tribute junk to Kyushu where they were placed in the care of Prince Thiztumar for forty-eight days. The prince was very curious about America and asked them many questions about the country and their treatment there.

From Kyushu they were sent to Nagasaki where they were joined by five more shipwrecked seamen, who had been for-warded from Honolulu to Japan via China. The group was de-tained in Nagasaki for thirty months. They were not lodged in prison but, on the contrary, enjoyed rather liberal privileges while under "house arrest." After two and a half years of cus-tody, they were finally allowed to proceed to their homes.

Manjiro went to Xicoco where his mother welcomed him joy-fully after his thirteen-year absence. She had not only mourned him for dead but had built him an impressive tomb. He re-mained with his sole surviving parent for three days and nights and was then ordered to Yedo with his boat *Adventure.* Here he was commissioned with an officer's rank in the Imperial Navy, with the privilege of wearing two swords.

Nakahama Manjiro remained in Yedo for several years, translating Nathaniel Bowditch's *New American Practical Navigator,* which he had brought on the *Adventure,* into Japanese—"A long and laborious task." He also built a number of boats upon the model of the *Adventure,* which was kept in a government storehouse in Yedo for many years. He was in the capital at the time of Commodore Perry's visit and was in charge of the delivery of some presents to him but was not introduced to any of the American officers.

In 1860 Manjiro was only thirty-six years old but held the rank of captain and commanded a vessel while at home. Because of his knowledge of the English language and American customs, he was detached from his regular post in order to accompany the *Kanriu Maru* to California. From the time the *Kanriu Maru* left Japan until she anchored off San Francisco's Vallejo Street Wharf, her battery booming the customary response to a twenty-one-gun salute from Fort Alcatraz, Manjiro had had *de facto* command of the ship. He asked questions of Lt. Brooke in English and shouted his orders to the crew in both Japanese and bastard Dutch.

The Japanese had bought the corvette from the Dutch for $70,000. She was built in the Netherlands and delivered to the Japanese by Dutch sailors who taught the Nipponese to man the rigging and manage the engines. The Japanese learned their seamanship and commands from the Dutch by rote. The ship was a floating Tower of Babel as "Mangeroo" tried to make sense out of a tangle of Japanese, Dutch and English. He did well in getting her to San Francisco at all, even with Brooke's help as pilot.

The San Francisco Board of Supervisors offered the keys of the city to Admiral Leami, plus the freedom of their council room in the City Hall—a privilege they did not accept though they could not have known that its nickname was "The Black

Hole." The supervisors dutifully inspected the ship, which had come as an advance guard for the Japanese Embassy to the United States. The ambassador and his large retinue had not trusted themselves to Leami's green crew and had sailed on the U.S.S. *Powhatan.*

The first modern naval vessel sent by Japan to any foreign country was not in the best of condition. She remained in port for eight weeks, six of which were spent at Mare Island Navy Yard where she was repainted, repaired and her rotted fore and main masts replaced with sound wood. She was also given a complete suit of sails, made by Harding & Linekin, Front Street sailmakers, upon a Navy contract. Eighteen men worked all-out to complete the job and in two weeks had the twenty-seven sails, 4,700 yards of hemp rope and four cotton deck awnings ready. The commandant of Mare Island would take no payment for the repairs, considering the corvette's returning of the *Fenimore Cooper's* shipwrecked crew to be a mission of mercy and recompense enough.

The Japanese, during their California stay, set themselves up in a three-story brick building on Mare Island and on the third floor of the International Hotel in San Francisco. During their visit, they toured the town and the bay, dutifully sketching (this was before the day of dangling Leicas) everything in sight, particularly the unfinished steamer *Chrysopolis.*

They tried their palates on ice cream, liquor and candy, and were honored at champagne banquets where ten of them over-ate themselves into the Marine Hospital. One died and was buried at Lone Mountain Cemetery but his remains were later shipped to Japan. Another sailor jumped ship at Mare Island and was hidden in the engine house of the floating dock by the engineer, David Wight, until the *Kanriu Maru* sailed.

For a time after the *Powhatan* arrived on March 29, 1860, with the Japanese Embassy officials on board, and before the corvette sailed, Americans on Mare Island were outnumbered by Japanese. San Francisco dignitaries and Governor Downey made the trip to Mare Island to call upon the exotic visitors. Everybody was delighted with the way things went except Captain Cunningham, Mare Island commandant, who was unlucky enough to walk past the old *Independence* as that antique receiving ship commenced firing a salute to the Japanese ambassador, who was going down-bay to San Francisco. Part of a charge from a gun on the old hulk hit Cunningham in the face and shoulder. He was hospitalized and the chore of entertaining the Nipponese fell upon David McDougall who, just two years later, was engaged in a running battle with Japanese shore batteries while commanding the U.S.S. *Wyoming.*

On May 2nd the admiral and his men rejoined the corvette, anchored off Clark's Point. Bright with new paint, she passed out of the Golden Gate with purring, reconditioned engines. She stopped in Honolulu on May 17, 1860, where Manjiro presented to his old friend Reverend Samuel Damon a copy of the Japanese Bowditch he had translated, of which only twenty copies had been made and all in longhand. None had been printed as yet.

In return, Damon helped Manjiro obtain a daguerrotype camera so that he could take pictures of his mother when he arrived back in Japan. A devoted son, he wanted it for that sole purpose and remarked, "and when that is done, it will be useless."

Nothing more was heard of Manjiro after he left Honolulu for Dai Nippon until 1865 when the United States Minister to Japan, Robert Hewson Pruyn, wrote that "on my arrival here, I made inquiries about Mangero but could learn nothing of him. After the arrival of the *Wyoming*, Commodore McDougall made like ineffectual inquiries, till one day we had a review of all the troops and saw the Japanese admiral, of whom the same inquiries were made, accompanied by Commodore McDougall's remark that he thought he had noticed him in the crowd of spectators. He was called forward. He had no swords, and said he was in disgrace and had not dared to come forward until called. We did not learn the cause of his disgrace."

In 1871, Manjiro had bounced back into court favor and was honored with six of his countrymen by being chosen to go to Europe to observe the Franco-Prussian War. On reaching the United States his health failed and he had to return to Japan, but only after visiting Fair Haven to see Captain Whitfield, who had rescued him so many years before.

When Samuel C. Damon visited him in Japan in the 1880's, he found him an invalid with a daughter and four sons. One of the latter was a physician and another an architect. Manjiro still possessed a copy of his *magnum opus*, the Japanese translation of the *Practical Navigator*. Damon still had his copy, in Honolulu, and learned that these were the only two left. The others were all burned when the Archives of the Empire were destroyed in a fire.

Manjiro was probably the first Japanese to acquire a knowledge of English. For two years he taught the language in a school in Tokyo which later became the University of Japan. Later in life he was respected but his fame forgotten, and Damon was told that Manjiro was dead when he first asked for him in Japan. Finally in Tokyo a Mr. Tsuda, an editor of an agricultural paper, obtained an interview with Manjiro for Damon. The former remarked to the Honolulu missionary-editor that he had been only "half-dead." Manjiro enjoyed this visit from Damon, never having forgotten the latter's kindness in advertising in the Hawaiian papers for benevolent persons to aid his expedition in the little *Adventure*.

Almost every year, Japanese seamen continued to be rescued, but their Government was very inconsistent in its treatment of repatriated sailors. Friedrich Gerstaecker, the wandering German who visited California in 1849, wrote:

A Japanese who can prove he was shipwrecked and taken aboard a foreign vessel, would not be condemned to death, but would be kept in an eternal prison and become, if not really, at least nominally, a dead man. The laws are so severe and merciless among this race that if a fisherman were known to have boarded a foreign vessel at sea he would almost certainly suffer death; and these poor fellows who have been picked up outside with their boats by European or American vessels always begged the captains, as I am told, to break their boat so that they might have a certain proof that there was no chance for them to save their lives but by asking help from the foreigners.

Typical instances of Japanese inconsistency occurred in 1846 when the *Manhattan* was kindly received on its mission of mercy while, on the other hand, Sir Edward Belcher, commanding H.M.S. *Samarang*, was told by Japanese authorities that they would not receive any shipwrecked Japanese from China and that a junkful of them had just been sent back to the Emperor of China.

California's second citizen of Japanese ancestry was Hikozo, or, as he was called in America, Joseph Heco. Born in Komiya on the Inland Sea in 1837, he thought he would like the life of a sailor and joined his father on the latter's junk *Sumiyoshi Maru* when she sailed in 1850 from Osaka for Yedo. He transferred to another junk, the *Eiriki Maru*, at the latter port and loaded cargo for the return to Osaka via Uraga. Just after leaving the last-named port, the *Eiriki Maru* was caught in a storm and her rudder disabled.

Manzo, captain of the junk, ordered two hundred bales of the cargo of barley and peas jettisoned but still she took in great quantities of water and the crew had to pump all the time. The tall, heavy mast made her roll so heavily that they decided to cut it away. They passed Ogashima Island in the Ryukyu group as they ran under a jury mast but were unable to reach the island. As they were swept farther out to sea they threw over

253

the side four hundred more bales of peas and barley and kept pumping and praying steadily.

They caught enough mackerel not only to feed themselves, but also managed to dry and salt a surplus. Their attempt to distill sea water for drinking, using a large rice-cooking pot, was successful but required such a large amount of fuel (it took ten hours to distill out one quart of drinking water), that they gave up the experiment. Fifty days after being blown out to sea, the crew sighted a ship which alarmed them as much as it elated them. In the words of Heco it was "a strange vessel, so huge and black, and the strange creatures on board her—for all we knew, no human beings at all." But they cried out to be saved and waved old clothes on the ends of bamboo poles.

Cigar-smoking Captain Jennings of the American bark *Auckland* received the seventeen seamen kindly and got his Chinese cook to write out the words *Gold Mountain* (the Chinese name for California) in Chinese characters. The Japanese could read the writing all right but imagined Gold Mountain to be the name of the ship rather than their destination. Forty-two days later, they saw small craft with three-cornered sails—pilot boats —darting about off a strange coast. A bushy-bearded man dressed in black and wearing a great gold chain on his chest and a beaver hat on his head, came aboard from one of the small boats. Besides a speaking trumpet, he carried a file of newspapers which Captain Jennings greedily accepted and instantly took with him to his cabin. By 10 A.M. of February 8, 1851, the bearded pilot had brought the *Auckland* to anchor at North Beach, under Telegraph Hill. Here Heco and his comrades had their first view of "Meriken" (America), of "Karuhoniya" (California) and of the great port city of "Sanfuranshisuko."

Sharp little Whitehall boats darted out to the bark and their occupants came aboard, men in flannel shirts and cloth pantaloons. To the wide-eyed Japanese, they were decidedly rough in appearance and they all either smoked pipes or chewed tobacco, and both categories spat continually. On the fourth day in port, the bark was moved to Long Wharf where Heco went ashore to gawk at such queer Western customs as the chain gang—some fifty prisoners, in irons, digging and carting away dirt—a roulette wheel and a masquerade ball at which the castaways, in native costume, were the guests of honor.

During the week the Japanese helped the crew transfer cargo to a hulk which served as a storeship and were then moved to quarters on the revenue cutter *Polk*, since the *Auckland* had to return to sea. They were put in the capable hands of a goodhearted Irish master-at-arms, Thomas Troy, who eagerly learned the language from them in hopes of visiting Nippon himself. The Japanese disliked idleness so they voluntarily helped the crew keep the ship cleaned up and waited on the officers in the wardroom. Because of their strict laws against learning foreign languages and customs, they did not pick up English. Heco was the only one really interested in learning the language but his elders warned him not to, and he gave up the idea, "for if I learned a foreign tongue and went home, I and they also would be put into confinement, besides suffering a very serious punishment, the exact details of which they were not certain of."

Upon the urging of the Japanese, Thomas Troy was transferred by Captain A. Webster from the *Polk* to the U.S.S. *St. Mary's*. The latter had been selected to transport the sixteen Japanese to Hong Kong to meet Commodore Perry's squadron. One of the men, Sentharo, chose to remain in San Francisco with Reverend Goble and joined the Perry expedition to Japan in 1853. He was known as Samuel Sentaro and as Sam Patch to Americans. Captain Manzo died April 3, 1852, in Hawaii and was buried in the graveyard at Hilo.

Manzo's crew was not very happy after they were transferred to the U.S.S. *Susquehanna* to await Perry in Macao. The warship's crewmen were all "old China hands," used to bullying and abusing the Chinese and inclined to do the same toward the proud Japanese. Some of the latter were so disgusted with their treatment that they attempted to go overland to Nanking in hopes of eventually reaching Japan. They did not get very far before they were set upon by bandits and robbed, and had to return to the *Susquehanna*.

Thomas Troy tired of waiting for Perry and decided to go to California "before the gold fever was over." He had little difficulty persuading Heco to join him, and two others decided to return with him to San Francisco. They were Kame, or Kamezo, and Tora or Jisaku. Troy spent what money he had to get them their passage ($50) to San Francisco on the British bark *Sarah Hooper*. They arrived in early December 1852 and found some of their friends from the *Polk* now stationed on the cutter *Frolic*. Heco sailed with the latter ship to Monterey and Catalina Island where, in Avalon Bay, the *Frolic* was careened. He stayed aboard on her cruise to San Diego and back to San Francisco, while Troy tried to line up a job for him.

Tora was getting $70 a month on the revenue cutter *Argus* at Benicia, under Captain Pease, and Kame was earning $60 a month on the surveying cutter *Ewing*. Heco left the *Frolic* and joined the *Argus* when Tom Troy was appointed master-at-arms of that vessel. Only fifteen years old, Heco managed to pick up a little money working in boardinghouses. In June 1853, Captain Pease introduced Heco to another of his countrymen, Kiutaro, supercargo and sole survivor of a two-hundred-*koku* junk's crew of eleven men. An American fruit schooner had found the hulk drifting in the South Seas.

Heco was a bright lad and he jumped at the opportunity when San Francisco's Collector of Customs, Beverly C. Sanders, offered to educate him. On June 15, 1853, he entered the service of the Collector of the Port and soon met Sam Brannan, Governor Gwinn, and other notables of California. When he went east with Sanders to be placed in a Catholic school in Baltimore he met the President of the United States.

Baptized Joseph Heco, he studied diligently under Brother Waters while Sanders was visiting Europe. Heco returned to San Francisco on November 28, 1854, and was placed by his guardian in a school until the financial panic of 1855 bankrupted Sanders. His schooling ended, Joseph Heco went to work for Macondray and Company on April 5, 1856. Tora, the second mate, became a clerk or porter for Wells Fargo until April 19, 1859, when he sailed to Hakodate via Honolulu on the American bark *Melita.*

Always ambitious, Heco next obtained an appointment as captain's clerk on Lieutenant J. M. Brooke's surveying expedition. Before the *Fenimore Cooper* sailed, September 26, 1858, Heco was called upon to interpret for a new group of ship-wreckees, a dozen Japanese rescued by the British ship *Caribbean.*

The *Cooper* took soundings and made scientific experiments on her way to Hawaii. All of this was interesting enough to Heco but the rolling and pitching of the ex-pilot boat kept him continually seasick and he left the vessel at Oahu. Here he visited two Japanese from Owari, who had been rescued by the whaler *Charles Phillips,* and a third man saved from a different derelict. Heco left Honolulu on the clipper *Sea Serpent,* commanded by Captain Jacob Whitmore, and made his way to Canton from Hong Kong. Here he came across "Dan," one of his comrades from the *Eiriki Maru.* "Dan" was employed by the British consul-general to Japan. Heco sailed on the *Powhatan* to Shanghai and continued on to Japan on the *Mississippi,* being careful to show his U. S. naturalization certificate to the new American Minister to Japan. Heco was proud of his U. S. citizenship. He found that his comrades from the *Eiriki Maru* had sailed with Perry for Japan but had been afraid to appear on deck and had returned to Shanghai where another ex-ship-wreckee, Ottosan, looked after them until a Chinese junk could take them home to Nippon.

Heco became a commission merchant in Yokohama, eventually employing his old friend and protector, Thomas Troy. When a few Russian sailors were killed in Yokohama and Admiral Popoff threatened to bombard the town, the U. S. consul intervened and suggested that Heco be engaged as an intermediary. The assassins could not be found but Heco managed to pacify Popoff by getting the Japanese Government to cede to the Tsar the northern half of Sakhalin Island.

Despite his achievements, Heco found his position in Japan disagreeable to his proud nature. Government officials in the Japan of that day looked down their noses at mercantile folk. Therefore, armed with strong letters of recommendation to important personages both in and out of Congress, he sailed on the *Carrington* for San Francisco. Arriving on October 16, 1861, he continued east to Washington where he met Secretary of State Seward and President Lincoln.

After a certain amount of the usual bureaucratic runaround and a farcical arrest—incredibly, he was mistaken for a Confederate general by what must have been the world's most myopic detective—he was appointed Interpreter to the American Consulate at Kanagawa (Yokohama). Allowed to wear diplomatic uniform and considered acting vice-consul in the absence of the consul, he now had plenty of the so-necessary "face," for as acting vice-consul he was equal in rank with the lieutenant governor of Kanagawa. Heco was allowed to transact private business as well, and the one-time shipwrecked boy of thirteen found himself in his later years influential, respected and well-to-do.

His last visit to San Francisco took place on May 5, 1862, en route to Japan with his appointment. He once again served as interpreter for shipwrecked Japanese seamen, this time a group of twelve brought into port by the *Victor*. Heco and the Japanese consul in San Francisco arranged for their passage to Kanagawa on the schooner *Ida*. On the 27th, Heco left for

Japan and arrived in time to be aboard McDougall's *Wyoming* when she had her running scrape with the batteries in Shimonoseki Strait.

The next San Francisco Japanese was Diyonoseke, the sole survivor of a fifteen-man crew rescued near Hawaii after seven months at sea. Diyonoseke was returned to the Land of the Morning Calm on August 14, 1854, when Captain Burrows brought the *Lady Burrows* into Simoda from San Francisco.

In November 1856, Captain Brooks of the American whaling brig *Leverett* arrived in San Francisco from Ayan, Siberia, to report having picked up an abandoned junk only nine hundred miles off the American coast. Two more junks were reported by American vessels in 1856, Captain Homer of the bark *Messenger Bird* telling of seeing one disabled at Guam, and Captain Jonathan C. Lawton of the brig *Prince de Joinville,* getting guano from Cedros and other isles, reporting a junk wrecked near Magdalena Bay, Baja California.

When Lt. Brooke took the *Fenimore Cooper* on its last voyage, he left a seasick Joseph Heco behind. He replaced him with another of his countrymen, however, named Marsakichi. His junk had been disabled and forced east though the crew lowered their anchor to act as a drag. The cable parted and they were helpless until rescued.

Although the Japanese were changing to more modern boat design, the sea still claimed its toll. In 1859 the bark *Gambia,* Captain Brooks, found the remains of a junk on Ocean Island and on the Fourth of July of the same year, not one but two junks were found stranded on the eastern, lagoon, side of Midway Island. In a heavy sea which prevented boarding, the bark *Yankee,* commanded by Captain Claxton, on May 11, 1862, passed a wrecked and waterlogged junk with one stump of a mast standing, the wood black with age. The sea was washing right over her; there was no sign of life.

Also in 1862, a junk stranded near Attu. In September, after

259

ninety days of drifting, three men, of a twelve-man crew, crawled ashore. They were taken the following year to Niko-layevsk on the Amur River and then to Hakodate by a Russian vessel. Earlier in 1862, Captain Crowell brought his ship *Victor* into San Francisco (May 4) with the eleven members of the crew of the *Io Maru*. She had left Kanagawa on December 21, 1861, for Owari and Hiogo, but, like so many of her predeces-sors, was trapped in the Kuro Siwo after being disabled on Jan-uary 5th. The *Victor* picked them up April 13th and took them to San Francisco where Joseph Heco interpreted for them. They were returned to Japan by the American schooner *Caroline E. Foote.*

A second *Sumiyoshi Maru,* or perhaps the very junk belong-ing to Heco's father, was found disabled at sea on February 2, 1871, by Captain Packer of the American ship *Annie M. Small.* He rescued the captain and three surviving crewmen and landed them in San Francisco on February 24, 1871. They had sailed for Shiroko with a cargo of wood for Osaka and were picked up after only seventeen days of drifting. Again in 1871 a rescue was made, this time by Captain W. B. Cobb of the Pacific Mail Steamer *China,* who picked up five of a sixteen-man crew of the wrecked *Sumiayee Maru* of Kobe. The captain died on the steamer after the rescue but the others were cared for by Charles W. Brooks, the Japanese consul in San Francisco, who returned them to Yokohama on July 1, 1871.

In 1873 Captain Cobb of the P.M.S. *China* made his second rescue of junk seamen, taking the crew off a derelict and landing them at Yokohama. On April 6, 1875, the *Game Cock,* com-manded by Captain T. C. Stoddard, fell in with the *Woonohi Maru,* cargoed with salt fish and seaweed. Her rudder was gone, her stern stove, and her crew of twelve eager to be off the hulk which they had coaxed into 1,500 miles of westering on a jury rig only to be blown east again and again as they fought to conquer the pull of the Black Current. The crew was landed in

San Francisco on April 27, 1875, and returned to Japan on the *Great Republic* by Mr. Takaki. For his trouble, the Japanese Government gave Captain Stoddard a gold chronometer.

In just over twenty years Nippon had reversed itself and was now honoring rescuers instead of punishing the rescued. The United States, for its part, never publicized these rescues even to its own people and it is not strange that Americans thought (and still think) that Japan was an unknown land until almost the end of the nineteenth century. At least threescore wrecks have been verified; how many junks and sampans were driven east and swallowed in the dread immensity of the Pacific no one will ever know. With the coming of the age of modern navigation—steam, detailed charts, buoys, bells, lighthouses, coast patrols and heavy oceanic traffic—the day of the derelict was pretty much over.

Only one derelict "junk" has been reported since the turn of the century, but she was found as recently as 1927! The American Mail Liner *Margaret Dollar* was steaming off Cape Flattery in November of that year when a fishing smack was spied two miles to starboard. With no sails set, she rolled wantonly in the seas. No life was seen aboard her. The *Margaret Dollar* turned off her course to investigate and found the fishing smack to be a derelict named the *Ryo Yei Maru*. Aboard were two bodies in a bunk in the crew's quarters and nine skeletons on deck.

The *Dollar* towed its grisly find into Puget Sound for a customs investigation. The *Ryo Yei Maru* turned out to be a spanking new boat, built in the spring of 1926. At one hundred tons, she was one of the largest fishing smacks ever built in Japan. From a diary kept by Suteji Izawa, and continued by Genosuke Matsumoto after the former's death, the officials learned of her tragic cruise.

On December 12, 1926, the crankshaft broke but the crew was not alarmed for there were other vessels about and they

261

were not even out of sight of the Japanese coast. However, they were unable to attract the attention of any of the other vessels in the fishing fleet and the one vessel they saw on the second day did not notice their plight, nor did the two boats seen on the fourth day.

The winter's monsoon is a land wind which blows steadily to the east and the *Ryo Yei Maru* was in its path. By the fifth day, no more fishing craft were to be seen and they realized that they were caught in the dread Black Current which was sweeping them on at about ten miles a day toward America. Izawa wrote in his diary, "We dare not express to each other our innermost thoughts—that we might sight a rescue ship, but this is in the hearts of all of us." The crew tried to make the Bonin Islands under sail but the great drift was too much for them and, after holding a conference, they decided to try to make the American coast before death claimed them. They celebrated New Year's Day of 1927 with dried bean cakes, praying to the god of sailors —"Konpira, have pity on us. Please pity us and forgive us."

The crew began to fall ill. Only one fish was caught and on March 6th, with the last of the rice gone, hope was gone. Three days later the first of the eleven men died. A bird was caught— to feed ten mouths. Five men died in March, including Izawa. From time to time the men would hoist sail and try to break out of the drift, heading anywhere in their despair, but the Kuro Siwo was too strong for their weakening efforts.

Three more men died, leaving only Matsumoto and the captain. On May 6th the former wrote that the captain was ill and on the 11th he wrote that he too was ill. There were no more entries. The end had come for the *Ryo Yei Maru*.

Chapter XI

WELLS FARGO'S GOLD BOAT

ONE of the crack steamers which, like the men of '49 and '50, heeded the siren call of gold in California was the *Antelope*. Built in 1849 for the run between New York and New Brunswick, in opposition to the *Raritan*, she steamed on the Lower Bay and Raritan River for just one season before she was purchased by George Law and sent to California. She put in a one-year tour of duty on Law's Line, running between Panama City and San Francisco, and was then bought by Captain John Van Pelt and restored to her original status of river steamer.

In 1854 the owner-captains of Sacramento riverboats met to put an end to the open warfare between them. The California Steam Navigation Company was born of this conclave and the *Antelope*, with Captain David Van Pelt in command, became the star of the fleet. She won a greater fame than her sister ships because of her clean lines and speed. This swiftness led to her being chosen by Wells Fargo & Company to carry their express and gold down the Sacramento to San Francisco. Gold dust, specie or bullion were transferred from dusty stagecoach boots or saddlebags to the green-painted iron strongboxes of the Wells Fargo offices in Sacramento's Transportation Block, down Second Street a way from the Orleans Hotel, the center of Sacramento social life and possessor in its bar of four famed gaslit chandeliers.

From the Transportation Block the money—commonly called "treasure" in those days—was transferred to the *Antelope* at the Embarcadero. She carried so much treasure that she soon won the nickname of "The Gold Boat," and the Wells Fargo messengers' compartment was called "the gold room," its floor specially braced against the weight of the heavy shipments. The *Antelope* also carried passengers and such prosaic freight as ink, paper and camphor, but she won her fame as a gold-carrier under such well-known captains as David Van Pelt, E. A. Poole, Albert Foster and Enos Fouratt.

One of her few accidents occurred when she was smothered in a dense fog opposite the mouth of Suisun Slough one day in October 1853. She proceeded cautiously toward San Francisco but another steamer, the *Confidence,* slid out of the low-lying haze and knifed into her amidships just forward of the gangway. The *Confidence's* engines were reversed and the *Antelope,* her guards cut and the bilge caissons breached, began to fill. The *Confidence* moved off without offering assistance but all hands fell to hammering oakum into the ruptures of the *Antelope's* hull and saved her from foundering.

No boats were lowered; indeed, the listing of the boat made that impossible. Some of the passengers panicked and the famed Lola Montez, who was aboard with her husband, helped to quiet them. The collision occurred at eight o'clock in the evening and it was not long after that the *Senator,* hearing the constant whistling of the *Antelope* for help, came to the rescue. People were panicky and some were bruised, but no lives were lost. The passengers were transferred to the Stockton boat at Benicia for the remainder of the trip to San Francisco.

On April 3, 1860, the first wiry rider swung into the saddle and galloped westward from St. Joe's Pikes Peak Stables, a special four-compartment *mochila* (saddlebag) covering his saddle. The Pony Express was born. That same day another rider sped out of Sacramento with eastbound U. S. mail brought upriver by the trim, well-named *Antelope.*

Then as now, publicity agents knew the value of a good stunt and they had James Randall ride a "nankeen-colored pony" from the Alta telegraph office in San Francisco to the docks where the *Antelope* awaited the *mochila,* labeled "Overland Pony Express," which contained between seventy-five and eighty letters at five dollars each. Randall galloped for the Embarcadero at 3:45 and the *Antelope* sailed on schedule at 4 P.M., to the cheers of a large crowd as horse and rider went aboard.

The *Antelope* reached Sacramento at two in the morning. Billy Hamilton rushed the mail east on the second leg of its journey. At one in the afternoon of the 13th, Warren Upson finished a rough Sierra crossing and handed the first westbound mail pouch to Billy Hamilton at Sportsman's Hall. The California Steam Navigation Company had agreed to hold the *Antelope* for the Pony Expressman provided that Hamilton would make Placerville by noon. What with his late start, Hamilton did not clear Placerville until two in the afternoon but the *Antelope* waited, expressing her impatience with wisps of steam trailing from her valve and the slow turning-over of her paddles. Flags flew all over Sacramento, balconies were crowded with women and roofs covered with men. The courts adjourned for the day, business was suspended and citizens rode out in droves to escort the Pony Express to the river.

Hamilton reined his sweating horse to a stop at the wharf and clattered aboard while captain and pilot sang out commands, deck hands loosened lines and the engineer sent the *Antelope* nosing eagerly out into the stream under a fine head of steam. The steamboat "put on all speed to accomplish an early trip" down the one hundred and twenty-five miles of twisting Sacramento River, reported the *Alta California,* and docked around midnight, April 13th. San Francisco had been alerted by announcements in all the theaters and the California Band had been blaring since eight o'clock, marching and countermarching from saloon to saloon in expectation of the *Antelope*'s arrival. Couples danced on the wharves and in the streets and plazas, the latter lit by bonfires.

Despite the lateness of the hour, a large crowd gathered as the steamer tied up and an impromptu parade was formed. Leading off were the men of Fire Engine Companies 2, 5 and 6; then came Ladder Company 2 and the California Band, tooting "See the Conquering Hero Comes"; then the hero and symbol of the hour—Bill Hamilton on his mount. Bringing up the rear were "citizens on foot and mounted." (The *Alta California* might well have added, "and citizens drunk and sober.") Speeches were delivered which, according to the papers, put both Hamilton and his horse to sleep. Then the letters addressed to San Francisco were taken from the sweat-soaked *mochila* and distributed from the steps of the Alta Telegraph Company office on Montgomery Street. The crowd finally broke up and went in the wee hours to bar or home to bed.

The Pony Express lost money from the start and was absorbed in a year and a half by Wells Fargo, but the sleek *Antelope* continued her steady mail and gold runs, just as she did before and during the pony-mail experiment. Because of her speed and tight adherence to regular schedules, she remained the favorite of river travelers. Five hundred and eighty feet long, she carried one hundred and fifty passengers in cabins and an equal number in steerage. She ran on Mondays, Wednesdays and Fridays from San Francisco, leaving her Pacific Street Wharf at 4 P.M. and alternating with the *Senator* or, occasionally, the *New World* or the *Chrysopolis*. Leaving Sacramento at 2 P.M., she would make the return trip downstream in the snappy time of eight hours.

In steamboat parlance, the *Antelope* was "a lucky boat." She never had a serious accident, explosion or fire and she always made money. During her first four years on the Sacramento River she earned more money for her owners than any other steamboat except the pioneering *Senator*. She also had the knack of making the newspapers, without getting into trouble herself. On September 5, 1864, she was steaming up the Sacramento near Rio Vista, followed by the *Washoe*. Suddenly at 9:30 P.M., without any warning, one of the *Washoe's* boilers exploded. Miraculously, Captain G. W. Kidd was not hurt, nor were pilots Baldwin and Easton. The mate, Bob Morrison, was blown up off the texas deck and down through a hole in the deck but escaped with only a few bruises and a severe shaking-up.

The *Washoe* was on fire in three places and beginning to fill. An alert lookout on the *Antelope* spotted her plight, relayed word to Captain Albert Foster and the latter pointed his craft back downstream, full speed ahead, toward the fiery vessel. He found the *Washoe* a shambles. Sixteen of her one hundred and fifty-three passengers were dead, thirty-six were badly injured and another fifteen were burned, scalded or slightly hurt. A fisherman had beaten Foster aboard the *Washoe* and was already treating the burned, using a sack of flour and a bottle of oil.

The *Antelope* loaded the dead and wounded aboard and steamed for Sacramento, her bell tolling the news of the tragedy as she approached the Embarcadero. She hung up for several hours on a mud bank but managed to reach the foot of R Street by 4:30 A.M. It has been estimated that 10,000 people, roused by the tolling of the town fire bell which answered the *Antelope's* signal, turned out to watch from the levee as the side-wheeler approached the east bank.

An emergency hospital was set up for the hurt in the Vernon House on J Street where they were quickly attended by doctors and volunteer nurses. Chief Engineer Anderson died cursing the "rotten iron" of his boilers which had not been able to stand one hundred and twenty-five pounds pressure. The dead were given a gala funeral and the *Antelope,* which had moved to her berth at the foot of K Street, resumed her schedule.

From time to time the little *Antelope* had to take physical beatings from bigger, bullying paddle-wheelers like the *Nevada.* They loved to bang into her sides, smashing her joiner work and railings into kindling. They were all jealous of her fine passages but her particularly arch-rival was the *Sacramento.* This boat was built by Peter Donahue for the express purpose of beating the *Antelope.* One day the *Antelope* left Sacramento a half-hour behind the *Sacramento* but caught up with her and tried to pass her where the northern end of Steamboat Slough meets the Sacramento River. The *Sacramento* "caught her suction" and forced the *Antelope* to crab sideways until she landed, ignominiously, on a mud bank. Captain Enos Fouratt pulled her off quickly and started in rapid pursuit. Some of his hot-blooded passengers were already checking the chambers of their sixguns but he calmed them down and assured them that he would even up scores before they reached San Francisco.

The two steamboats stopped at Rio Vista and Fouratt quickly jammed the *Antelope*'s bow into the *Sacramento*'s starboard quarter. The pilot of the latter rang "Full Astern" in the hope of raking the side of the *Antelope* and perhaps carrying away her paddle wheel. Fouratt was more than ready for him and was already warming the *Antelope*'s engines up to full speed ahead. All the *Sacramento* could do was to swing herself across the "Gold Boat's" bow. The *Antelope* thereupon pushed her rival merrily down the river, broadside on, before letting her off. The next day, Captain Fouratt was arrested in San Francisco on a charge of malicious mischief. The legalities cost him "some slight delay and expense" but he felt his victory well worth the cost. Some time later, Fouratt was hauled before a grand jury twice for assault with a deadly weapon (another steamboat) when he rammed an obnoxious rival on the river and a passenger was killed.

Although Donahue's *Sacramento* was built to beat the *Antelope* and did so, Donahue eventually was so captivated by the fine side-wheeler himself that he bought her. He kept David Van Pelt on the texas deck, knowing that he would get the best out of her.

Peter Donahue was attracted by the rich stands of virgin redwood forest north of San Francisco, beyond the reach of any railroad. He set out to correct this by buying the Sonoma County Railroad Company, which existed on paper only, and began building a line which he called the San Francisco and North Pacific.

Grading crews and gandy dancers made the adobe fly and the rails ring. By 1870 Donahue had a right-of-way terminating at the bleak, tule-grown bank of Petaluma Creek. Here, forty miles from San Francisco by water, he built a wharf, railroad station, roundhouse and shops, and a hotel called the Sonoma House. This booming, bustling beachhead he named Donahue. In 1871 the line reached Healdsburg at the edge of the redwood country and Donahue transferred the swift *Antelope* from the Sacramento River run to the Petaluma Creek Line. Captain David Van Pelt still commanded her until he took over the new *James M. Donahue* which replaced the aging "Gold Boat."

The *Antelope* led a quieter life on San Francisco Bay and Petaluma Creek, with no more fires or rammings. About the only excitement furnished the crew and passengers was the uninhibited conduct of the two mules which the wharfinger at Donahue, David Walls, drove. When he would unhitch them from the horsecar, the two beasts would gallop to the end of the dock, happily jump off into midstream and circle back to shore.

In 1884 Donahue moved his rail terminal and townsite to Tiburon on San Francisco Bay, cutting his water route by thirty-four miles. He packed up depot, houses, *Antelope*, Sonoma House and swimming mules and left Donahue Landing just as he had found it, an uninhabited creek-bank of tules and rushes. Only the wharf and track remained to mark the ghost town.

The *Antelope* did not long outlive her Petaluma Creek port-of-call. In 1888, only four years after the move, the old "Gold Boat" of Wells Fargo Express days was turned over to the wreckers to be broken up.

Chapter XII

ABANDON SHIP!

TALES of shipwreck have a strange fascination for man, perhaps because they serve to document and point-up so forcefully man's unending struggle against the sea. There were dozens of voyages out of San Francisco which have ended in shipwreck and any one of these would make a good story. However, not all shipwrecks have the component parts for the perfect wreck story—drama, courage and cowardice, hardship. Some involve drifting boats, thirst and cannibalism. Others have their desert isle castaways, either in dire circumstances or in relative comfort. Among the best are those in which there is an after-chapter which often exceeds in interest the events of the shipwreck itself. This epilogue is usually concerned with an attempt to seek help by means of long small-boat voyage. Two stories in this category are worth recounting. One occurred only ten years after James Marshall discovered gold at Coloma, the other took place only forty-three years ago. The latter technically does not come within the period under consideration but the wreck is anything but typical of the pre-World War I days and is much more like adventures which befell seamen all too often in the nineteenth century.

The *Wild Wave* was a splendid medium clipper built in 1854 at Richmond, Maine. During her entire, brief career she was in the hands of one man, Captain Josiah N. Knowles. Knowles took her first to England, on to the Chinchas and then to Genoa. Finally her figurehead nodded toward the Golden Gate and on January 23, 1858, she arrived in San Francisco. On February 9th she sailed out in ballast for Valparaiso with a crew of thirty and ten passengers. She was something of a treasure ship, for she carried two boxes of gold coin valued at $18,000.

At 1 A.M. on March 5, 1858, the *Wild Wave* was cruising along at thirteen knots, twenty-four days out of San Francisco. Easterly winds had forced her far off her normal track and a lookout scanned the strange seas into which she had wandered. Suddenly, but too late, a cry of "Breakers ahead!" from aloft sent all hands to their stations. Knowles fought to put her about but she mis-stayed and, wearing, struck a coral reef. Within five minutes the $65,000 clipper had bilged to lie on her beam ends full of water. The sea broke right over her, wrenching off her copper sheathing and casting on deck raw-edged, deadly sheets of it perfectly capable of decapitating the hurrying seamen. Spars, rigging and tackle rained on the deck but, miraculously, no one was killed.

Captain Knowles ordered the topmast cut away to ease her but it did little good. Soon all three masts were gone entirely. The ripening dawn revealed that the *Wild Wave* had run upon a reef of Oeno atoll, in latitude 24° 01' S and longitude 130° 53' W. The chart position of the tiny island was some twenty miles in error. Knowles had placed his faith in the co-ordinates for Oeno shown on his chart and thought himself sixteen or eighteen miles safely offshore when the clipper struck.

As the morning light grew, the captain saw how lucky he and his men had been. The *Wild Wave* had struck on the smoothest part of the entire reef, some two miles out from the beach. Had they been wrecked on almost any other part of the reef, all hands would have almost certainly been lost. The men landed on the half-mile circle of brush-covered sand which constituted the lonely, uninhabited island, and worked all day boating ashore provisions, navigation instruments and sails. They set up two big tents, one for the officers and passengers and the other for the crew. On the atoll they found plenty of sea birds and eggs and they obtained water by digging shallow wells. At the end of a long day's work the steward cooked a supper and all hands turned in to get what sleep they could. Land crabs clacketed about, occasionally pinching a sleeping form like angry lobsters. Rats from a wreck visible on the reef also ran about on nocturnal foraging forays.

The captain knew that Pitcairn Island, about eighty miles distant, was inhabited by the descendants of Fletcher Christian's *Bounty* mutineers of 1789. He hoped to move from Oeno to the inhabited island but, of the first ten days on the atoll, there were only two when they could even board the wreck because of the heavy surf. On the 13th the gale subsided, and the surf with it. Knowles and his mate, James H. Bartlett, of Binghamton, New York, launched the boat they had rigged with a sail and, with five seamen, set out for Pitcairn. They took the treasure with them and gave orders to the second mate, left in charge of the Oeno party, to follow them if help did not reach him in four weeks. Knowles took sea birds from their nests, hoping that they had the homing instincts of pigeons so that he could send messages by them to Oeno. They sailed away as those on shore gave them a ringing three cheers.

High seas, thunder and lightning threatened them the first night, the boat leaping so wildly that Knowles could not even read the compass. He shortened sail and next morning the men found themselves ten miles farther from Pitcairn Island than when they had started. The wind continued to blow so hard that they could not carry a swatch of sail, so they rowed until the captain's hands, long unused to such toil, became raw and blistered. They hoisted a bit of sail from time to time and

273

finally raised Pitcairn Island at dusk. They were on the wind-ward side of the steep isle so they could not land and had to lay on their oars all night.

The next morning they ran in. After landing, they crossed a wooded mountain to the settlement on Bounty Bay where their spirits were dashed when they found it deserted. Notices tacked up on the abandoned houses informed them that the *Bounty* descendants had all packed up and gone to Norfolk Island, about 3,300 miles west-by-south of Pitcairn. Knowles and his men trudged back over the mountain to their boat to release the birds, bearing messages. They threw themselves down on the ground to fall instantly asleep, enjoying their first rest in fifty-six hours. Knowles and Bartlett split the gold between them and buried it under their sand "pillows."

The surf was too high the next day to sail to Bounty Bay so they went overland again and managed to capture a goat and a number of chickens which they cooked and ate. Returning to the beach, they were dismayed to find that their boat had been smashed by a tremendous sea, although they had hauled it far above what they supposed to be high-water mark. They were now hardly better off than they had been at Oeno. On the atoll they had at least had a boat in which escape was possible. Burying the gold again under a flat rock near the ghost town of Botany Bay, the captain and his men decided to make the best of a trying situation. They scrounged a great number of oranges, bananas, coconuts and breadfruit, and were able to capture sheep, goats, chickens and even bullocks left behind by the Pitcairn Islanders. The captain fitted up a deserted house for himself where he read a cast-aside copy of *Jane Eyre* when he was not worrying about his young wife back in Brewster, Mas-sachusetts.

Finding an old musket barrel, a crewman mounted it on a rude stock to hunt goats. One man would aim the piece while a shipmate fired it with a match in the most primitive matchlock style. The clumsy arm was so effective that on March 24th Knowles wrote ruefully in his log, "Nineteen goat meals this week."

The captain hoped to be picked up by the whaling fleet in February or March but, to be on the safe side, he had his men search the village for tools for the construction of a small schooner. Unfortunately, although a few rusty axes, planes and augers were discovered, no saws were found so that when a tree was felled it had to be hewn into a single plank. The men were forced to use many wooden pegs, although they burned down several small houses to obtain the nails used in their construction.

Rains slowed them down but they made good progress once the captain's hands had healed. On April 5th, one month after the wreck, they had the stem and keel hewn out. April 20th passed without any sign of the second mate and his party. A week later they killed a wild hog and salted the pork for the voyage and the following day the planks were all finished and stood against the wall of the church to dry. After a truly tremendous amount of labor, they were at last able to lay the keel.

While some worked on the hull or shaped spars, others, including the captain, picked oakum from old pieces of rope (inside the church during the frequent rains) and, improvising a rope walk, made forty-five fathoms of cordage. Another group dug a charcoal pit and burned charcoal to make up a fuel supply for the boat's passage. The Swiss Family Robinson had nothing on the *Wild Wave*'s crew when it came to desert-isle ingenuity. On May 22nd the captain amused himself by trying to shoot some goats with his revolver but they were too quick for him. Four days later he celebrated his twenty-eighth birthday with a meal of chicken, coconut milk and the ubiquitous goat meat.

On June 4th the hull, thirty feet long, eight feet wide and four feet deep, was finished. It was painted with paint found in a house and was calked but had to be recalked when the green wood shrunk. Old barrels were transformed into water casks, and from the hangings of the church pulpit—together with an old white shirt, blue dungarees and bunk curtains—an ensign was made. A small pump was rigged, a copper kettle became their stove, an anvil their anchor. Schooner-rigged, her three sails were composed of the lifeboat's canvas plus some sailcloth and stray rags found on the island. From a bucket of tar and several pounds of resin they found in a hut, the men payed the bottom seams and painted the others with refuse white lead. One mast was salvaged from the *Wild Wave*'s lifeboat, the other was the village flagpole from Bounty Bay.

A constant lookout was maintained while the boat was being built but no sails were sighted so Knowles decided to make an attempt to reach Tahiti. Letters were written to be left behind and the craft, named the *John Adams* in honor of the venerable old settler of Pitcairn Island, was launched on July 23rd. She was laden with fruit, including 1,200 oranges, with chickens, goat meat and salt pork, water and a few hoarded cans of preserved meat. Knowles dug up the $18,000 in gold once again and put it aboard the *John Adams*. He then bade farewell to the three men who remained behind at their own request. They preferred to await rescue on the island rather than trust their lives to the crude craft. Just after noon on the 24th, the captain set sail for Tahiti under jib, foresail and mainsail.

The wind was dead ahead for Tahiti and soon turned into a wild northwest gale. Knowles accordingly changed course and made for the Marquesas Islands, 1,300 miles away, planning to stop at Oeno en route. But three days of contrary winds prevented him from calling at Oeno to contact the other castaways. The *John Adams*, though a staunch vessel, was a poor sailer and while logging 120 to 125 miles a day, she made everyone aboard her seasick with her wallowing and lurching. After an eleven-day passage they spoke "Ohitahoo" (Tahuata) Island in the Marquesas. Here, on August 3rd, they found no Europeans but plenty of warlike natives at Resolution Bay. The savages invited them to anchor and land but Knowles did not like their looks and decided to press on for Hiva Oa.

Stopped by a calm, they reconsidered again and changed course to run into Nukahiva. Here on August 4th, to their great delight, not to say surprise, they discovered the U. S. ship-of-war *Vandalia*. Knowles sold the *John Adams* to a missionary for $250 the same day that the *Vandalia* sailed under Captain A. Sinclair for Oeno via Tahiti. She arrived at Papeete with the castaways six days later and left the next day with Mate Bartlett to rescue the Oeno group. They found that the second mate's party had built a boat so large that all efforts to launch it were unsuccessful. One of the group had died but the remainder were in good health and boarded the *Vandalia* which then proceeded to Pitcairn and picked up the three men left there.

At Tahiti, Captain Knowles accepted the invitation of Captain Pichou, commander of the French sloop-of-war *Eurydice*, to sail to Honolulu. After a pleasant trip of sixteen days he reached the Hawaiian capital. From there he sailed in the bark *Yankee* to San Francisco, bringing the specie and the home-made colors of the *John Adams*. (The flag, together with his pistol, is in the possession of the California Historical Society and since 1955 has been on display as a loan to the Maritime Museum of San Francisco.)

Knowles was greeted upon his arrival in San Francisco September 29, 1858, as one risen from the dead. His old boatman cried out, "My God, is that you, Captain Knowles?" Knowles learned here for the first time that he was a father. On October 6th he caught the first available steamer for Panama, the *Golden Gate*, and went home to Brewster. From 1863–1865 he ran to San Francisco with the clipper *Charger*, dodging Confederate cruisers and later (1874–1876) took Douglas McKay's one hundredth vessel, the *Glory of the Seas*, into the San Francisco-Liverpool grain trade. In the *Glory of the Seas* he made one passage from New York to San Francisco in ninety days which was very good time indeed. So good, in fact, that it was never beaten after that date. He also made the all-time record run between San Francisco and Sydney—thirty-five days anchor to anchor. He averaged eight knots over the 7,062 mile course to Australia although he wrote in his log "Ship very crank, so cannot carry as much sail as otherwise would."

He also commanded the *Kentuckian* and the first steam whaler out of San Francisco, Goodall & Perkins' *Bowhead*, making a very profitable first voyage in the whaleship. In 1880 he entered the shipping business in San Francisco and was identified with the Golden Gate City from that time on. The *Glory of the Seas* was laid up after he left her, but in 1885 Captain Joshua S. Freeman put her back into operation in the Pacific coal trade. Knowles became one of the major shipping figures in San Francisco and died at his home in Oakland on June 10, 1896, at the age of sixty-six.

A later shipwreck which had much of the drama of the *Wild Wave's* adventure involved the *El Dorado*. Her story was good enough to make the *Saturday Evening Post* in 1914, and later appeared in the form of a little paperbound book titled *The Log of the El Dorado* which was published in San Francisco in 1915. The author, Captain N. P. Benson, was master of the four-masted San Francisco lumber schooner *El Dorado* which loaded a cargo of rough fir lumber in Astoria for discharge at Antofagasta, Chile. Benson and his mates helped the longshoremen get the deckload lashed on March 13, 1913, and took on water and provisions. Next morning a crimp herded a gang of men out on the wharf. They had all signed for the voyage before the Deputy Shipping Commissioner.

Benson noticed that all had suitcases instead of seabags and that they did not come aboard howling drunk. This stamped them as landsmen and not sailors. Benson turned to his mate, Mr. Wilson, and said, "They're a bad lot. Not a sailor in the outfit." This kind of talk was just so much wind in the rigging, for Benson was ready to take anything the crimps sent him to make up a crew. Most real sailors by the turn of the century preferred the steam coasting schooners with their $50 a month pay, lots of leisure in port between trips, only two or three voyages a month, and a payday at the end of each trip. In the eyes of deep-water skippers the men were becoming maritime laborers instead of sailormen. Windjammers had to be content with the leavings, and when the crimp handed over eight greenhands for the price of eight A.B.'s, Benson took them gladly. Luckily, the *El Dorado* was a schooner and all sails could be worked from the deck. He would not have to send some hayseed aloft as the case would be on a square-rigger.

The second mate took the wheel while Mr. Wilson counted off the watches and a tug towed them halfway to the lightship. The tug cast off and Wilson came aft to report that half of the crew had become seasick immediately upon crossing the bar. From the look on Benson's face Wilson knew the old man was wondering if his Friday sailing would really prove to be a jinx.

By the time the *El Dorado* had reached the South Pacific the crimped farmers and lumberjacks could steer and lend a hand with some idea of their duties. The *El Dorado* ran south in a great arc which took them out of the southeast trades and then came about to make the run into Antofagasta, with westerlies to push them the 2,700 miles.

On June 11th the sky seemed to go into eclipse, becoming a solid wall of blackness. The barometer fell and the sea, whipped by a mounting wind, began to run high. Benson took in and made fast the topsails and spanker. By the greasy dawn of the 12th the *El Dorado* was laboring heavily in a terrible sea. The mate sounded the well and reported that the schooner was making a little water so Benson put a couple of men on the pumps. The wind wheeled around to the northeast and increased to gale violence, straining the *El Dorado* so that her seams opened. The watch on deck stayed at the pumps all of the time. Benson ordered the mainsail taken in but was spared the trouble when it was blown away by the steadily increasing gale. Finally he ordered the *El Dorado* hove to under double-reefed foresail, mizzen and spanker.

Despite the steady sucking of the hand pumps and the steam pumps, by nine at night there was five feet of water in the hold and the angry seas were shaking the schooner as a terrier worries a rat. To make matters even worse, the deckload began to shift. When Benson checked it he found that it had worked eight inches to starboard. He also found that the starboard side of the poop deck was separating from the poop rail, the interstice gulping water thirstily. The captain decided to wear her around because of the heavy starboard list. This relieved her shortly but then the deckload shifted to port and the *El Dorado* began to go to pieces.

At midnight the second mate reported to Benson and Wilson on the poop. The pumping crew had been driven out of the well when the water reached their shoulders. The steam pump was still throbbing away but it alone could not keep the schooner from becoming waterlogged. Benson decided to make a bold maneuver. He was not going to wait for the seas to maul his schooner to pieces. If they were going to drown, they might as well make a run for it. Under a wisp of foresail they scudded along although the schooner was so low in the water that the seas broke over her continuously. Benson had had lifelines rigged, however, and not a man was lost.

About four in the morning, as Benson waited for daylight ("it seemed easier to die in daylight"), his Japanese cook miraculously served hot coffee and sandwiches to the crew. Benson commented, "How he managed this is a mystery wrapped in his Oriental soul, for I didn't think there was anything dry or warm on that ship." He was glad his cookie was Japanese rather than Chinese. He was sure a Chinese would

280

have gone to pieces and left the crew to starve while praying to his gods.

Friday the thirteenth of June, Benson ordered the deckload jettisoned to lighten her, but after a few hours of devilish work the seas came into the galley and donkey room, putting out the fire under the donkey engine. The steam pumps stopped and the *El Dorado* lay helpless in the most terrific seas Benson ever saw in his thirty years of navigating. He described a Japanese typhoon he had been through when a cabin boy on the *W. H. Lincoln* as a "cupful of wind," compared to the South Pacific-style hurricane which was smashing the *El Dorado* to pieces.

It was impossible to launch a small boat but around eleven o'clock the wind moderated and the sun came out. By noon, wind and sea had gone down and Benson gave the order to abandon ship. He emptied the ship's medicine chest and dumped into it his sextant, navigation books and charts, and ship's papers. He picked up the chest and rushed it into the lifeboat slung in the spanker-throat halyards. The crew dashed for their personal possessions while Benson placed blankets, clothing and oilskins in the boat. The cabin and galley were death traps, for the bulkhead threatened to collapse at any moment and let the seas flood in. A particularly high sea lifted the schooner up, tons of water raced aft and the bulkheads finally smashed. Benson was able to escape with only a case of corned beef and a box of soda crackers.

The green crew stood up well and were game. They stood waiting to abandon the wallowing schooner, some without southwesters or even coats, some shoeless. It was impossible to enter the ship's cabin but since the lifeboat had no food (though plenty of water), Benson made his way to a little locker in the aftercompanionway where he kept a supply of canned foods. He got thirty-eight cans of soup, thirty-two of condensed milk, four jars of jam and three of tongue. These, with his twelve one-pound tins of corned beef and the box of Saltines were the only provisions for eleven hungry men faced with the prospect of a thousand-mile voyage in a twenty-two-foot lifeboat.

It was no easy matter to launch the boat and Benson was not too sure he could do it, but the schooner was going to pieces underfoot so there was no choice. He ordered Mr. Wilson and Johansen, the second, into the boat which hung in the spanker-throat halyards on the portside. He told the crew to lower away when he gave the word, but not a second before. Climbing up on the wheelbox, he studied the sea. Suddenly he saw a smooth spot and he knew he had about twenty seconds before another sea would come crashing into the *El Dorado*. He shouted "Lower away!" and the men let go the tackle. The two mates got in two powerful strokes of their oars before the sea hit them. Two crewmen, aft on the schooner, gave a tremendous pull on the boat's painter and the lifeboat shot toward the ship's stern. Even then the boat was not out of danger for the over-hang of the stern came down on top of her, almost smashing the boat under the surface. Wilson managed to shove her clear with an oar, which he lost in the process, and the lifeboat floated free off the stern.

Benson crawled out on the end of the *El Dorado*'s huge spanker boom and made a rope fast to the end. Then, one by one, the crew crawled out and slid down the rope into the waiting boat. Wilson and the "Swede" tried their best to ma-neuver the boat under the boom but several of the men dropped into the water rather than in the boat. All were grabbed up safely. Benson, as master, was last to leave his doomed ship and he made a perfect landing, dropping from the boom not only squarely into the lifeboat but in the very stern-sheets, his proper position to command the boat. The mate wasted no time on the captain but shouted to the crew to pull clear. The *El Dorado* was left foundering in any ugly sea littered with fresh lumber from her deckload and old black timber from her hull.

The men rowed for all they were worth to get the little lifeboat clear of the threat of the floating lumber which could easily hole her. She sat low in the water with her load of eleven men, showing only ten or twelve inches of freeboard above the angry water. As they took leave of the rolling *El Dorado,* her decks awash but her spars still standing, Benson sized up his crew of landsmen, all of whom were a little green around the gills. He always remembered that moment:

> No skipper leaving Columbia River ports in April for a voyage to the West Coast [of South America] need expect a crew worth while, for sailors at that time of year are very scarce. They go north to the Alaska fisheries for the season. However, a man is a man to those that deal in sailors. Fit or unfit, the blood money is just the same, and if a skipper doesn't like the men the crimp sends him, he has the privilege of sending them back— and lying idle in the stream until his owners fire him. I took what I could get and made the best of it—and now, in that twenty-two-foot lifeboat, tossing from crest to crest of those huge seas, I cursed that crimp to the deepest hells—and made the best of it.

The captain and his two mates tried to cheer up the crew. Benson announced that they would make Easter Island, seven hundred miles away, in eight or nine days at the latest. Then he remembered that the chronometer was lost when they abandoned ship.... He consulted with his mates over the charts before dark and they agreed that the boat was about 2,700 miles off the coast of Chile and some 560 miles southeast of Pitcairn Island. Since it was the stormy midwinter season of prevailing westerlies, Benson gave up any idea of running for Pitcairn. Easter Island, 700 miles northeast by east, was their only hope. With no chronometer to tell him his longitude, Benson would have to run out the latitude first and then keep on eastering until he fell in with the island. This would make the distance to traverse more like 900 miles of open ocean.

Their second sleepless night was a hard one. Most of the crew were seasick, they had to bail all the time, and the cold salt spray swept over them constantly. It rained very hard and they dared not go to sleep. Benson agreed with his mates that whenever one would see one of the other two falling asleep he would kick him awake. Benson was proud of his mates, especially Wilson who quoted that "God helps those who help themselves" and believed every word of it. They stepped the mast and bent on spreadsail and jib on the 14th, Benson's birthday. The lifeboat, built on the design of a whaleboat, flew over the waves and Benson figured she would make a hundred miles every twenty-four hours. Benson's birthday dinner was two soda crackers, a cup of soup and one-eleventh of a one-pound can of corned beef.

The mates and Benson took turns at the tiller while the crew huddled under wet blankets in the bottom of the boat. Because of the frequent squalls which buffeted the overloaded boat, Benson posted two men to stand by with buckets to bail and appointed another man to handle the sail. On the 15th he got an observation, finding that they were in latitude 24° 49′ S. They ran before a gale that afternoon but by ten at night the wind hauled around to the south and the boat was in constant danger of being swamped. They kept her stern to the wild seas, breaking one oar in doing this. By daylight they were almost exhausted from their exertions and lack of sleep.

Next day she almost swamped several times for they could not keep her end-on to the waves and the boat would swerve broadside in the troughs, almost rolling over. Benson contrived a makeshift sea anchor of six heavy wool blankets rolled up and tied to a three-inch line fifteen fathoms long. There was a great strain on the line but the device worked instantly, keeping the boat stern-on to the sea. The spray made continuous bailing necessary but there was little danger of swamping now.

The captain kept two men at the oars although they had steerageway of about three miles per hour before the storm.

These men took up the slack in the line to their precious sea anchor. By the sixteenth of the month, Benson and the mates could not keep their eyes open though they did not dare sleep. They existed in a stupor. Both mates' minds wandered. One spoke of shallow water and the other of green fields and trees which he thought he saw. For his part, Benson saw mirages of every port from Valparaiso to Seattle.

The gale broke at 2 P.M. and the seas went down. When the sea anchor was hauled in, the blankets were wrung out and the men tried to sleep under them. The three officers dozed during the night though they kept to their agreement and tried to kick one another awake. They did not trust the boat to the green crew. Benson let Wilson sleep two hours while he and Johansen glared and kicked at each other. When Wilson awoke, the other two officers slept. The boat made good progress next day and the weather bettered. Benson got several observations and they began to sleep in relays although, after a week in the boat, their hands and feet were swollen and their hips, buttocks and knees raw from the chafing of salt-crusted clothing.

The gale moderated early on Friday the 20th and Benson set a rag of sail which sent them bounding across the sea in such a cloud of spray that it kept the men sputtering and gasping for breath. Although the boat was pitching and rolling badly, Benson got a shot at the sun and found that they were in 27° 08' S latitude, a good position for a run for Mission House or Cook's Bay on Easter Island. He now had to maintain a due east course and steering became a matter of life and death. They had come nine hundred miles safely but there was every likelihood they would run right past the island unless their navigation was correct and their lookouts sharp-eyed. If a gale should come up, they could never get back to Easter Island once having passed it. They were too weak and emaciated.

The wind hauled around to the southeast so Benson put on every scrap of canvas she could carry and they clipped along with a lookout constantly scanning the sea for a sign of land. The captain got another observation on Saturday the 21st and corrected his course for the northward drift of the boat. The whole crew was growing weak since Benson gave out only enough food to keep them alive. He had to keep some in reserve in case they missed Easter Island and had to go on to the mainland of Chile, 2,100 miles away. Their meals were salt water-soaked soda crackers mixed with fresh water and condensed milk to make a mush. This was issued, a cupful to a man, every noon.

Sunday was clear and warm and most of the crew slept in the unaccustomed luxury of the sun. A young fellow who was lookout called to Benson as the latter crawled forward to rig a canvas cover as a sail. Benson called the crew and they all stared at something just visible on the horizon, two points off the port bow. Benson knew that the highest point on Easter Island was 1,767 feet, so he figured that they were about thirty miles out. He broke out a double ration of grub to celebrate their landfall and bent on the canvas cover to give the lifeboat more speed.

By midafternoon the island was close and the men got out the oars so they could land before dusk. But about five it began to grow dark, with the point of land for which they were making still seven miles away. Benson and his boat crew ran for cover before a gathering gale could strike. At eight they hove to on the south side of the island in the lee of a great cliff which seemed to be a thousand feet high.

All night long they lay on their oars, holding the boat just outside the line of breakers. They laughed at the gale from the protection of the island's lee, and watched the clouds scud along in the moonlight. Then the wind shifted to the south and the laugh was on them and they had to run before it, from Southwest Cape to East Cape. They did not see a single landing place anywhere along the fifteen miles of cliff coast, just spray dashing against the feet of precipices, and lines of curdling breakers.

They lay under the lee of East Cape until the wind abated in the morning. They then pulled for the coast, again looking for a beach. They poked into an inlet and found a steep beach about one hundred yards wide and covered with big boulders. Benson thought that landing there was out of the question so they started to pull on the oars again against the wind and sea. Shortly, Benson realized that his men had reached the end of their endurance and, in desperation, they ran for the beach. The crest of a huge breaker carried them in and, luckily, deposited them gently on a sandy spot between spray-soaked boulders. The men went overboard and eased the boat up the beach on the dead water of the next breaker. They did not want their boat stove in case they should need it again.

The men found that they could not walk after the eleven days of being crowded together on the boat so they crawled on hand and knees. After resting a few hours, all had a double ration of the soda-cracker slop. Still, most of the crew, Benson included, could not walk. Though their feet were in bad shape, the two mates managed somehow to climb the cliff and set off for help. Benson later got four of the strongest men remaining to haul the boat up to safety and then to make a shelter in a small cave at the base of the bluff. Here they were protected from the wind and rain. It was not cold but they were hungry and sore.

Soon all could walk except Benson and two other men. Six tried to go up the cliff. Four made it and two slid back down to the beach where the others were huddled in the cave. The men on the top of the island stumbled and fell over the lava rocks as they searched for a trail. Twenty-four hours after they left the crew, Mates Wilson and Johansen found the only settlement on the island. They had covered fourteen miles through underbrush and lava malpais and were in terrible shape.

The men were still huddled together in the cave after an uneasy night when they heard a noise on the top of the bluff. They crawled out to see ten *kanakas* coming down the cliff, having left their horses at the top. They spoke to the castaways in Spanish. Benson, having run for years to Chilean and Mexican ports, was able to answer in passable *castellano,* explaining that they would need help to get up the bluff. With a *kanaka* on each side, the crewmen were, one by one, pushed, pulled and dragged to the waiting horses and lifted into the saddles.

The horseback ride was no pleasure jaunt, Benson feeling that he was back on the hard thwart of the boat again. But, thirteen miles later, they were at the residence of P. Edmonds, an Englishman. When they passed through the native settlement of Hanga Roa, or Cook's Bay, their arrival created quite a stir among the *kanakas,* who greeted and congratulated them in Spanish. There were only about one hundred and fifty natives left on the volcanic island. In 1863 Peruvian blackbirders raided the island and the next year an estimated fifteen hundred natives left with Catholic missionaries. In 1867 the population was down to nine hundred. In 1878 another five hundred were removed to Tahiti and missionaries took three hundred converts to Mangareva.

After the three weeks it took the seamen to get back in good shape, they rode horseback, visited with the natives, explored the island and romanced the native girls. Benson had lost twenty pounds on the trip and two of his crewmen, Carlson and Tassaman, nearly lost their minds. The former had had only a cotton shirt and dungarees for protection against midwinter in the South Pacific when they had abandoned ship. He was still shaking a week after landing. But Benson was right, "A sailor is hard to kill and a Scandinavian hardest of all."

Benson, Wilson and Johansen lived with Edmonds while the crew lived in the deserted mission house at Cook's Bay, a mile and a half from Matavai. They all took part in the big cattle roundup and sheep and wild horse drives to keep themselves amused, but Benson began to tire of the humdrum life on Easter Island. (He had no native "wife" like some of his more contented crewmen.)

Since no vessels had called he decided to pack up and leave. He did not want to wait a year for a ship. It was almost September 1st and the winter practically over, so he thought he could make the passage to Tahiti, 2,500 miles, in the boat safely. Edmonds thought he was crazy and did everything he could to aid him. Benson was determined to go if no vessel touched at Easter Island by October. The captain checked his watch and Edmonds' timepiece for thirty days when he took his 4 P.M. observation. One he found absolutely accurate, the other lost only half a second daily. He overhauled the boat and learned to make fire by rubbing sticks together, since there were no matches on the island. He persuaded Drinkwater and Simanour from his crew to accompany him and taught them the native trick of making fire. Wilson and Johansen flatly refused to go with their captain. They had had quite enough of lifeboat travel. Benson cut up an oil drum to make a crude galley stove. He put aboard kegs of water, wood, jerked beef, sweet potatoes, taro, eggs, potatoes and a side of bacon.

His perfect watch broke its mainspring as he wound it the day he planned to leave, October 6th. However, he still had the other watch which he had rated so carefully. It was blowing too hard that day to leave, so he laid over until the 7th and left Cook's Bay at noon with a spanking southeast breeze filling the boat's sails. He deliberately chose his sailing date so he would have moonlit nights in order to steer and read the compass. Benson laid his course for Mangareva in the Gambiers, 1,600 miles distant. Unsuccessful in starting a fire with a lens, he and his two companions resorted to the firesticks and soon had bacon and eggs for breakfast. They made good progress for a week, then had gales and again fine weather until the 18th. From then on, gales and good weather alternated until they reached Rikitea, Mangareva, on the 23rd. It had taken them sixteen days, an average of one hundred miles a day. The three men were kindly received by the French and especially by Captain Hoffman, the trader. They stayed just two days to stretch their legs and clean up, then were on their way again.

Benson made the nine-hundred-mile run to Tahiti without incident except for a shark which scraped the boat a few times and followed them for forty miles after leaving Mangareva. He lashed a sharpened marlinespike to an oar and harpooned the beast between the eyes with the crude weapon. The shark made a great splash and disappeared. Just before they sighted Tahiti a swordfish attacked them for almost two hours. Its sword grazed the boat and Benson expected to be scuttled at any moment. The fish finally left and on November 5th they reached Tahiti, where the U. S. consul placed them in an hotel.

Three weeks later Benson sailed on the *Moana* for his home port of San Francisco, arriving on Friday, December 5, 1913. He brought with him his lifeboat to turn it over to the owners, Sanders & Kirch. They told him to keep it as a souvenir. A few months after Benson left Easter Island, a British steamer called there and took the *El Dorado*'s crew to Sydney, where they caught a British boat home to Port Townsend, Washington. The adventure of the *El Dorado* was over just a few years before the days of sail were completely ended by World War I.

Chapter XIII

SHANGHAI DAYS IN SAN FRANCISCO

THE anything but gentle art of crimping seamen was by no means confined to San Francisco during the nineteenth century, but no port—Valparaiso, New York or Liverpool—bore quite so evil a reputation for crimping as it did. The Golden Gate city so far excelled her competitors that a new term for crimping was coined on the Embarcadero, a term which made its way into the English language, including dictionaries, as "shanghaiing."

A miserable fishing port seventy-five years ago, Shanghai was less often the destination of a slugged or drugged seaman than was Canton or Mejillones, but a "shanghai voyage" or a "shanghai passage" grew to mean a long, roundabout, and usually involuntary deep-water cruise. Later the term was applied to crimping of any sort, such as for the coastal trade or for arctic whaling out of San Francisco.

Crimps everywhere were a pestiferous lot, as hard to shake as leeches. In New York harbor, to discourage a tenacious crimp, a just-arrived captain in the mid-nineteenth century had to drop a small anvil through the bottom of the ruffian's boat as it lay alongside his vessel. A Captain Williams wrote that Boston boardinghouse landlords came aboard ship with bottles in their pockets before the sails were even furled. They enticed the seamen ashore and held their clothes for a week's board. By the end of a week or so, Jack's funds would be low and he would get an advance on his wages in order to get out of the boardinghouse with his duds. When not literally robbed by the boardinghouse master, a seaman would be at least "pillaged of all his extra clothing and the advance of another shipment, and then brought down in a state of intoxication, and put on board ship for her voyage."

This simple system, developed on the East Coast by professional crimps, was extended to all major American and many foreign ports. A war was fought in 1812–1814 over the impressment of naval seamen, but the poor sailors of the American merchant marine had to put up with this even more vicious form of impressment, a servitude which approached peonage at best and slavery at worst, until 1915 when the Seamen's Act was finally passed by the United States Congress.

As early as 1834 the Boston *Recorder* was damning the "Boarding House and Landlord system, a traffic in human beings whom it brutalizes in order to render fit subjects for the traffic." The *Recorder* claimed that "nine-tenths of the sailor landlords in this city are foreigners of the vilest class." A statistical study of merchant seamen on American vessels of the period, however, would not have been too dissimilar.

The whole system of near-slavery for merchant seamen was dealt a powerful blow in this period when the Savings Bank for Seamen was founded in Boston in 1834. At least Jack Tar had a place to put his money, a place safe from the greedy crimps, their hired floozies and the grasping boardinghouse masters. In the first six months of 1834, seamen deposited $10,000—no mean sum in 1834—in the Boston bank. Although the establishment of sailors' banks was a shock to the crimps and their kind, it was in no sense a death blow. The dockside predators rolled with the punch and continued preying on merchant seamen for the next seventy years.

Even with the low wages which prevailed in the American merchant marine prior to the California Gold Rush, a ship's payoff after a long voyage averaged several thousands of dollars and attracted all sorts of human vultures. The latter were ready to use prostitutes, shell games or knockout drops to separate a sailor from his swag. Once a seaman was in their power, the boardinghouse keepers would maintain the poor fellow in a sort of wretched serfdom by furnishing him board and room while they bled him of his money. At last they would deliver him up to a shorthanded skipper for a sizable sum of "blood money" plus an advance of the man's wages to pay (all over again) for his board and room.

The *Sailor's Magazine* in February 1839 picked up and reprinted a case history of crimping from the Boston *Mercantile Journal* which was just as apropos of San Francisco a decade or so later as it was of Boston. A sailor who came into Boston from a Baltic voyage boarded at a waterfront lodging and entrusted his wages to the landlord for safekeeping. Within a fortnight he found himself bundled off to sea in debt, even though his hosteler had secured his advance wages. The sailor came into Boston again and, having learned nothing from his experience, went to the same boardinghouse master. When he sobered up this time he found himself crimped into the U. S. Navy without a cent to his name or a second shirt for his back. After serving on the U.S.S. *Erie* he returned to the same Boston landlord and was again shanghaied out, dead drunk and broke. When he returned from this third voyage, he refused to drink any more grog but he still gave the same landlord his money for safekeeping. When he asked his host for money to buy clothes, he was told that he was already $20 in debt. When the sailor could not pay up, he was thrown into jail. After spending four or five weeks in prison, he was only too happy to be conveyed aboard a ship by his enterprising landlord, losing his advance wages of $15. When he came back to New England for the fifth time, a few of the facts of life had penetrated his thick skull. He refused to put up at his old landlord's and kept perfectly sober. However, the seaman found it impossible to win out over a boardinghouse master, for the latter simply charged him with a debt of $50 and had his wages attached. No court would take the word of a seaman against that of a "businessman."

Newcastle, New South Wales, and Sydney both had bad reputations for crimping and the Sydney *Morning Herald* of August 17, 1906, reported on the cruel treatment of sailors in the two ports. During a debate in the New South Wales Parliament it was stated that 70 per cent of the boardinghouse masters and saloonkeepers of Watt Street and environs were connected with shanghaiing activities. It was San Francisco, however, which pioneered in crimping or shanghaiing to lead the way on the Pacific Ocean. John Masefield, the sailor-poet laureate of England, recalled of the city: *San Francisco was not a good port for a ship to enter, because in those days the crimps used to entice the incoming crew out of their ship and then sell them for what they would fetch to the captains in the bay in need of crews.*

It is believed that as early as 1852 some twenty-three gangs were engaged in the profitable business of shanghaiing seamen out of San Francisco. The other ports of the western American littoral were not remiss in reaping a harvest of profits from this efficacious form of labor recruitment. In Pisagua, Chile, seamen were given doped pisco and the *British Isles* in 1906 was easily able to get fourteen men from the crimps of the miserable little port. In Iquique, Chile, shanghaied seamen went at ninety pesos a head, the same year.

In Portland the chief boarding masters were Jim Turk, the Grant brothers, and Mysterious Billy Smith. Captain James P. Barker of the full-rigged Britisher *Dovenby Hall* paid Larry Sullivan $105 a head blood money in 1902 for twenty men of whom only one had ever been to sea before. The remainder were shanghaied ex-soldiers, lumberjacks, farmers and cowboys who had wandered into Portland for a good time. Joseph (Bunco) Kelly won fame, however fleeting, in the Pacific Northwest when he shanghaied eight corpses aboard a sailing vessel at Portland, passing them off as drunks and collecting fifty dollars a head blood money from the outbound hell ship.

Kelly used to brag that he had sent to sea at least two thousand bona fide seamen, a thousand landlubbers, and one cigarstore Indian. The last Kelly had wrapped in a blanket himself and carried aboard a British four-masted wheat ship as a drunk. Kelly was but five feet tall, of about the same beam, and built like a fire hydrant. He possessed enormous strength but was a softhearted scoundrel who could not bear to beat a tar's brains in personally. Instead, he relied on his special prescription of knockout drops, on standing order at a Burnside Street drugstore.

Although Seattle had skid row crimps and sailors' boardinghouses as well as John Consodine's box houses, it took a back seat to Port Townsend. William H. S. Jones, second mate of the limejuicer *British Isles,* remembered the town as "one of the most notorious ports for crimps." Captain C. H. Haug of the Hamburg-American Line put into Port Townsend in 1899 in the bark *Plus.* Of the Puget Sound crimps he said: "They nearly killed me and one of my shipmates because we took a beachcomber on board without their consent. We shipped farmers, miners and soldiers and had to pay blood money—I believe fifty dollars a head—and three months' advance. The poor beggars had nothing coming when they paid off in Dublin. It was at the same time when Mac Levi took off two different crews of the American ship *America* and intercepted two more on the road from Frisco to Seattle. The captain of the *America* had a bet that he would get a crew without Mac Levi's help, but he lost. He had to buy his crew back from Levi, after going to the expense of sending three crews from Frisco to Seattle."

Buckman Pasha, the Yankee Nova Scotian who became an admiral in the Turkish Navy, had a younger brother who hit Port Townsend in the winter of 1893 and landed on the beach. Young Buckman found the sailors' red-light district located between the tide and Water Street south of the slough. Adjoining the cribs with their half-breed hostesses was Tom Saunders' honky-tonk with a convenient trap door for "recruiting" seamen who had been given a Mickey Finn. Next door was Limey Dirk's boardinghouse and across the street lay Limey's Pacific Hotel.

Limey Dirk was an Englishman, an ex-pug who was as tough spiritually as he was physically. He had a Turk's-head for a heart. The sailors of Port Townsend eventually tired of his bullying and shanghaiing and under Ben Dixon organized the Sailors Union of the Pacific. The major plank in their platform was a demand for union wages, an increase of five dollars to bring their monthly pay to $25. While the men were on their stayaway strike they put up at the Highland Hotel and ate at a decent restaurant kept by a Mrs. Olsen. They spurned resolutely Limey's enticing free eye-opener of a shot of rotgut at his hotel and boardinghouse. This show of moral strength was made easier, it must be admitted, by the lack of appeal of Limey's foul coffee. This brew, concocted in the main from burnt breadcrusts, passed for "breakfast" in his establishments.

The sailors began to tire of passive resistance, which they felt did not become them, and one night went down to the beach to fill their pockets with stones. They then bombarded Limey's windows. Dirk charged out of the building with a gun in each hand, shooting wildly at shadows while the howling sailors hid behind the whorehouses up the street. Night after night this waterfront guerrilla warfare went on. Luckily for the sailors, Limey was no marksman and never did succeed in hitting anyone with his pistols. The sailors' aim was better, for one night a rock clipped the English crimp right on the head and laid him out cold. Next day he was back on the job, however, boarding up his shattered windows, his head swathed in bandages.

Hjalmar Rutzebeck, a young Dane whose alias was Svend Norman, made the mistake of celebrating his desertion from the German hell ship *Osterbeck* with a chance acquaintance in a waterfront saloon in Victoria, British Columbia, around the turn of the century. It was only a matter of a couple of draughts of beer before the pub began to wobble around like an eccentric carousel. When Rutzebeck, alias Norman, awoke, he found himself sprawled in the forecastle of the *Osterbeck*'s sister ship, the *Tarpenbeck,* bound for Antofagasta. With him were two Texas cowhands, a mulatto named Jorge, two Polack laborers and an old Norwegian sailor named Haakon. All seven had been shanghaiied on Victoria's waterfront.

Rutzebeck, Jorge and the Norseman managed to jump overboard when the German bark lay at anchor in the harbor of Caleta Coloso, the tiny Chilean nitrate port nine miles south of Antofagasta. The Dane's escape attempt was successful, but like so many sailors, he had not learned a thing from his experience. He signed up in Callao as a boarder with a fellow Dane called Jimmy the Pig. After Jimmy the Pig had possession of Rutzebeck's seabag and chest and had given him three weeks' board and room, he shanghaiied his countryman out in the smooth system which he had pioneered on the Pacific Coast of South America with Johnnie the Rogue of Pisagua and Paul the Diver of Antofagasta.

The South American crimps worked closely with the corrupt police. Drunken sailors were customarily rounded up by the constabulary and jailed a day or two before their ship was scheduled to sail. The ship's officers, rather than pay the exorbitant fines fixed for their misdemeanors, would consider them deserters. As was done in Rutzebeck's case, they would confiscate the seamen's wages and gear and then purchase other men from the shipping shark's "pool." Jimmy the Pig demanded a blood-money payment of £16 for each man delivered. The vicious Dane was an expert in out-and-out slaving.

Many seamen were shanghaied two, three or even more times, like the nameless Bostonian of 1834. A friend of Bill Coffman, named Fitz, was slugged and robbed of thirty pounds in Antwerp. Being stone broke he took refuge in a sailor's boardinghouse with the understanding with its master that he would be shipped on a coastwise vessel. He awoke one morning to find himself aboard the British four-master *Peter Iredale* in the English Channel, bound around Cape Horn for Portland, Oregon.

He deserted the *Peter Iredale* in Portland. The old "slow coach" later went on the beach at Clatsop spit and can still be seen there. Fitz freely abandoned his eight months' wages to escape the clutches of the Limey mates and worked his way south to San Francisco. He was on the beach there only two months before he awoke again from a drugged sleep to find himself, with a splitting headache, bound for Cape Horn and Europe on the *Belfast*. Fitz, like Rutzebeck, eventually learned his lesson the hard way. He was never again trapped by slick talk and cheap whisky. "All boardinghouse runners looked alike after that." He steered clear of them.

No crimp left his memoirs and few shanghaied seamen were in any position, literary or financial, to sit down and pen recollections of waterfront druggings and sluggings by the informal press gangs. Little more is known of the major San Francisco crimps, runners, and boardinghouse masters of Drum, Davis, Front, East and Pacific streets than their names and an occasional anecdote. Bob Pinner and Jimmy Laflin were said to prefer shanghaiing whalers from their headquarters at 35 Pacific Street. Horseshoe Brown was doing well in the game until he killed himself and his wife in front of his Kearny Street place. Shanghai Brown was said to have fallen prey to his own profession, being kidnaped in 1896 and shanghaied by the brassbounders (apprentices) of the windjammer *Springburn* and sent on a winter voyage around the Horn.

The gentler sex was represented among the Embarcadero crimps by two tarts named Miss Piggott and Mother Bronson. The former was even further distinguished by her choice of a runner. Finns were rare enough in San Francisco seventy-five years ago but Miss Piggott enjoyed the distinction of employing a Lapp as a runner for her house, surely the only Laplander in California, if not America.

The ladies got the leavings, however, the men being more characteristic of the trade. One of the most notorious runners was Johnny Devine, the Shanghai Chicken. The San Francisco *Call* named him as "one of the most dangerous of the habitués of the Barbary Coast." He had been shanghaied out of New York himself when he was twenty years old in 1859 and showed up in San Francisco about 1861. He was a pimp as well as a crimp, with seven girls walking the streets for him, and he also dabbled in burglary and pickpocketing. It is said that he was arrested twenty-seven times in nine months but received no more punishment than a grand total of fifty days in jail. This came as a result of his being hired for $50 to slug an enemy of his employer. He worked the man over so well that the victim had to spend several months in the hospital. The Shanghai Chicken spent his time in the county jail.

When he was new to San Francisco, Devine posed as quite a boxer and, in fact, defeated Patsy Marley in a Point Isabel bout. A little later he took on Soapy McAlpine and found him not only a Tartar but a better prize fighter. McAlpine extended his advantage over the Shanghai Chicken—no Marquis of Queensbury man himself—by knowing and employing far more roughhouse techniques. He not only outboxed Devine but also outfouled, outgouged, outbit and outkicked the Shanghai Chicken. Devine was soon lying unconscious on the floor.

When Devine was able to walk again he publicly proclaimed

that he was through with the ring. He became a runner for crimp Johnny Walker and later became a sort of roughneck *maître d'* for Shanghai Kelly. Devine did not observe even the slack code of the crimps and felt no guilt in hijacking sailors already captured by competitive runners. He had little trouble most of the time in his intramural raids until he tried to take a drunken salt away from Tommy Chandler. Chandler, a runner for Shanghai Brown, was a sometime pug who had whipped Dooney Harris, the English boxer, and Billy Dwyer. Chandler knocked Devine down with one punch on the jaw. The Shanghai Chicken got to his feet and, after immobilizing the sailor with a slung shot, drew his pepper-box pistol and shot Chandler in the chest and right hand. Chandler recovered from the chest wound but never regained the complete use of his right hand and this spelled an end to his prize-ring days. He resumed his crimping, however, and refused to press charges against the Shanghai Chicken, so Devine went scot-free.

On July 13, 1868, Devine and Johnny Nyland, another runner for Shanghai Kelly, got looped and attacked a handful of men in Billy Lewis's saloon, knifing and shooting several, but none seriously. They then took on the clientele of the bar attached to Billy Maitland's boardinghouse on Front Street near Vallejo Street. Nyland cut up two men with the big knife which he claimed to have taken off the corpse of a waterfront policeman. The Shanghai Chicken, for his part, made a target range of the whisky bottles displayed at the rear of the bar, and snapped a shot or two at the barkeep himself.

Billy Maitland, a huge bear of a man, heard the shouted curses and crashing of glass and rushed into the barroom. With almost one motion he took the knife away from Nyland and kicked him out into the street. He turned on Devine, to find the Shanghai Chicken aiming his pistol unsteadily at him. Maitland rushed him and Devine dropped the gun to raise his arm to protect his throat. The heavy knife in Maitland's hand sliced

300

through Devine's left wrist like a cleaver and cut off his hand. Devine screamed in pain but Maitland ignored his cries and tossed him out in the street alongside Nyland. The Shanghai Chicken propped himself up, got to his feet and, between curses, cried out, "Hey, Billy, you dirty bastard! Chuck out me fin!" Maitland accommodated, opening the saloon's doors and tossing Devine's severed hand on the board sidewalk. Nyland helped Devine to Dr. Simpson's drugstore at Pacific and Davis where the Shanghai Chicken tossed his bloody hand on the counter, saying, "Doc, stick that on again for me." Then he collapsed.

Simpson sent Devine to a hospital where his left arm was amputated above the wrist. After he recovered, he was fitted with a piratical-looking iron hook which made him more dangerous than ever in a rough-and-tumble fight, for he sharpened the point to a needle edge.

Devine began to drink too much and Shanghai Kelly found he could no longer depend on his lieutenant. He accordingly decided to shanghai him out of San Francisco. Several attempts were abortive but finally some of Kelly's toughs got him down to a boat landing. There, however, Devine slipped out of the ropes that bound him and lit into the other crimps with his wicked hook. After the men fled, Devine rowed Shanghai Kelly's boat down to another wharf where he sold it to a rival crimp.

Devine kept going downhill, spending more time rolling drunks than shanghaiing seamen. He was given a year in the county jail in 1869 for larceny. His thefts became so petty that in 1871 he was committed for thirty days for stealing three pigs' feet from a lunchroom.

In May 1871, only a few weeks after being released from his ludicrous pigs'-feet punishment, the Shanghai Chicken shot and killed a German sailor, August Kamk, at Bay View in South San Francisco, for his money. He then threatened to kill a woman when she refused to hide him. The next morning he was caught by policeman John Coulter who found him on board the steamer *Wilson G. Hunt* which was ready to sail from Meiggs Wharf. He was found wearing the German's cap. He made no attempt to clear himself, saying to Coulter: "John, you're a damned good fellow, but I'm afraid you'll have me hung." "Why so?" asked the patrolman. "Well, I shot a son of a bitch at Bay View yesterday, and I think they'll make me swing for it."

Devine did swing and was buried in old Calvary Cemetery near Masonic Avenue, just outside the poor plot and barely within the "respectable" graveyard. Curious visitors found the Shanghai Chicken's tomb framed with the blank crosses of the pauper dead. His own cross had fallen by the 1880's and its number—5608—was hidden by the grass and nettles which flourished there. Had he been a crimp alone, he would have been entitled to space with the other business folk of the graveyard. But since his was a murderer's grave, it was set apart from the others. Someone wrote his epitaph in pencil, long afterward, on his fallen cross—*Chicken Devine got his neck broke, Because he shot another bloke.*

In San Francisco crimps laced their liquor with opium and laudanum but also pioneered in the use of chloral hydrate—"knockout drops." Every crimp, runner or boardinghouse master was required to be able to mix a potion which would put a man safely to sleep but which would not ship him to Fiddler's Green. It used to be said of cowboys that they would be dead drunk twenty minutes after hitting a town. A deep-water sailor freshly arrived in San Francisco could cut that time in half. He would wander the streets a bit as a spectator boyishly interested in everything and ready to participate in any manner of merrymaking. Chances were, however, that he would not stray far from the Embarcadero. The waterfront was his native habitat, his world. He liked to spend his time ashore with the kind of people he understood and was used to, his shipmates. Naturally, he was an easy mark for Embarcadero crimps with doped liquor.

There was plenty of amusement for a seaman in Victorian San Francisco, the "hoyden city." He did not have to go far from tidewater to reach one of the forty-eight houses "kept by bawds" which the *Christian Advocate* reported in 1853. Most of them were on Jackson, Pacific and Commercial streets. Cementing them together were gambling hells and pawnshops ready to take whatever money or valuables might be left after the fandango houses were through with him. An historian of the day claimed that there were five hundred and thirty-seven establishments serving liquor in San Francisco that year of 1853. Not all were saloons, to be sure, for restaurants, gambling dens, billiard parlors and bagnios catered to the drinking man. In any case, no sailor need ever go thirsty. The unmistakable sounds of popping corks and shaken dice and the purring whir of roulette wheels supplied the background music for the fleecing of naïve sailormen in San Francisco.

To be sure, there were a few honest boardinghouse masters, men like Captain Palmer B. Hewett. Called Don Pedro by everyone, he kept a decent place on Montgomery Street beyond Broadway, on the first rise of Telegraph Hill. However, more typical were those on the pattern of Patsy Corrigan, Johnny Fearem, Daniel Swannack, the brute who ran the boardinghouse called the Sailor's Home, or Calico Jim.

One balmy summer's eve in 1899, two young sailors named Hiram Bailey and Ben MacFarlane strolled down Glen's Alley near Battery Point. They dropped into Calico Jim's place, joining some of their new friends from the *Royalshire, Benares, Queen Margaret, London Hill, Lancing* and the *Washington.* Some of the sailors claimed over glasses of beer that the *Washington,* a notorious hell ship thanks to a bluenose bucko mate, was putting to sea with a crew of thirty, of whom nine were shanghaied landsmen—four farm laborers, three bartenders and two clergymen. Four of the lubbers were said to be lying in irons already after tangling with the big-fisted Nova Scotian mate who had been forced to make up a crew at a time when sailors were scarce because of the Klondike gold rush.

Calico Jim was a square-jawed, high-cheeked Chilean with a soft-silver voice which disguised his true nature. The latter was revealed by his adder eyes. Ben and Hiram ("Shorty") enjoyed several drinks served them in person by a solicitous Calico Jim or his Negro runner, then they remembered no more. The two men were kicked awake and found themselves in the forecastle of a four-masted steel bark. Bailey, who wrote up his reminiscences, thought prudence and caution to be the better part of valor and called the ship the "General Gordon" which was not her name. She was bound from Mission Wharf for Sydney, sailing via Mazatlán, Mexico, and Iquique, Chile. At the latter port she was to take on a cargo of nitrates for New South Wales.

The "General Gordon's" captain hailed from Sausalito where he kept a big house, complete with flagpole. His daughter stayed at home in Sausalito but his son sailed with him, and Hiram Bailey found himself detailed to teach "Sonny" his algebra. The apelike mate, a Nova Scotia bluenose (was this the Washington?) was a real brute. He hit an old seaman named Senn viciously across the chest with a belaying pin when the man tried to slip ashore on the last barge at Mazatlán. The mate then strung Senn up by his thumbs in the forecastle. The captain finally cut the man down.

By this time, the crew was on the verge of mutiny. The colored cook took his cue from the mates and tried his hand at lording it over the shanghaied landsmen but MacFarlane beat him up. Then the mate took Ben on but MacFarlane whipped him roundly, although the Nova Scotian used spiked knuckledusters. While the two were slugging it out, Hiram and a pal named Baltimore removed all the belaying pins from the fiddle and fife rails so that the bleeding mate could not find a weapon

304

with which to bash in Ben's skull. The mate finally tugged at a revolver in his pocket but its hammer caught in the lining. When Ben knocked him down and out before he could free the pistol, the crew raised a cheer. The captain watched the affair without saying a word.

Some of the crew dragged the mate along the deck and dumped him into the pig's trough where he lay for three quarters of an hour. When Ben MacFarlane climbed into his bunk that night, sore and bloody, he found that the crew had placed the mate's sixgun and knuckle-dusters under his blankets. The bluenose, who had bitten off the tip of his tongue in the fray and who had had a couple of ribs smashed, made himself scarce on deck for many days and the men were able to have a bit of fun when they celebrated in symbolic fashion their having worked off the dead horse.

It was a Friday when their month's debt slavery ended. Their crimps had boarded them for 20¢ a day but had charged them $1.00, drawing the money—the seamen's first month's pay—from the shipping agent the day the bark sailed. If a man did not ship, the crimp got nothing for his pains, so he saw to it that every manjack was aboard at sailing time. After a full month, the crewmen of the "Gordon" were finally working for themselves and not for the crimps. To celebrate the occasion, they fashioned a horse out of barrel hoops and canvas. They may have stuffed it with the scorned tracts placed on board many ships outbound from San Francisco. Cheering, singing and just yelling, they heaved the mock horse over the rail.

On a Saturday in November 1899, they arrived at Iquique, joining the *Chrysomene* in the harbor. Here, Senn immediately jumped ship. After taking on a load of nitrates, the "*General Gordon*" put to sea again. All went well until the bark was caught in a hurricane one night in the South Pacific and the mate shouted to Old Man Smith on the lee arm of the crossjack yard. The tongue-nipped Nova Scotian did not have the articulation he had once possessed and whatever command he gargled was lost in the noise of the gale. Smith either did not hear him or failed to understand the command.

The mate cursed and grabbed a belaying pin from the rail. Sticking it in his belt he started up, dropping a stream of oaths into the spindrift behind him. He laid along the footrope of the crossjack yard like a huge spider. He made his mistake as he passed Ben MacFarlane and Hiram Bailey. The bluenose yelled at Ben, "I'll send *you* to hell in a moment!" Ben and Hiram went after him. The mate reached Smith and instead of helping him to free the gasket from the clew garnet, beat him in the face with his fists. MacFarlane caught up to him and struck him one blow, then dodged, waiting for the deadly whish of the belaying pin. But none came and Ben swung again in the darkness. His fist cut only air and he almost lost his footing. His lucky punch had knocked the mate off the yard. No one suspected it and the crew, in any case, simply muttered good riddance and "may he roast forever." They assumed that the hated Nova Scotian had been washed off the deck when the "*General Gordon*" was pooped by the hurricane seas.

During the rough weather MacFarlane was almost scalped in a fall. The captain managed to patch him up though he put the piece of scalp on backwards. The Old Man then ordered Chips aloft to nail a silver dollar to the fore topmast (the lower masts were of steel) as a prize for the first man to spy a landfall. Smith won and soon a bearded Sydney pilot clambered aboard the "*General Gordon*," forty-nine days from Iquique. They made fast to a harbor buoy near the old colonial clipper *Sobroan*. A great ship, her skipper used to say that "only birds could pass her." At this time her salad days were over and she was doing duty as a reformatory for Aussie "throw-outs."

The "*Gordon's*" crew scattered to the winds but there was no problem in replacing them. Men stood in line to get a bunk in her forecastle. No shanghaiing was necessary in Sydney in the year 1900. The Klondike lay in the direction from which the bark had come and in which she would return. After loading coal at Newcastle, New South Wales, the *"Gordon"* sailed for Spreckels Wharf, San Francisco. The eastward passage was uneventful except for the death of Old Man Smith. Just sixty-four days from Australia, the tug *Sioux Chief* pushed the bark up to the wharf.

Crimps came out to the bark promising her crew comfortable boardinghouses, women and good food and drink. The mate and second officer tried to keep them off, but since they had to help work ship and argue with the tugboat captain, some "water rats," as the crimps were called, got aboard. They handed out stogies, passed a bottle of rye around and soon the dusty-dry sailors were singing and dancing to the accompaniment of a pock-marked crimp who sat on a sea chest, playing a mouth organ.

The *St. Elmo,* bound for Hong Kong, was shorthanded. Her skipper would pay $50 a head blood money and the crimps had to work fast. Aloft, the surly starboard watch was furling the topsails. At the foot of the shrouds paced the Old Man and the mate, standing guard with drawn revolvers. Calico Jim's Negro helper came aboard and quickly got in a row with Slush, the ship's colored cook. Their battle royal ended when, like billy goats, they butted heads. The runner stayed down with a fractured skull, as the groggy and battered cookie staggered to his feet.

Bailey hired a crimp to take him ashore for $2, but a drunken Irishman named O'Brien upset the skiff. Hiram swam against the tide until he reached a wharf. He hung on to a piling until some of his strength came back and pulled himself up onto the dock. After spending three days in the hospital on San Bruno Avenue, he found himself free.

Bailey quit the sea to become an engineer, never wanting to see the *"General Gordon"* again. However, he did spot her once again when, in 1915, she lay in Liverpool harbor. We are not sure just what vessel the *"Gordon"* was nor are we agreed as to whether Bailey was afraid to correctly identify her because of fear of retaliation, libel or violence, or because he wanted to protect his pal, Ben MacFarlane, perhaps a pseudonym, who had killed the mate.

Bill Coffman was a turn-of-the-century sailor who doubled as a saloon entertainer. One night, after his act at The Cove closed, he offered to escort two foreign seamen on a tour of San Francisco Barbary Coast night spots. The three had successfully negotiated the Nymphia on Stockton Street, the Bella Union at Kearny and Washington, the House of All Nations and Purcell's Negro dive, the So Different. Coffman was walking down Jackson Street toward East Street (the Embarcadero) when he suddenly felt his thirst rising. He ducked into a waterfront saloon and stood at the bar. His last recollection was that of his knees losing their lock. He felt himself crumple to the sawdust on the floor.

Coffman was awakened by his own vomiting. He found himself face down on a cot in a pitch-dark room, his head aching. It was apparently nighttime though there was no sign of a window or skylight. He stumbled about the room until he found a door and began to beat on it. A voice cursed him and told him to keep quiet. When Coffman continued to pound away, the door suddenly opened and a pair of hands grabbed him and threw him onto the cot, which immediately collapsed. Coffman lay there a long time with his stomach cramps and pounding head for company, but around daylight a man came into the room and poured steaming coffee into him.

Coffman asked for a doctor as soon as he could speak. The reply was that a "sawbones" had seen him the day before and had said he would be O.K. When Coffman asked where he was and what had happened to him, the man only told him that he was in Mr. Brewer's boardinghouse on Steuart Street, that he had been there two days and already owed Brewer $12 for medicine, food, lodging and the doctor's visit. Advised that he had better pay, Coffman groaned that he had not a cent to his name. Brewer's runner said, "We'll see about that." He brought Coffman hot coffee laced with rum and led him to a washbowl, ordering him to clean himself up. Still dizzy, Coffman followed the crimp down the stairs, through the saloon and out into the street where he was hauled into a delivery wagon. He lay in the wagon, dizzy and miserable, while the driver guided his horses over the rough cobblestones of the waterfront.

When the driver reined up, Coffman was helped down from the wagon and pushed into a room. His guardian gave Coffman's name and nationality to a man behind a counter and stuck a pen in the sailor's hand. Coffman scratched his name on the paper and was rewarded at the wagon with a shot of rum. By this time he was so far gone that he was carried upstairs at Brewer's bodily and dumped in his room.

Next morning his two companions of the day before came into the room. "Get going," they ordered. Coffman found five other men in the wagon, besides himself and Brewer's two crimps, who both carried heavy sticks as "persuaders." They were driven down to the foot of Howard Street and hustled out on a dock. Coffman and three others were shoved down a ladder to a rowboat and the two others, dead drunk, were swung over the wharf by the boardinghouse runners and dropped into the arms of the waiting boat crew. The two toughs then jumped into the boat and shoved off.

Coffman aroused himself at the cry of "Ahoy, the *Belfast!*" from one of the oarsmen. He saw three sailing ships in a cluster, two of them flying the Union Jack. Coffman clambered up the rope ladder, stepped on the broad rail but slipped and fell four feet to the deck. He was hauled erect by the second officer who asked him if he was a sailor. When Coffman gasped out that he

309

had sailed on a schooner, the second mate shouted at him, "If you've sailed before, why don't you say Sir?" Without waiting for an answer he sunk his fist in Coffman's midriff, knocking all the wind out of him and sending him gasping like a stuck fish in the scuppers. The other men came aboard and the two drunks were thrown on deck where "second" gave them a good booting before turning away.

A sailor helped Coffman out of the scuppers and led him to the forecastle where he gave him coffee. He was a Scotsman named Arthur Gribble. From him Coffman learned that the *Belfast* was loaded with 2,500 tons of Port Costa wheat and was bound for Queenstown, Ireland, for orders. When Coffman learned the passage would be something like five to seven months, he told Gribble he had been brought aboard against his will and asked if it would do any good to complain to the captain. The Scot answered by asking him if he had signed anything. With a shock, Coffman remembered that he had. Gribble told him that the mates would never let him get aft in any case. They would take no chances on losing men. An officer was on anchor watch and would allow no craft to close with the *Belfast* except the expected boarding master's boat with another load of shanghaied seamen.

Of the sixteen A.B.'s and two ordinaries who had shipped in Cardiff, eight had deserted in Hong Kong and were replaced— at blood-money rates—but these eight had then jumped ship in Port Costa. With them went four A.B.'s and one ordinary seaman. Captain J. E. Davies was left with only five of the original crew, all men with wives and families in Britain like Gribble. Were they to desert they would lose all right to sail on British ships in the future. It would mean losing their livelihood. They made the best of a bad bargain. Davies paid $75 blood money to the San Francisco runners for Coffman and the other four men and just after the pilot came aboard he got three more hands. They were passing Meiggs Wharf in tow of a tug as the crimp came out of the captain's cabin, having settled his bill. He grinned at his recruits and said, "Goodbye and good luck," and clambered over the side to his boat. The shanghaied men cursed him and wished him aboard for the duration. Coffman kept clear of the mates who were brutally hazing the new men. He learned that the United Kingdom would be a dead-end for him. It was almost impossible to ship out of Britain without agreeing to a clause in the ship's articles calling for a hitch of three years and return to the United Kingdom. All the landlubbers on the *Belfast* were called "farmers," as was the custom, but two of the men shanghaied in San Francisco were actually farmers. They were two French Canadians from Quebec, Felix and Celle, who had wandered into the wrong saloon at the wrong time. They had never seen the ocean before arriving in San Francisco and the kicks and cuffings of the British mates only made them more bewildered with their situation.

Usually a crimp threw a dunnage bag after the "body" of a new seaman before collecting two months' pay from his victim, but he had slipped up in Coffman's case. The latter had to buy his gear at the slop chest, signing a note for hip boots, southwester, oilskins, underwear, two flannel shirts, two pairs of dungarees, cotton blankets, a tin plate and pannikin, a knife, fork and spoon. On the first day of October 1902, Coffman found himself one day at sea and already three months in debt. He also discovered that ersatz coffee together with hardtack, dunked in the java, was breakfast, and tea and hardtack the evening meal. Lunch was more substantial, consisting of a pannikin of soup made of dried peas and salt beef or salt pork. "Fresh" meat was served on Sundays to break the monotony. This was actually tinned Australian mutton, all the juice of which had been squeezed in making Bovril. On the Queen's birthday the crew was given a treat of sixteen ounces of brown sugar and a little marmalade for each man. Later, the lime juice was broken out and a cup served to each sailor every day to prevent scurvy. The menu was approved by the British Board of Trade as official issue for deep-water ships and the document to that effect was posted in the forecastle.

Every mistake the green men made meant a beating, and they made plenty in the stormy passage south in the 1,800-ton, three-masted bark. The nineteen-year-old Coffman, like every other "farmer" aboard, longed to get even with the second mate, Mr. Atkins. Christmas Dinner off the coast of Argentina—the usual pea soup and salt horse—came and went without an opportunity and one hundred and fifty-three days after leaving the Golden Gate, the *Belfast* put into Falmouth. The captain had decided to call there for orders rather than at Queenstown. The *Belfast* then proceeded to Cork, where the cargo was delivered and the crew was paid off. Coffman had earned £26 12s, but after paying off Brewer's blood money, £10, plus £4 4s for slop chest charges and 4s for bumboat purchases in Falmouth, he had only £7 4s, or $36 U. S., to show for almost six months of hard work at sea.

After jumping ship a few times and beating the daylights out of Captain D. J. "Crazy" Killman of the four-masted schooner *Lyman D. Foster* in the midst of a wild storm, Coffman finally got back to San Francisco. He put up as a boarder at the Excelsior on the Embarcadero, run by George Larson and his son Willie. They were not above shanghaiing a man or two when a $50 advance note would cancel an overdue board-bill, but they got more play from the real sailors, especially those in the coastwise trade, who liked a short spell ashore between trips.

Some seamen shot their entire pay the first night ashore. With a raft of IOU's clogging Larson's cash drawer, they would have to give in to his urging that they settle for a "dead horse" on some tub making north toward Grays Harbor. When Coffman's credit ran out, Willie Larson tried to get him to sign an advance note. Coffman noted the ship was British and the destination

Antwerp. He declined with thanks and was thrown out of the boardinghouse, his duffle being seized for back board.

In 1907 Coffman found that a new San Francisco was building on the ruins of the old, but many of the old dives reappeared—Spider Kelly's, the Montana, the California, the O. K., the Crutch, Cowboy Mag's, Parenti's and Fat Daugherty's. The crimps were still around but Bill Coffman was smarter than most sailors. He turned his back on both the sea and the bottle and, swallowing the anchor, went on to become a business leader in San Francisco, a great figure in sports and the founder of the famous East-West Shrine football game. But he never forgot the old, but not good, Shanghai Days in San Francisco.